Whiskey
&
Philosophy

Other books in the Epicurean Series, conceived by
Fritz Allhoff:

Steven D. Hales, ed.
*Beer & Philosophy: The Unexamined Beer
Isn't Worth Drinking*

Fritz Allhoff and Dave Monroe, ed.
Food & Philosophy: Eat, Think, and Be Merry

Fritz Allhoff, ed.
*Wine & Philosophy: A Symposium on
Thinking and Drinking*

Whiskey & Philosophy

A Small Batch of Spirited Ideas

Edited by Fritz Allhoff and Marcus P. Adams

John Wiley & Sons, Inc.

Published by John Wiley & Sons, Inc., Hoboken, New Jersey

Published simultaneously in Canada

Design by Forty-five Degree Design LLC

The results from the experiment conducted at Stanford University Business School that appear on page 47 are cited with permission.

For general information about our other products and services, please contact our Customer Care Department within the United States at (800) 762-2974, outside the United States at (317) 572-3993 or fax (317) 572-4002.

Wiley also publishes its books in a variety of electronic formats. Some content that appears in print may not be available in electronic books. For more information about Wiley products, visit our web site at www.wiley.com.

Library of Congress Cataloging-in-Publication Data:

Allhoff, Fritz and Marcus P. Adams.

Whiskey and philosophy : a small batch of spirited ideas / Fritz Allhoff, Marcus P. Adams.

p. cm.—(Epicurean series)
Includes bibliographical references and index.
ISBN 978-0-470-43121-4 (pbk.)
1. Whiskey. I. Allhoff, Fritz. II. Adams, Marcus P. III. Title.
TP605.A45 2009
641.2'52—dc22

2009007425

Printed in the United States of America

10 9 8 7 6 5 4 3 2 1

Contents

Foreword

Much abused, by its addicts and traducers alike, it is
a complicated simple, the whisky, pure in essence, but
diverse in effects; and against it none can prevail.

—*J. P. McCondach*

Whisky (or 'whiskey', to use the spelling adopted in this book)
is both an idea and a reality, and between the two, as T. S.
Eliot observed, lies the shadow.[1] It is far more than liquor in a
bottle: it embodies tradition and high craft, social history and
topography, poetry and song. In other words, it comes with a
pedigree, unlike less noble spirits, laden with associations that
even the most cunning salesman cannot overlook. It is, quite
literally, elemental, made from cereal grains (the quintessential product of the earth), brewed with water, made ethereal
by fire, and matured by the action of air upon wooden casks.
Distillation was one of the earliest of the alchemists' secrets;
the key words associated with the art— 'alcohol', 'alembic',
'alchemy'—all derive from Arabic. The first use of distilled
spirits is likely to have been in religious rituals: Dionysian
rites of baptism by fire in the fifth century BCE, early Christian
Gnostic cults, heretical medieval sects like the Bogomils and
the Cathars.[2] A lot to think about here.

To look at it another way, whiskey is a reincarnation. The
coarse and heavy cereal grains are sublimated, the spirit leaving
that earthly body, purged and disinfected, all but vanishing into

pure nonbeing; then, by heavenly metempsychosis, returning to the world as a perfectly pure and impersonal liquid. Placed in an oak cask, a further transformation occurs, this time a metamorphosis, still today not fully understood by chemists. Dr. Jim Swan, a world expert on maturation, described it elegantly to me: "Think of the new-make spirit as a caterpillar, and of the cask as its chrysalis. After three or five or fifteen years in the wood, it emerges as a butterfly."[3]

With such a pedigree it is not surprising that whiskey has a potency and directness that other drinks lack, a quality of "spiritual instancy." Aeneas MacDonald, whose seminal book *Whisky* was much admired by Eliot, wrote: "Some might say that whisky is a Protestant drink, but it is rather a rationalistic, metaphysical and dialectical drink. It stimulates speculation and nourishes lucidity. One may sing on it but one is as likely to argue. Split hairs and schisms flourish in its depths; hierarchies and authority go down before the sovereignty of a heightened and irresistible intuition. It is the mother's milk of destructive criticism and the begetter of great abstractions; it is disposed to find a meaning—or at least a debate—in art and letters, rather than to enjoy or to appreciate; it is the champion of the deductive method and the sworn foe of pragmatism; it is Socratic, drives to logical conclusions, has a horror of established and useful falsehoods, is discourteous to irrelevances, possesses an acuteness of vision which marshals the complexities and the hesitations of life into two opposing hosts, divides the greys of the world rigidly into black and white."[4] I quote MacDonald at length, since his words serve well as an introduction to what you will find in this book! More by implication than expressly, he also alludes to whiskey's "dark side."

The "shadow," to return to T. S. Eliot, was seen by MacDonald and others as being associated with those who drink "not for the pleasure of drinking nor for any merits of flavour or bouquet which the whisky may possess but simply in order to obtain a certain physical effect."[5] No doubt there are benefits in mitigating a cold climate and a Calvinistic theology, but his enemies are the "let's-have-a-spot" and "make-it-a-quick-one" gentry, who regard whisky not as an end in itself but as a means to an end, "who have not organs of taste and smell in them but only gauges of alcoholic content . . . who dwell in a darkness where there are no whiskies but only whisky—and, of course, soda."[6]

It has all to do with appreciation, and of all alcoholic drinks, I maintain, whiskey deserves to be appreciated: it rewards consideration, contemplation, and reflection. It is, after all, the most organoleptically complex spirit known to humans. Professor David Daiches summed up the opposite approach in his book *Scotch Whisky*: "The trouble with any alcoholic drink is that it can be drunk by people who dislike the taste and who are simply out for the alcoholic kick. It used to be standard practice in Hollywood films for actors to indicate when they were taking an alcoholic drink by the grimacing gulp which accompanied its rapid ingestion, the implication being that it tastes horrible but you drink it for social reasons or because it makes you feel good."[7]

This way lies perdition, through the extreme darkness of alcohol abuse and addiction; these are not limited to whiskey, although whiskey is often considered the most boastful demon in the temperance reformer's Hades. As a result, politicians have been able to impose ever-higher duties and taxes, ever more stringent licensing laws, smug in the assumption that they are saving us from ourselves. Today, the spirits industry looks nervously at the phenomenal success of the antismoking lobby, which has managed to pillory and persecute a large sector of the community in almost every Western country, and which, make no mistake, now has its sights on "booze."

What's required here is honesty and a sense of perspective. Single malt Scotch and limited batch bourbon are not the drinks of choice of teenage binge drinkers; indeed, it is rare that a taste for whiskey is acquired before the age of about thirty. The alcohol consumption guidelines, proposed by the Royal College of Physicians of England in 1987, soon became "benchmarks" and then "limits" set in stone. In the United Kingdom, men drinking over twenty-one units—or women over fourteen—are branded hazardous drinkers; yet a unit of alcohol in the United Kingdom is 8 g compared to 12 g in France, 14 g in the United States, and a hefty 19.75 g in Japan. No less an authority than Richard Smith, former editor of the *British Medical Journal*, confessed that "those limits were really plucked out of the air. They were not based on any firm evidence at all. It was a sort of intelligent guess by a committee."[8]

I am often asked: "What is the correct way to drink whiskey?" The answer is that there is no correct way to drink; you should enjoy it as you like, with or without ice, water, mixers, and so on. But *appreciation* is a different matter. To appreciate whiskey to the fullest, you use your nose as much as your palate. You savor aroma as well as taste; never forget that 'flavor' is, by definition, a combination of the two. As a result, an appropriate glass is essential, one that has a bowl so you can swirl the liquid, and a rim that narrows slightly so as to direct the aroma up your nose. You don't add ice (this closes down the aroma), but you do add a little still water, since this both opens up the aroma and makes the spirit easier to taste.

The appreciation of whiskey has been rediscovered only recently. I have already quoted MacDonald, and will do so again: "The notion that we can possibly develop a palate for whisky is guaranteed to produce a smile of derision in any company except that of a few Scottish lairds, farmers, game-keepers and bailies, relics of a vanished age of gold when the vintages of the north had their students and lovers."[9] This was in 1930. The "vintages of the north" were malt whiskies, which had all but disappeared by then, every drop of malt whisky made going into blended Scotch. The situation was only slightly better in 1980. The then editor of *Decanter* magazine, Tony Lord, wrote in one of its supplements: "In 1981 Scotch whisky means blended whisky. Only one bottle in a hundred is malt, the original whisky. . . . Sadly only about half [of 120 operating distilleries] are bottled as single malt whiskies, and many of these are in such miniscule quantities as to be almost unobtainable."[10]

But the situation was already changing. The owners of Glenfiddich Distillery had resolved as early as 1963 to bottle and promote their malt as a single. During the 1970s, a number of other distillers, mainly independent companies, followed suit, albeit in a small way—Macallan's entire promotional budget in 1978 was £50 (then about $90)! This became a steady trickle in the 1980s and a rushing torrent in the 1990s, prompted by consumer demand and media interest in malts. In the late 1980s, and for the first time, books began to appear devoted to the evaluation of whiskey by flavor, again prompted by consumer interest. And so we reach the present, where there are more whiskeys deserving of appreciation than ever before in history—not only single malt Scotches, but single malts from Japan and Ireland, deluxe blends and small-batch bourbons.[11]

Whiskey & Philosophy is a perfect companion to the appreciation of these magnificent drinks, and I commend it to you unreservedly! In this spirit, let us now toast to what I hope will be for you a long-lasting marriage of two excellences, whiskey and philosophy. "The proper drinking of Scotch whisky [and of bourbon, Japanese, Irish, and Canadian whiskeys!] is more than indulgence: it is a toast to civilization, a tribute to the continuity of culture, a manifesto of man's determination to use the resources of nature to refresh mind and body and enjoy to the full the senses with which he has been endowed."[12]

—*Charles MacLean*
Edinburgh, September 2008

NOTES

The epigraph is from J. P. McCondach, *The Channering Worm* (Edinburgh: Canongate, 1983), p. 46.

1. "Between the idea/And the reality/Between the motion/And the act/Falls the Shadow . . ." T. S. Eliot, "The Hollow Men" (1925), http://poetry.poetryx.com/poems/784 (accessed October 1, 2008).
2. C. Anne Wilson, *Water of Life: A History of Wine-Distilling and Spirits, 500 BC to AD 2000* (Totnes, Devon: Prospect Books, 2006).
3. Jim Swan, personal communication (August 1992).

4. Aeneas MacDonald, *Whisky* (Edinburgh: Porpoise Press, 1930), pp. 18–19.
5. Ibid., p. 13.
6. Ibid. Whiskey was often drunk with soda in the 1930s.
7. David Daiches, *Scotch Whisky: Its Past and Present* (London: André Deutsch, 1969), p. 149.
8. Andrew Norfolk, "Drink Limits 'Useless'," *Times Online* (October 20, 2007), www.timesonline.co.uk/tol/life_and_style/food_and_drink/article2697975.ece (accessed October 1, 2008).
9. MacDonald, *Whisky*, p. 14.
10. Tony Lord, *Harrods Book of Whiskies*, 4th ed. (London: Decanter Magazine, 1981), no page numbers (p. 17 if counting manually).
11. See, for example, Michael Jackson, *The World Book of Whiskies* (London: Dorling Kindersley, 1987).
12. Daiches, *Scotch Whisky*, p. 163.

Acknowledgments

This book would not exist without the contributions and support of many people. First, we thank our contributors, whose essays compose this volume. There was a tremendous response to the call for papers, and we are thrilled with the contributors who ultimately made it into the following pages. They endured multiple rounds of edits, often in response to our inane comments and prodding. We hope that the essays are stronger for these but, regardless, we appreciate their fortitude. Most of these people we have never met, and it is somewhat strange to develop such relationships by e-mail. Nonetheless, we look forward to meeting them eventually and sharing some great whiskey.

Second, we thank our publisher, John Wiley & Sons, and the fantastic people there with whom it was such a privilege to work. Connie Santisteban received far more questions from us than she might have liked, but her feedback was always just what we needed; we very much appreciate her help. We also thank Eric Nelson and Kimberly Monroe-Hill. This book follows two of Fritz's others, *Wine & Philosophy* and *Food & Philosophy* (the latter in collaboration with Dave Monroe); these came out with Blackwell Publishing, before its subsequent acquisition by Wiley. Jeff Dean, the philosophy editor at Blackwell, worked tirelessly on these books and without their success, this one would not have been possible.

ACKNOWLEDGMENTS

When we started this book, neither of us really knew all that much about whiskey, aside from the fact that we both liked to drink it. The original idea for the book was actually Jeff's; Fritz's background was in wine, and Marcus had the budget of a graduate student that would have precluded him from having much of a background in anything. Nevertheless, the challenge seemed like a worthy one, so off we went. Along the way, there were many people who helped us understand whiskey; for their help, we now consider ourselves reasonable enough authorities to have our names on the cover. Ian Buxton, one of our contributors, was brilliant in terms of helping us find the appropriate contacts and in answering our numerous questions about Scotch. Chuck Cowdery offered great support with bourbon. Bill Owens, of the American Distilling Institute (ADI), got us in touch with craft distillers around the United States. The ADI 2008 meeting (Louisville, Kentucky) was a great event that gave us a chance to meet many of these people directly.

And then there are the people from the industry who supplied samples of their products as well as the associative brand literature. We were not able to mention all of these products in the book, though we have offered reviews of some of our favorites at the end. But we learned so much through interacting with these people (and drinking their whiskey!); all of this played an important role in our understanding of whiskey as manifest, for example, in our ability to vet the essays that made the cut and are included in the volume. We therefore thank the following: Lorne Mackillop (Angus Dundee Distillers); Beam Global Spirits & Wine; Derek Hancock and Matt Chivian (Benromach and Gordon & MacPhail); Yanni Kehagiaras and Brian Sheehy (Bourbon & Branch); Tracy Frederick (Brown-Forman); Mark Reynier (Bruichladdich); Angela Traver (Buffalo Trace); John Mac Lellan (Burnstewart); Craig Pakish (C&C Shine); Dan Tullio and Mark Wilson (Canadian Club); Roseann Sessa (Castle Brands); Lara Karakasevic (Charbay); John Glaser and Debbie Burke (Compass Box); Rick Wasmund (Copper Fox Distillery);

Sari Brecher, Craig Chester, and Nick Morgan (Diageo); Nick Clark (Four Roses); John Grant (Glenfarclas); Stuart Nickerson (Glenglassaugh Distillery); Larry Kass (Heaven Hill Distilleries); Seth Fox (High Plains Distillery); Roderick Mackenzie (Ian Macleod Distillers); Karen Walker (Inver House Distillers); Andrew Dixon (Kella Distillers); Hunter Chavanne (Kentucky Bourbon Distillers); Lars Lindberger (Mackmyra); Andrew Dixon (ManX); Sarah Zeiler (Michael Collins); Henry Preiss and Alison Thomas (Preiss Imports); Anne Riives, Russell Patton, and Nick Pishko (Morrison Bowmore Distillers); Lindsey Tauer (Phillips Distilling); Jennifer D'Aponte (Rémy Cointreau USA); Kevin Richards (Sazerac Company); Peter Currie (Springbank Distillers); Lucy Farber (St. George Spirits); Jess Graber (Stranahan's); Stephan Berg (the Bitter Truth); Julie Camp (the Classic Malts Collection); Lisa Cifuentes, Amy Felmeister, and Morgan Perry (the Thomas Collective); the Macallan; Toby Maloney (the Violet Hour); and Rory Steel (William Grant & Sons).

During the tastings, Shannon Bernard-Adams and Cari Calder put up with our obnoxious requests for blind presentation, exact pours, rinsed glasses, and all the other trappings of insanity. Zvi Biener, Arthur Falk, Richard Glatz, and Peter Distelzweig also participated in the tastings (see the results in appendix A); we thank everyone for their contributions.

And Fritz thanks Marcus, and Marcus thanks Fritz: this was an amazing project to work on, and we really enjoyed doing it together.

Finally, we thank you, the reader, for your interest. Cheers!

—*Fritz Allhoff & Marcus Adams*
Kalamazoo, MI & Pittsburgh, PA

INTRODUCTION

Start Up the Still

Fritz Allhoff and Marcus P. Adams

> So long as the presence of death lurks with anyone who goes through the simple act of swallowing, I will make mine whiskey.
>
> —*W.C. Fields*

As you sit down to read this introduction, pour yourself some whiskey, whether a wee dram or something more substantial. Our recommendation would be bourbon or, failing that, something from Islay (pronounced *EYE-la*), but choose whatever you wish. Depending on your mood, you might try one of the whiskey cocktails we present at the end of the book. All that really matters is that you have whiskey in front of you. We certainly did while working on this project, and we suspect that many of our contributors did as well. As much fun as it can be to think about the philosophical dimensions of whiskey, it is important to never get too far away from whiskey itself. The essays in this book range from the conversational to the abstract, but they are all unified by homage to the glory of whiskey. So, while we think about whiskey, let's not forget to drink it!

There is no better place to start a philosophical discussion of whiskey than to consider its name: 'whiskey' derives from the Gaelic '*uisge beatha*', which translates as "water of life." The Gaelic underwent various metamorphoses through the 1600s and 1700s before the contemporary appearance of 'whisky' in the mid-1700s.[1] Debates rage as to whether Ireland or Scotland should properly be regarded as the home of whiskey, though it is uncontroversial that a license to distill within the Irish district of Bushmills was granted under the authority of King James I in 1608, and that this was the first such license ever issued. In some sense, this gives priority to the Irish, but surely there was whiskey before there were licenses; references to it appear in various forms as early as the 1400s.

Given this long tradition, as well as the rivalry between the Scottish and the Irish, it is inevitable that differences would be had, and the basic spelling of the word is one of the most fundamental. Most of you already know that Scottish whisky and Irish whiskey have different spellings, though this convention is probably more recent than most people think; references to Scotch whiskey appear as recently as the early 1900s.[2] And, of course, whiskey is now made around the world, and distillers have to figure out how to spell the word that eventually makes its way onto their bottles. Canadian whisky caught a strong foothold in the industry through American Prohibition and follows the Scottish spelling. Japanese whisky—currently the darling of several international whisky competitions—also uses the Scottish spelling. Conventional wisdom also holds that American whiskey is spelled with the Irish spelling, though this is not always true; one of the most famous American bourbons, Maker's Mark, is labeled "Bourbon Whisky."[3]

Most whiskey literature uses 'whisky' as the generic term, making exceptions for American and Irish whiskeys. This is undoubtedly because of the enormous influence that single malt Scotch has exerted over the whiskey world, an influence that is surely deserved. Irish single malts have made great progress in recent years, though their more common blended variants pale in comparison to much of the whisky on offer from Scotland;

with few exceptions, even Ireland's single malts are less regarded than their Scottish counterparts. Traditionally, there is little doubt that Scotland's single malts are nearly alone atop the pinnacle of great whiskeys.[4] Why then, is this book titled *Whiskey and Philosophy* rather than *Whisky and Philosophy*? While acknowledging the ubiquity of the Scottish spelling for generic uses, we nevertheless have adopted the American spelling for present purposes, and for several reasons. For one, our publisher hated the idea of using 'whisk(e)y', which had been our first inclination in the interest of being inclusive. Aside from being invisible to those searching for 'whisky' or 'whiskey' books, the syntax is just unwieldy. Therefore, we had to pick, and the American spelling resonated with us.

While whiskey has a long tradition in the United States, it is clearly undergoing a renaissance. American drinkers have become far more discriminating in recent years, and whiskey bars have begun to open around the country; many of these are throwbacks to the Prohibition-style speakeasy. Small batch and single barrel productions—higher-quality whiskeys than the standard bottlings—are increasingly more widely available and more highly sought. For example, between 2002 and 2006, sales of bourbon and Tennessee whiskey rose just over 12 percent overall, while sales of whiskey in the $20–$30 range rose over 27 percent. In the same time period, though, sales of so-called super premium bourbons ($30) rose over 60 percent.[5] It is also worth noticing that these bottles were not even produced until about twenty-five years ago, with Blanton's release of the first single barrel bourbon in 1984. Other distilleries soon followed, but American bourbon has hardly been produced at a high level for anywhere near as long as Scotch whisky.

Both of us are Americans, and we are excited by the prospects of bourbon's future. Though this book is being distributed worldwide, most of its sales will be in the United States, and we wanted to acknowledge that. But most important, we think that American whiskey is really, really outstanding. Why is it that single malt Scotch is so celebrated and American whiskey so routinely denigrated, at least comparatively? The biggest reason, it seems to us, is consumers' lack of exposure to high-quality American whiskey.

One of us was recently in Europe talking to some friends about whiskey and was surprised to hear the near consensus in the room that American whiskey was just not very good, especially compared to some of the great single malts from Scotland. What American whiskeys are these? Some names were thrown about, nearly all of which were under $20 a bottle and aged for only a couple of years. It is certainly not surprising that a great single malt, like Lagavulin 16, is more highly regarded than these. This is an obviously unfair comparison, but one that really gets to the heart of a lot of the misconceptions about American whiskey. First, we would put up a $20 bottle of American against any single malt Scotch sold at that price. The latter, of course, barely even exist and for those that do, the verdict is hardly obvious.

And second, there are some fantastic American whiskeys, and people should get out there and drink them! One of the most amazing bottles of whiskey that we have ever had is the A.H. Hirsch Reserve 16; sadly this amazing stuff, which came from the now-defunct Michter's Distillery, is almost completely gone. Surely this bottle can stand up to some of the great single malts, even if the style is obviously different. As the supplies dwindle, the price of Hirsch Reserve 16 has approached $300, but it is worth noticing that the original release price was no more than Lagavulin 16 (about $80). There are other fantastic bourbons—many of which are made by small producers or in small quantities—that stand up to the best that Scotland has to offer. And this was another reason that we chose to use 'whiskey' rather than 'whisky': to celebrate some of the great whiskeys that are being made in the United States.

These previous comments are hardly meant to be irrelevant to some of the central philosophical issues that are engaged in this book, though we will lay out those issues more directly in the second half of this introduction. For now, though, let us identify two issues already broached. First, orthography is hardly trivial. How we spell 'whiskey' is emblematic of myriad historical, cultural, and, indeed, philosophical themes. Notions of identity, supremacy, and patriotism are all bound up in that simple 'e' that is either elided or included. Had American whiskey chosen an alternative convention, would it be able to rival Scotch for greatness or would it forever be subservient to it? What ultimately matters, of course, is what is in the glass, though the underlying connotations are significant.

And the rivalry between bourbon and Scotch—or at least the one that we hope to hype and promote—gives rise to deep philosophical issues about aesthetics, objectivity (or subjectivity) of taste, commensurability of values, and so on.[6] To wit: which is better, bourbon or Scotch? Are questions like this even coherent? Likely not, given the wide range of whiskey that either category has to offer. Go back to the comparison between Hirsch and Lagavulin; is this comparison any more tractable? It probably depends on whether you are sitting in Frankfort, Kentucky, or Islay, Scotland. Lagavulin begs for violent, stormy nights on Scottish Isles, whereas Hirsch could be perfect during a summer sunset in the American South. Hirsch is for weddings and Lagavulin is for divorces. Hirsch is as upbeat and happy as Lagavulin is dark and brooding. They are so different stylistically that all sorts of exigencies dictate which one is more appropriate for the occasion. But there are limits to this subjectivity as either of those wonderful bottles would always be welcome over lesser whiskeys.

But what if people simply disagree about whether something is any good, full stop? One of us was once drinking in Australia with a friend from St. Andrews, arguably the epicenter of single malt Scotch. The best bottle of bourbon available at this Melbourne bar was Woodford Reserve, which is hardly bad stuff. Nonetheless, the Scot, clearly well versed in whisky, alleged that "there's no future for this." The comparison between a $30 bottle of Woodford Reserve and various

$60 single malt Scotches is already unfair, but what of the blanket smugness and thinly veiled implication that Kentucky has nothing to offer? Surely this cannot be right, but what are two people who disagree so fundamentally about aesthetic value supposed to say to each other? A widely heralded Latin proverb says *de gustibus non est disputandum*, which colloquially means "there is no accounting for taste." Really? Don't we want to say that our dear friend from St. Andrews has it wrong? As surely he must. Great philosophers, though, from David Hume[7] to Immanuel Kant[8] have wrestled with this question, yet disagreement still abounds.

Sticking with bourbon and Scotch, it is worth emphasizing just how different these sorts of things are. Aside from both being whiskeys, they otherwise have fairly little in common. Bourbon, of course, has to be made from at least 51% corn (by weight, in the mash bill), though most bourbons are made of around 70%–75% corn. The remainder of this is rounded out by other small grains, principally rye, though wheat and barley are sometimes used as well. Bourbon has to be aged in charred new oak barrels, though the aging requirements widely reported are a mistake.[9] Compare these features to single malt Scotch, which is made from 100% malted barley and aged in reconditioned barrels, predominantly ones that had previously held bourbon. Tabling other differences in production—such as stills, water, and so on—it is not surprising that the finished products taste quite different.

In fact, these differences make it virtually impossible to confuse the two, unlike what once was the case with Old World and New World wines (i.e., wines from Europe and those from anywhere else). In a now-familiar story, one of the most important events in American wine took place at a tasting in 1976, when a California cabernet sauvignon and a California chardonnay outpointed some of the top red Bordeaux and white Burgundy, respectively.[10] At the time, Californian wines were nearly universally regarded as inferior to their French counterparts, and this tasting—which was presided over by French judges—was a catalyst for the Californian wine industry.

In the intervening decades, Californian wines have dramatically increased in stature, though many purists still favor the French. Is some similar recognition possible for bourbon? Probably not, and for the reasons discussed earlier: bourbon would never be confused with a single malt Scotch, and, therefore, tasters would easily be able to discriminate between them. Bourbon is too opulent, too sweet, too oaky, or so the critics would say. It lacks structure and finesse. And so on. Ironically, those are the same things that contemporary critics say about Californian wine, which has transformed stylistically since the 1976 tasting toward bigger, more fruit-forward styles. Part of this has to do with chasing the palates and scores of a few well-known wine writers; Bordeaux is probably even shifting toward California in this regard. The point, though, is that confrontations like this are only possible insofar as the products are similar; in wine, this was once possible and might eventually be again, but with whiskey it never would have been possible in the first place.

So, where does this leave us? In the first part of this introduction, we wanted to raise some general philosophical issues pertaining to whiskey, and we chose two that were related: how to spell 'whiskey' and how to think about comparisons of different whiskeys. There was an agenda in both of these discussions, which was to indicate an excitement about American whiskey, and to challenge some of the orthodoxy regarding the supremacy of Scotch. Undoubtedly this will be controversial in certain circles, though we encourage everyone to try some of the best that America has to offer. Much of the discussion thus far will be furthered by the essays in this book, though far more topics will also be broached. In the second half of the introduction, let us more specifically cover the contents of the book and its layout.

We have organized the book into five units: "The History and Culture of Whiskey"; "The Beauty and Experience of Whiskey"; "The Metaphysics and Epistemology of Whiskey";

"Ethics and Whiskey"; and "Whisky: A Sense of Place." The first unit is designed with two goals in mind: first, to provide a broad discussion of the historical background of whiskey through detailed accounts of its key figures and early producers; and second, to provide analysis of contemporary cultural issues relating to whiskey enjoyment. The next three units have been organized to cover the relationships among whiskey and many of the primary disciplines within philosophy. A few of the disciplines upon which these essays touch are aesthetics, philosophy of perception, philosophy of language, logic, metaphysics, epistemology, and ethics. Though the essays in these units argue for substantive (and in several cases quite original!) philosophical theses, these units have been designed to be accessible and engaging. The final unit has been organized around three key geographical regions, where many believe that the whisky produced is directly tied (or not in some cases) to the region in which it is produced. While we suggest reading the first and fifth units each as a cohesive unit, the essays in units two through four could be read independently since each essay in these units argues for a specific thesis. In the remainder of this introduction, we will provide a brief overview of each unit and the essays within each unit.

The first unit, "The History and Culture of Whiskey," covers a great deal of ground by providing interesting accounts of whiskey's origins and the culture surrounding whiskey enjoyment. Though few whiskey drinkers today would realize it, whiskey is quite unique as a distilled spirit; it has a much more detailed history than many other spirits such as rum or vodka. Not only does it have a rich history, but the production process is quite detailed and requires more care in the case of whiskey than in the case of other spirits. To begin the unit, Andrew Jefford, an accomplished whiskey and wine writer,[11] masterfully details whisky's origins by first considering what sort of product it is: is it agricultural or industrial? Next he discusses issues of geography, asking whether the place where a whiskey is produced leaves its mark, or *terroir*, on the resulting spirit. Jefford discusses many more topics relating to the origins of Scotch whisky and to its present form due to control by conglomerates; this essay makes not only a great start to the unit, but also to the volume as a whole.

The next essay, from Ian Buxton, attacks two ideas about whisky that permeate not only the marketing of whisky but also strongly influence how many people evaluate a particular whisky's quality and desirability: provenance and authenticity. By first detailing the background related to the rise of whisky brands around the turn of the twentieth century, Buxton shows how in most cases claims to a whisky's authenticity and references to a particular whisky's provenance serve as merely emotional appeals in a corporate marketing strategy. As Buxton argues, these references are often only thinly based in history. Given that it is nearly impossible to find a Scotch whisky brand (and most brands of other types of whiskey) that doesn't make reference to at least one of these concepts, Buxton's essay plays an important role in evaluating the claims companies make. The third essay, by David Wishart, highlights various key points along the development of whisky. Here Wishart underscores the variegated groups who have had control of Scotch production, from the Guild of Surgeon Barbers to Monks. His essay is a unique contribution because of his account of how the best whisky in the 1820s happened to be secretly produced contraband whisky (which eventually was legalized because King George liked it so much!).

Next, Ada Brunstein provides a penetrating analysis on the topic of women and their participation in whiskey production, and how more recently women have an increased market share in whiskey consumption. Brunstein's wit makes this essay quite enjoyable to read, but it also provides some novel ideas—especially her theory on why both women *and men* get past the "burn" and keep drinking whiskey after their first encounter with it. Wrapping up the first unit is Hans Allhoff's essay, which discusses two approaches to a classic whiskey cocktail: the Manhattan. Here, Allhoff compares approaches to the Manhattan to womanizers' approaches to women, using an account from Milan Kundera[12] as a springboard for his philosophical reflections. What follows is a lighthearted but substantive argument that also provides many useful notes on crafting an excellent Manhattan for one's own consumption.

In the second unit, "The Beauty and Experience of Whiskey," we start exploring topics within the traditional philosophical disciplines of aesthetics and philosophy of perception. The essays in this unit cohere around two central themes: first, what sort of experience it is to drink a whiskey; and second, what makes a particular whiskey a good one. These topics are fitting to consider whether one is an accomplished whiskey taster or a novice; after all, when we taste a whiskey aren't we often inclined to step away and consider both the experience of tasting it as well as the qualities that make it a good one? With these themes in mind, the unit begins with Robert Arp's essay on pleasure and whiskey enjoyment. Here Arp explores the hedonistic paradox in the context of whiskey drinking and living a wild lifestyle. Whiskey drinking is a great context to discuss the hedonistic paradox, which is when one seeks pleasure but ends up finding pain, because of the association people have of whiskey drinkers with wild living—especially those whiskey drinkers who, as Arp discusses, "gulp" their whiskey. To resolve the paradox for whiskey drinkers, Arp provides a solution from the philosopher John Stuart Mill, and in the end Arp inspires us all to be more reflective whiskey drinkers.

The second essay in this unit, by Mark Waymack—a philosopher who has written extensively on whiskey[13]—ventures into the philosophical discipline of applied aesthetics as he explores the topic of why we choose certain whiskeys over others. Waymack's account is derived from his response to a question he often hears when someone finds out he writes about whiskey: What is the *best* whiskey? Rather than presuming a *particular* whiskey to be best or that there is some

Platonic form of whiskey, in this essay, Waymack provides his answer to that question. His account first details a few of the three basic elements that allow us to enjoy a whiskey: first, we must be receptive to it both physically and psychologically; second, it must be well made; and third, we must prefer the taste profile. Next, Waymack tells how our choice of whiskey is related to the things we associate with it. Some of his own associations are his encounters with individuals in the whiskey industry such as Bill Samuels (president of Maker's Mark), Jimmy Russell (master distiller of Wild Turkey), and Jerry Dalton (master distiller of Jim Beam). Finally, Waymack argues that these associations influence our experience of whiskey, but this is not to say that we enjoy bad whiskey as a result; rather, his account shows that they can enhance the richness of our experience.

The next essay, from philosophers Douglas Burnham and Ole Martin Skilleås, continues with aesthetics as the language that professional whiskey tasters employ when appraising whiskeys is analyzed. Here, Burnham and Skilleås argue that such appraisals are *not* merely subjective, but that they have an intersubjective status. To defend this claim, they examine tasting language from two distinct schools: first, a descriptive school that employs terms like 'dried apples', 'butter', and 'toast'; and second, the evaluative school that makes use of terms like 'abrasive', 'weak', 'bold', and so on. Burnham and Skilleås conclude by arguing that both of these schools implicitly depend upon aesthetic judgments.

Next, Thom Brooks brings in the philosophy of nineteenth-century philosopher G. W. F. Hegel to help us judge among different varieties of Scotch (though his account is applicable to other types of whiskey), and especially to be able to do so when advice from whisky reviewers can be quite variegated. Here, Brooks makes use of what Hegel calls his "logic," a system designed to help us distinguish and order various features of things we are examining such as whisky. Brooks argues that the ideal, or best, Scotch is the one that possesses all the flavor notes he describes and one that does so in a particular order.

Brooks concludes the essay by discussing what he believes is an example of such an ideal whisky—the Macallan. His discussion from Hegel and detailed account of flavor notes is sure to enhance one's whisky experience as well as provide a unique system by which to evaluate the Scotch. In the final essay of this unit, philosopher Harvey Siegel provides a biographical account of his experiences with whiskey, especially detailing time he spent in Scotland as he discovered his love for Scotch. Here he recounts a memorable occasion when he stood at the intersection of two famous whiskey rivers: the Spey and the Fiddich. As he details this time, he recounts how his experience at this intersection can only be described as "spiritual."

The third unit, "The Metaphysics and Epistemology of Whiskey," deals with issues relating to two of the major disciplines within philosophy: metaphysics and epistemology. This unit, though accessible, contains some of the more esoteric essays in the volume. The first is by philosopher Tom Polger, who talks about an important topic in metaphysics: natural kinds. Here he considers whether whiskey—like gold, silver, cats, and dogs—is a natural kind. Another way of phrasing this question is whether whiskey "carves nature at its joints." Along the way, Polger considers whether various types of whiskeys might make good candidates for being natural kinds, focusing especially on bourbon. In the end, Polger concludes that considerations about whether whiskey is a natural kind have raised more questions than they have answered, but the essay is an enjoyable read that brings many issues from metaphysics to the forefront in discussing whiskey's place in the world. The next essay, by former Jim Beam master distiller Jerry Dalton, explores connections between whiskey tasting and the German physicist Werner Heisenberg's Uncertainty Principle. Like Waymack, Dalton recounts how he is often asked what the *best* whiskey is (specifically bourbon); however, unlike Waymack's account of his answer in terms of aesthetics, Dalton looks to physics and chemistry to investigate the relationship between the taster and the thing being tasted. What follows is an intriguing account on the uncertainties involved with tasting from a recognized bourbon expert.

The third essay in this unit, from philosopher Steven Geisz, explores how the Buddhist theory of no-self could impact one's decision to drink whiskey in the present, especially *how much* whiskey one should drink in the present. The primary question he considers with regard to the self is whether, if the Buddhist theory of no-self is correct—i.e., the view that there is no continually-existing self—we can drink all we want in the present and just let our future self worry about the consequences. After all, if there is no self that continues across time, the person who wakes up tomorrow will be a different person! Ian Dove's essay on informal logic wraps up the third unit, and here he provides a method for comparing tasting notes from experts. Throughout the essay, Dove provides side-by-side comparison of whiskey tasting notes from experts such as Michael Jackson and Jim Murray and discusses how one might evaluate differing opinions from such experts. Following these comparisons, Dove concludes with recommendations to the whiskey buyer who stands in the store wondering what to buy.

For the fourth unit, "Ethics and Whiskey," we explore how ethical considerations relate to whiskey. In the first essay, philosopher Richard Menary provides an account of what it means to be virtuous, something philosophers have discussed since the ancient Greeks. Here, Menary notes three types of virtue: the moral virtues, the intellectual virtues, and the aesthetic virtues. As Menary argues, the virtuous whiskey drinker exhibits all three. Menary's essay will help you think about ways both to live well and to drink well! The next essay, from philosopher Dave Monroe, explores a question about whiskey and ethics: Does whiskey make people immoral? This is an especially provocative question because of the manner in which whiskey drinkers are often portrayed in movies and novels such as the Clint Eastwood movie *Unforgiven*,[14] which Monroe discusses. To answer the question, Monroe ponders whether whiskey might have a special property that causes people to be immoral (what he calls the mean property thesis, or MPT), concluding that whiskey does not have such a special property but also arguing that we should work to dispel the myth that whiskey causes people to be immoral. The final essay in this unit is from Jason Kawall, a philosopher, who draws comparisons between arguments in environmental ethics about preserving species and arguments for preserving distilleries. Should we be concerned if a distillery like Port Ellen closes? Kawall's essay looks at distillery closings and argues that we should value distilleries. But what if whiskey produced elsewhere tastes the same? Should we then care if a particular distillery has closed? Yes, Kawall argues, and this is because our enjoyment of whiskey is enhanced through knowing about its history and origins—these are lost forever when a distillery shuts down.

The fifth unit, "Whisky: A Sense of Place," closes the volume by providing detailed discussions of three key whisky regions that have historically played a major role in the whisky industry: Islay, Japan, and Speyside. The first essay is from Kevin Sweeney, an aesthetician. In the essay, Sweeney weaves together two distinct elements: first, he provides philosophical discussion of an important issue relating to whether taste is cognitive, that is, whether we have control over our tastes; and second, he provides a biographical account, which also serves as an example in Sweeney's essay, of how he and his wife, Elizabeth, traveled to Islay to explore its whiskies and countryside. To tackle these twin objectives, Sweeney recounts how Elizabeth found Islay whiskies repulsive, so they decided to travel to Islay to see if she would come to like them. Sweeney argues that taste can be based on a cognitive attitude, and his wife, to some degree, is a case in point of this view: because of their time on Islay, her taste in whisky changed, even if "only modestly." For those who are well acquainted with the wonder of Islay whiskies, or for those who are novices, this essay provides an excellent overview of the enjoyment of Islay whiskies as well as a detailed discussion of what it means to acquire tastes.

The second essay, which is from Tokyo-based journalist Chris Bunting, surveys an area of the whisky market often unknown to whisky drinkers, Japan. As mentioned earlier, Japan has recently won numerous awards for producing excellent whisky in the Scotch style, but it still has limited international availability and exposure. Bunting's essay fills this lacuna by providing a detailed account of whisky's origin in Japan from its early days to its award-winning expressions today. Along the way, Bunting also provides an account of the Japanese whisky brands that have emerged by referencing the French philosopher and social critic Jean Baudrillard's work on the words we use to refer to products like whiskey. Bunting's essay is one of our favorites in the volume, and one that must be read by anyone unfamiliar with the story of whisky in Japan. The final essay in this unit, from Susie Pryor and Andrew Martin, examines two of the most renowned whisky regions in Scotland: Speyside and Islay. In their account of these regions and the whisky from them, Pryor and Martin argue that the enjoyment of whisky is influenced to a great degree by certain experiences that whisky companies promote, such as festivals and at distilleries, among others. Through personal interviews of individuals on Islay and on the Malt Whisky Trail in Speyside, Pryor and Martin illustrate how events such as these influence how people think and talk about whisky. Pryor and Martin help us consider the ways in which corporations (and their brands) influence how we perceive a product— our view of a particular whisky is not as simple as merely an interaction between us and a drink! Accordingly, their essay is an excellent close to the volume as they help us think about the influence of corporate branding strategies and the whiskies we love to drink.

Enjoy, and don't forget to drink good whiskey during your voyage! Especially if it's bourbon.

NOTES

The epigraph is taken from W. C. Fields and Richard J. Anobile, *Drat! Being the Encapsulated View of Life* (New York: World Publishing, 1968), p. 82.

1. Charles MacLean, *MacLean's Miscellany of Whisky* (London: Little Books, 2004), p. 12.
2. Ibid., p. 16.
3. George Dickel Tennessee Whisky, which dates to the late 1800s, is also an exception to the standard American spelling. Wasmund's Single Malt Whisky, made in Virginia, also uses the Scottish spelling, though for obvious stylistic affinities.
4. We will use 'whiskeys' as the plural of 'whiskey' and 'whiskies' as the plural of 'whisky'. Any unqualified use of 'whisky' will be a reference to Scotch whisky, and other uses will be qualified (e.g., 'Japanese whisky').
5. Eric Asimov, "Bourbon's Shot at the Big Time," *New York Times* (November 28, 2007).
6. For discussion of these issues in the whiskey context, see Jerry Dalton, "Heisenberg's Spirits: Tasting Is More Uncertain Than It Seems" (this volume), pp. 195–207. For closely related discussion pertaining to wine, see George Gale, "Who Cares If You Like It, This Is Good Wine Regardless" in *Wine & Philosophy: A Symposium on Thinking and Drinking*, ed. Fritz Allhoff (Oxford: Blackwell Publishing, 2007), pp. 172–185.
7. David Hume, "Of the Standard of Taste" in *Essays, Moral, Political and Literary*, ed. Eugene F. Miller (Indianapolis, IN: Liberty Classics, [1757] 1987).
8. Immanuel Kant, *Critique of Judgment*, trans. Werner S. Pluhar (Indianapolis, IN: Hackett Publishing, [1790] 1987).
9. See the "Standards of Identity for Distilled Spirits," http://edocket.access.gpo.gov/cfr_2002/aprqtr/pdf/27cfr5.21.pdf (accessed September 15, 2008). Incidentally, there are a lot of myths about bourbon: that it has to come from Bourbon County, Kentucky; that is has to be made with at least 51% corn and less than 80% corn (lest it be corn whiskey instead of bourbon); and that it must be aged a minimum of two years. The geographic requirement has largely been debunked though still persists at some levels. The aging requirement is for straight bourbon, not bourbon simpliciter; this former is, technically, a different category. The 80% corn limit simply doesn't exist, as the Standards of Identity indicate. Corn whiskey can't be aged in charred new oak barrels and that's what distinguishes it from bourbon, not the corn content. Or, to say

it another way, if bourbon had 80%-plus corn and was aged in charred new oak barrels, then it would still be bourbon; it just turns out that bourbon is traditionally made with less corn. This error regarding corn limit is still fairly common and is even made by such authorities as our illustrious foreword writer! See MacLean, *Miscellany of Whisky*, p. 32.

10. See, for example, Orley Ashenfelter, Richard E. Quandt, and George M. Taber, "Wine-Tasting Epiphany: An Analysis of the 1976 California vs. France Tasting" in Allhoff, *Wine & Philosophy*, pp. 237–247. See also George Taber, *Judgment of Paris: California vs. France and the Historic 1976 Paris Tasting That Revolutionized Wine* (New York: Scribner, 2005).

11. See, for example, Andrew Jefford, *Peat Smoke and Spirit: A Portrait of Islay and Its Whiskies* (London: Headline, 2004).

12. Milan Kundera, *The Unbearable Lightness of Being* (New York: Harper & Row, 1984).

13. See M. H. Waymack and J. F. Harris, *The Book of Classic American Whiskeys* (Chicago: Open Court Publishing, 1995).

14. *Unforgiven*. Dir. Clint Eastwood, Malpaso Productions, Los Angeles, 1992.

UNIT I

The History and Culture of Whiskey

I

Scotch Whisky
From Origins to Conglomerates

Andrew Jefford

When *Homo sapiens* was a primate of restricted distribution, members of the species sought, fought for, and found the food and drink they required to sustain their existence in the contingent natural world. The advent of agriculture, after 190,000 years of this 200,000-year story, marked the first human step back from these contingencies. Nourishment could be assured by use of the natural cycle; it was no longer exclusively nature's gift. A garden had been cut on nature's back. Human agricultural activity over the subsequent 10,000 years has been frenzied. It has been marked by successful domestications of wild species and by increasing sophistication in the preservation of foods.

Let us now briefly imagine a shopping basket of some daintiness. It contains one mackerel, one apple, and one can of cola. The mackerel is preagricultural. It has been snatched from marine autonomy. Its bright eye will quickly dim; its silver blue iridescence will fade and tarnish; it will soon stink, rot, and attract a different set of species from our own.

The apple—large, fleshy, and attractively pigmented—is classically agricultural. It is bred over decades, then carefully grown, harvested, stored, transported, and stickered with the name of its variety and country of origin. It is, as an object, still a gift of nature: it requires a particularly patterned growing season and will show seasonal variability, which, together with its precise origin, condition its finer qualities. It will quickly decay if not preserved by controlled atmosphere storage.

The can of cola is a postagricultural triumph. Its contents are a mixture of modified natural products (such as extract of spent coca leaf, extract of vanilla, extract of cinnamon, and caramel) and chemical products (such as caffeine and phosphoric acid). The drink on which it is modeled, Coca-Cola, is produced as a concentrate, then shipped to packagers for manufacture and sale in over two hundred countries. The Coca-Cola ideal is that the drink should be uniform, consistent, and stable wherever it is sold. Such an ideal is more industrial than agricultural. It will, admittedly, decay, but so do machines; the rate of decay, though, is far slower than for any equivalent freshly grown agricultural products whose nutritive function is mimicked by soft drinks, such as apples, plums or pears.

Dainty; yet this basket is a gauge of human development. Let us add a bottle of Scotch whisky. Where in this spectrum does it fall, and what are the implications of its nature on those who produce and consume it?

Whisky: Agricultural or Industrial?

The ingredients of Scotch malt whisky are simple: malted barley, water, and yeast. Scotch grain whisky extends the ingredient list, but not by much (wheat, corn). Blended whisky is a mixture of malt whisky and grain whisky. Plain caustic caramel (EU additive E150a) can be used to adjust the color of Scotch whisky.

The growing of barley is an agricultural activity. Yields vary by season and variety. The barley (and other grains) used to make Scotch whisky can be grown anywhere in the world. No variety is specified by law, but large distillers tend to use a very narrow range of specified varieties. Some claim that barley variety and origin is significant; others counter that provided a strain capable of giving the correct flavor profile and desirable alcoholic yield is used, the significance of exact variety and origin is sentimental.[1]

The brewing water used by some malt whisky distilleries could be described as agricultural in origin, in that it is "wild" loch water, burn water or spring water. Other distilleries use untreated municipal supplies.[2]

Yeast is a microorganism farmed and harvested by manufacturers with consistency as an avowed aim.

Whisky distillation takes two forms: single or continuous distillation (for grain whisky) and double distillation (for malt whisky). Both are closely monitored industrial processes whose aim is consistency in the quality of the "new make." The creation of flavor in these freshly distilled spirits remains, even today, imperfectly understood, but distillers assiduously duplicate the exact form and design of still components during maintenance programs at individual distilleries so as not to jeopardize this prized consistency.

The aging of whisky, by contrast, takes place in secondhand casks. These casks are often further reconditioned to extend their lives. No two casks, thus, are alike, and their effect on new-make spirit of consistent quality is to render it inconsistent. The removal of these inconsistencies is one reason that most whisky is blended. Even single malt whiskies are, when sold by the brand owner, blended to achieve a consistency that can be recognized and cherished by the consumer.[3]

It may be disagreeable to most whisky lovers, then, but it is hard to reach any conclusion other than that a modern bottle of whisky is, like a can of cola, a postagricultural triumph whose ideals are more industrial than agricultural. Its ingredients may be simpler and more uniformly agricultural in origin than those of cola, yet whisky aroma and flavor are overwhelmingly a consequence of the processing of those raw ingredients (malting, brewing, distillation, wood aging) rather than the ingredients themselves. Industrial consistency rather than the qualitative speckling more typical of agricultural products is the ideal in each of these four operations. The diversity offered to consumers in the range of Scotch on sale seems likely, thus, to be more directly a consequence of manufacturing techniques and brand-building endeavor than of earth, stone, and sky.[4]

Whisky and Origin: A Chimera?

There is no more contentious topic in the study of Scotch whisky than the extent to which origin may or may not affect whisky flavor. 'Origin', in this context, is roughly analogous to the concept of *terroir* ('placeness') in wine. It refers to any factor related to the origin of the ingredients from which a whisky is made, or to the natural conditions prevailing in the locations in which that whisky is made and aged, which leave a palpable sensory stamp on the finished spirit.

Scotch whisky must, by law, be distilled and aged in Scotland. Most would agree that Scotch has a recognizable aroma and flavor. Is that aroma and flavor related to the Scottishness of its origins or rather to the whisky-making recipes, equipment, and practices prevalent in Scotland? The question is hard to answer conclusively since no other whisky-producing country possesses identical equipment or follows identical practices. Where determined efforts have been made to mimic that equipment and those practices (as most famously in Japan), the results have been close enough, labels concealed, to leave tasters nonplussed as to which is which.[5] Japanese malt whiskies, indeed, have "outscored" Scotch malt whiskies.[6]

By contrast, few, if any, Scotch whiskies could be confused by even untrained palates with bourbon. Bourbon, though, is distilled principally from corn in column stills and aged in new and usually highly charred casks. These differences (especially the third, since the first two are shared by many grain whiskies) have dramatic flavor consequences. These differences, though, derive from practice rather than origin.

Aging whisky in the cool, moist, temperate climate of Scotland rather than in the much warmer and drier climate typical of bourbon-producing regions of the United States does indubitably have an effect on the flavor of the spirit. This effect can, in part, be calibrated by the fact that bourbon loses more volume than does Scotch during maturation, and that bourbon gains strength during maturation whereas Scotch loses strength during maturation.

The "Scottishness" of the average bottle of Scotch, thus, is based on a mixture of non-*terroir* factors (recipe, equipment and distilling and aging techniques) and one *terroir* factor (the climate in which the whisky ages).

Blended whisky dominates world sales of Scotch.[7] Blended whiskies mix grain whisky with malt whisky, habitually in a ratio of around 60:40. Distillers of grain whisky make no claims that the character of their product is affected by origin.

Distillers of malt whisky do make such claims. Blended whiskies, by contrast, are usually composed without any overt reference to their character deriving from the precise origins of their malt components.[8] The only origin claimed for most blends is Scottishness and, as suggested above, this is likely to be more a consequence of recipe, equipment, and process than origin, though both play a part.

How legitimate are the claims made that malt whisky reflects origin? The creation of flavor in finished bottled whisky is a hugely complex equation. Given that it is a complex matter, I hope that the following abbreviated summary of the industry consensus may be forgiven.

Differences in barley, yeast, and water are usually regarded as being of minor significance in flavor creation, with the exception of peating levels and the kilning of the malt itself, which are evidently major factors in flavor creation. Differences in brewing practices are regarded as being of minor significance. Differences in still shape, condenser design, and distillation practice are regarded as being of major significance. Differences in wood-aging regimes are regarded as being of major significance. The precise location within Scotland in which wood aging takes place is regarded as being of minor significance. The major flavor factors, thus, are the peating (or lack of it) of the malt, distillation itself, and wood aging.[9] None of these is affected by origin. Malt peating levels are a recipe decision; distilling is an industrial technique of considerable refinement; and wood aging is a question of stock management with flavor implications. Origin could only play a role via the precise source and variety of the barley, the water supply, or the atmospheric conditions in which the whisky passes its aging period. The industry consensus is that these are relatively unimportant matters—though those who disagree with this consensus do so energetically.[10] If the consensus is correct, the impact of origin in the creation of malt whisky flavor is, indeed, largely chimerical.

The Whisky Distillery and Its Customers

The distillation of Scotch whisky first flourished on farms and was practiced by farmers as a way of using and preserving surplus grain at quiet moments in the farming cycle.[11] What sort of an entity is a distillery today?

Recently there has been a small renaissance in farm distilling,[12] but most grain and malt whisky distilleries have no farming dimension whatsoever. Widespread farm distilling drew to a close when it was rendered illicit by licensing legislation; this favored larger production units.[13] The invention of the continuous still and the commercial innovation of blended whisky that followed hastened this process.[14] Distilleries, today, are factories for turning cereal grains into potable spirit, albeit factories often located in picturesque locations. Raw materials are delivered, transformed on site, and dispatched for aging or bottling elsewhere. The prime concern of most distillery managers is efficiency in producing a consistent product to an agreed specification. Innovation (other than maximizing efficiency) does not figure in their job description.

Given that 89 percent of all Scotch is sold in blended form, custom for the vast majority of Scotch whisky distilleries, malt distilleries included, comes from large whisky blenders. Even comparatively well-known distilleries producing spirit of recognized high quality sell a tiny proportion of their production to the public in bottled form under the distillery name.[15] The product known by most consumers as "Scotch" is finished by the blending process. Whisky distilleries, therefore, are factories producing large quantities of a semifinished, unpackaged product largely sold to other commercial clients.[16]

Whisky and Time: The Sleeping Cask

Scotch whisky has a fourth ingredient in addition to grain, water, and yeast: time. It comes into being only after three years' cask aging. (Prior to that, it is "Plain British spirit.") Most standard blends have an average age of about five to nine years. Most malts are sold between their tenth and twentieth birthdays. The average length of time stocks are held before sales within the industry as a whole is six years. In 2007, 1,135 million bottles of Scotch were exported, and a further 102 million bottles were consumed in the United Kingdom; much of this total would have been distilled prior to 2002, and been sitting in the cool darkness of a cask in a Scottish warehouse ever since. Total whisky production for 2008 is estimated to be around 443 million liters of pure alcohol.[17] UK Customs & Excise does not publish stock figures, but the overall stock of Scotch is thought to be well over 3,000 million liters of pure alcohol. Financing these colossal stocks requires major capital investment. The necessity of aging whisky before selling it means that the return on capital for those producing whisky is slow. It is, as a consequence, hard for smaller entities to compete with larger ones in the distilling and aging of Scotch.[18]

Selling Whisky: The Inescapable Brand

Almost all Scotch whisky is sold under a brand name. Brands provide the mental map that enables consumers to make choices among different whiskies. Brands promise universal consistency and reliability. In this, they are predicated on an industrial ideal rather than the agricultural ideal of winning provisional and temporary excellence from the variability and contingency offered by nature.

Within a free market, the chief means of bypassing the power of the brand is by offering generic products of one sort or another to the consumer. Supermarket label products purport to do this, though it could be argued that they are in fact products carrying the supermarket's own brand. Drugs are sometimes made available to the impoverished needy on a generic rather than brand name basis. And wine, too, is widely sold by type rather than by brand via the use of appellations. Appellations are not brands; they are, rather, guarantees of origin (and sometimes of more than that: alcoholic strength, varietal composition, and production practices, for example). Although they are not brands, appellations function as brands for the brandless. Small producers with no market presence or reputation and no possibility of creating either are nonetheless able to render their products intelligible and desirable to consumers by the use of an appellation. The wines of a competent but not outstanding wine grower with four hectares (approximately 9.88 acres) of vineyard in Sancerre will never acquire notoriety in New York. But, sold as Sancerre, his wines will find a ready market among New York's fish lovers.

Appellations do not yet exist for Scotch whisky, though five "regional names"—Highland, Lowland, Speyside, Campbeltown, and Islay—are due to receive legal definition in a forthcoming revision of Scotch Whisky Regulations, expected to be on the statute book in early 2009.[19]

Appellations would have little to offer the creators of blended whisky, which as we have seen accounts for nine out of every ten bottles sold worldwide, since blends mingle grain whisky with a wide spectrum of malt whiskies.

If, as suggested above, the impact of origin in the creation of malt whisky flavor is largely chimerical, appellations would have little to offer malt whisky either. The whiskies of Islay come closer than most to incarnating an origin-derived generic ideal susceptible to purchase by appellation rather than brand. Yet, even on Islay, brands are dominant because there are stark flavor differences among Islay whiskies, and because those differences are derived from recipes and production decisions rather than the nuances of origin.[20]

Malt whiskies are origin-coded brands, whereas blended whiskies are fantasy brands of occasional historical pedigree. Whisky producers prefer the freedom of brands predicated on blends to those which commit them to a single distillery of origin for obvious reasons: the size of distilleries is finite, whereas blended brands can continue to expand almost indefinitely to soak up market need. For example, in December 2003, Diageo redefined its Cardhu brand from being a single malt made at the Cardhu distillery to being a vatted (blended) malt "inspired" by the character of Cardhu. (Cardhu is a core malt for the world's most successful blended whisky brand, the Johnnie Walker family. It was also hugely successful as a single malt on the Spanish market.) To Diageo's surprise and discomfiture, the move was widely criticized, underlining at least a sentimental attachment to the notion of origin for malt brands. Sales of Cardhu fell, and the move was reversed in 2006.

The whisky world has many brands but relatively few powerful brands. Those powerful brands are, at present, growing still more dominant at the expense of smaller rivals. Audited, or "official," figures are unobtainable, but the leading industry source estimated that for 2004, the Famous Grouse Finest had 3.4 percent of the total whisky market; 100 Pipers, 3.42 percent; Chivas Regal brands, 3.92 percent; Dewar's White Label, 4.92 percent; Grant's, 5.17 percent; Ballantine's brands, 7.02 percent; J&B, 7.48 percent; and the dominant Johnnie Walker brands, 21.49 percent of the market.[21] Since 2004, Johnnie Walker's global sales have grown further—by over three million cases.[22]

Whisky and Difference:
The Comfort of Consistency

The play of brands, large and small, within the worlds of malt and blended whisky purport to offer the consumer a wide spectrum of aroma and flavor differences. Do they deliver this?

The uniformity of ingredients and processing techniques used to make Scotch whisky gives the drink a much narrower organoleptic spectrum than, say, French wine or Belgian beer. Nonetheless, for the tiny percentage of consumers purchasing single-cask bottlings of malt whisky, those aroma and flavor differences are real. The provocatively elaborate tasting notes of the Scotch Malt Whisky Society, for example, are not fiction. The sensorial wonderland of allusions they promise can be discerned by attentive and enthusiastic tasters.

Distillery bottlings of malt whisky, too, offer aroma and flavor differences to consumers, though perhaps fewer than the plethora of malt brands would suggest. The ingredients used to make malt whisky are almost shockingly uniform (two yeast suppliers' strains dominate the industry, as does unpeated malted barley in which variety plays no discernable organoleptic role). The now-dominant use of secondhand ex-bourbon white American oak casks in preference to the much more expensive ex-sherry European oak casks has added a further note of homogeneity. The differences in packaging between two single Speyside malts of middling reputation are often starker than the differences in their contents. The recent popularity of finishes for malt whiskies (a final aging period in intensely flavor-bearing casks to add an overt aroma or flavor note to the malt) is indicative of an often-frustrated thirst for character among malt-whisky drinkers.

Finally, the aroma and flavor differences among similarly priced blended whiskies are, frankly, slight, despite the claims of those advertising them, selling them, and, sometimes, writing about them. I have passed a disconcerting percentage of the last two decades tasting beer, wine, and spirits and describing the sensorial differences among them, and there is no more challenging tasting than a blind comparison of leading brands of blended whisky. Quality is good and the products are satisfactorily constructed and nuanced, but the differences among them are feathery emphases rather than the forceful and often dramatic contrasts encountered in similar wine or beer tastings. The loyal consumers of blended Scotch whisky are evidently comforted by consistency.

Buying Whisky: The Flight from Complication

Some 90 percent of Scotch whisky is exported from its country of origin, and 89 percent of that total is blended whisky sold by brand name. For most global whisky drinkers, Scotch is an aspirational intoxicant. The circumstances of its production are ill understood (most brandy consumers know that they are drinking distilled wine, whereas few whisky consumers realize they are drinking distilled beer). Even its unadulterated taste, I would suggest, is often ill liked, making it the most paradoxical of commercial successes; this explains the fact that it is customarily drunk as a mixed drink. I have drunk Johnnie Walker Black Label, perhaps the greatest of all blended whiskies, mixed with cold green tea poured from a waxed paper carton in a Hangzhou nightclub. This was an act of great generosity on the part of my host, a tea merchant with a sensitive palate; few drinks on offer were more expensive, and an entire bottle was purchased for our small party. Cold green tea was the standard mixer for the club's whisky-drinking clientele; elsewhere it would have been cola, ginger ale, lemonade . . . The whisky on its own was considered undrinkable, though the luster of its name shone brightly through the smoky nightclub gloom, and its effect brought those drinking it into a temporary communion.

Under these circumstances, complications of offer are, for the majority of whisky purchasers, profoundly undesirable. Aspirational products perform best when there is a comprehensibly limited range of brand names to aspire to. Labels and bottle shapes need to be recognized from afar within the nightclub shadows. Flavor is a tightrope: you need enough to satisfy the minority who genuinely enjoy the product itself, but not so much as to deter the majority who don't. Malt whisky may eventually replace blended whisky in the affections of the global whisky-drinking public, but if so, it will be in spite of rather than because of its complications.

The Necessity of the Conglomerate

Let us resume our discoveries. Whisky is a predominantly industrial product, most of which is sold in blended form that effaces its origins and inconsistencies. Distillery customers are overwhelmingly fellow distillers and blenders acquiring large volumes for blending purposes. The whisky business, because of its time lines, is capital intensive. The "difference" purchased by customers when they choose one whisky rather than another is chiefly external and superficial, rather than internal and profound. The blended whisky market is an international one dominated by a few brands, and the notion of the brand is cherished and valued more highly by producers than any notion of the origin of its component parts. Most consumers of whisky need simple choices and do not want distinctive or challenging flavors.

These six factors create a commercial climate conducive to participation by conglomerates (defined as large commercial entities with a substantial capital base, undertaking a range of diversified activities in a wide number of countries and continents). The subsidiary divisions of such entities (production, aging, blending, distribution, and sales and marketing) can mesh and interlink their activities on whisky's global market, achieving economies of scale as they do so. Further synergies accrue when these whisky-making and whisky-marketing activities are linked to other activities undertaken by the conglomerate elsewhere in the drinks business, or in the luxury goods business more generally. Only conglomerates, it could be argued, have the financial power and the distributive muscle to create, support, maintain, and sustain global blended whisky brands.

This does not mean that smaller entities have no role to play in the whisky market.[23] Smaller companies are highly effective service providers to conglomerates. Blended whisky has some niche markets accessible to smaller players (such as Compass Box), though not many. Small and medium-size companies with a long-term whisky pedigree and a predator-resistant ownership structure have survived in unconglomerated form thus far, and they may continue to do so. (William Grant and the Edrington Group are the two major examples.) It is, though, malt whisky above all that offers the potential for the nonconglomerate to perform and prosper. This is because the malt whisky offer is one in which there is room for complication rather than simplicity, where intense and characterful flavors are seen as an attractive trait by a minority of consumers, and where origin and difference is prized and valued. Strong malt whisky brands, indeed, can help carry the blended whisky brands of unconglomerated companies via existing international distribution arrangements. It should be noted, though, that despite its internal vivacity, the malt whisky market occupies a mere 9 percent of the total whisky market. Most malt whisky distilleries, too, are owned and run by conglomerates (often highly effectively) because the destiny of their whiskies is overwhelmingly the blending vat. These are the reasons that Scotch whisky is conglomerate dominated and will remain so.

Conglomerate for Good or Ill

Let us now contrast the actions and status of conglomerates with those of smaller companies. It may be inevitable that Scotch whisky is at present conglomerate dominated, but is it desirable?

The Scotch whisky market is healthy. Between 2006 and 2007, for example, the volume of Scotch exported grew by 8 percent and the value grew by 14 percent, attaining all-time record figures in both cases.[24] For the first time since the early 1970s, new distilleries are being built (e.g., Diageo's colossal Roseile and William Grant's Ailsa Bay) and derelict or "mothballed" distilleries are being restored (such as the long-silent Annandale Distillery in Dumfries and Galloway, as well as the Speyside pair of Tamnavulin and Glenglassaugh). Despite repeated overstocks within the industry and financial recessions outside it, world consumption of whisky has risen steadily over the past three decades.[25] This may be an inevitable concomitant of global economic growth, but at the very least it seems fair to say that the conglomerates involved in Scotch whisky have not acted as a check on the industry's development. Most believe, indeed, that they may be credited with both steering and satisfying the global demand for Scotch whisky astutely. The fact that the value of exports is increasing disproportionately to volume suggests, too, that the conglomerates are drawing drinkers into consuming better-quality whisky rather than simply consuming more whisky of indifferent quality: morally a sound strategy, and commercially a sane one.

Conglomerates are financially secure. Their ownership structures, names, and addresses may change and modulate, but as features of the commercial landscape, they are enduring.

This is politically, socially, and economically desirable. (Scotch whisky accounts for two-thirds of Scotland's food and drink exports, employs forty thousand people directly or indirectly, and invests £700 million (approximately $1 billion US) with Scottish suppliers of goods and services every year.)[26]

The marketing and distributional strength of the conglomerates involved in Scotch whisky is much admired and provides a model for the spirits business more generally. Conglomerates commit major financial resources to whisky marketing, a gesture from which the entire sector benefits. In general, the all-important heritage and image repertoire of Scotch whisky is well respected by its leading conglomerates. Scotch still appears Scottish, even when (as in Johnnie Walker's case) the ideas are created in Amsterdam, and that very broad sense of origin is strongly attractive to consumers.

The distilling and aging standards of conglomerates are high, though these are at all times industrial rather than artisanal in intent, and are designed to help create the ideal of consistency on which blends are founded.

Conglomerates, by contrast, are often poor stewards of the weaker distilleries and brands in their care. A structural flaw in any industry dominated by large players is that those players will sensibly want to put most of their energies into a relatively small number of products or brands rather than dissipate their energies over a large number of products or brands that may compete with others in the same stable. The historical outcome of this is that great malt whisky distilleries have been lost forever (St. Magdalene, Port Ellen) and others seem unlikely ever to return (Rosebank, Glenury Royal).[27] Once powerful and much-loved brands can have their destiny changed during a single strategy meeting and become inaccessible to loyal consumers overnight (the Antiquary, Haig, or Vat 69, to name just three); others are reformulated or disappear entirely.[28]

Conglomerates tend to vaunt origin when it suits their marketing strategy, but they tend to ignore it when it doesn't (as in the case of Cardhu, cited earlier). Origin, in any case, is loosely defined by conglomerates. What little Caol Ila (pronounced *cool I-la*) is sold as a single malt is emphatically marketed as an Islay whisky by Diageo, despite the fact that it leaves the island by tanker two weeks after distillation and passes the rest of its many years of prebottling life in warehouses in central Scotland. Conglomerates, moreover, are deeply conservative in terms of innovation and experiment in brewing, distilling, and aging techniques. Most distilleries are run along the strictly uncreative lines established by precedent. The only welcome innovations are those that might reasonably result in lowered costs or increased productivity. If Scotch whisky can seem overly staid and industrial to those, for example, nourished on the structural creativity of the wine business, conglomerates must take much of the blame for this.

Smaller, nonconglomerate entities have, of course, also played a key role in the present health of the Scotch whisky industry, though their importance as stakeholders has diminished in recent years. They are less financially secure than conglomerates; indeed the rise to prominence of the conglomerates has in part been built on the financial fallibilities of smaller rivals. Paradoxically, when smaller rivals are successful, their rising value also renders them vulnerable to acquisition by conglomerates, as Glenmorangie's acquisition by LVMH (Louis Vuitton Moët Hennessy) shows. In the blended whisky market, many smaller companies feel that the only commercial strategy left to them is to compete on price; such is the marketing and distributive power of conglomerates.

Much of the creativity in the malt whisky area, by contrast, has been driven by medium-size or smaller companies such as Glenfiddich, Glenfarclas, and Bruichladdich (pronounced *brook LAH-dee*), or like Glenmorangie prior to its takeover, as well as by independent merchants and bottlers. Indeed, the pioneering of single malt as a category was initiated in modern times by independents (Glenfiddich from 1963 and the Macallan from 1973). The conglomerates had to respond, though they would perhaps have been happy to sell blends alone had competition not forced them to review this policy. Origin is taken with unrivaled and thoroughgoing seriousness only by small, independent distillery owners (Bruichladdich, Springbank, and Edradour are the only three malt distilleries to dispatch finished product from the distillery door). The radically innovative raw material and distilling experiments undertaken in recent years by Bruichladdich are unique.

The good of conglomerates, in sum, is that Scotch whisky is in a healthy state and is a desired product in almost every market in the world that welcomes alcoholic drinks (as well as some that don't). The ill of conglomerates is that Scotch whisky is a less innovative and diverse product than it might be, and that the fugitive and easily bruised notion of authenticity and origin in Scotch whisky has been further eroded as the conglomerates have risen to their present position of dominance. The global nature of the Scotch whisky market and the fact that blends have driven this global expansion mean that domination by conglomerates is inevitable. The stimulus and input of smaller, nonconglomerate companies within the whisky industry, though, provide the oxygen that nourishes the Scotch flame.

NOTES

1. On this Mark Reynier of Bruichladdich Distillery (Islay) notes, "We have 100 percent of our barley direct from specific fields and farms. Fifty percent is organically grown. Each batch is harvested, malted, milled, fermented, distilled and matured in total isolation. By nose alone, at zero age, a layman can distinguish between variety, terroir and harvest" (Mark Reynier, personal communication). Contrast this with the view of Douglas Murray, process technology manager, Diageo, Alloa: "There are thousands of barley varieties globally, and we know that they either have very poor yields or give flavors we do not want and are therefore not considered for use in the Scotch whisky industry. The chemical makeup and therefore yield and flavor of the varieties we do use are similar: that's why we use them" (Douglas Murray, personal communication). Barley variety and origin are almost never mentioned on whisky packaging.
2. Oban is one malt distillery example; all grain distilleries use municipal supplies.

3. Some malt whisky distilleries do not relish this use of the word 'blend'. As Robert Ransom of Glenfarclas notes, "Blend is a misleading term because it has different, yet similar, meanings in different contexts. . . . We prefer to say we 'marry' or 'vat' casks together to produce an expression of Glenfarclas, rather than blend casks together" (Robert Ransom, personal communication).

4. David Williamson, public affairs manager for the Scotch Whisky Association (SWA), dissents from this view: "Industrial or agricultural? We would suggest agricultural. It is important to remember that the Scotch Whisky Act and Order require that the finished spirit has the 'aroma and taste derived from the raw materials used in . . . its production'" (David Williamson, personal communication).

5. Michael Jackson et al., *Whisky* (London: Dorling Kindersley, 2005), pp. 248–249.

6. Ibid., p. 250.

7. Global volume sales in 2007 were 89 percent blended whisky compared to 9 percent malt whisky and 2 percent grain whisky, according to the SWA.

8. Even where blends do make such claims, they are usually expressed in terms of no more than an inspirational keynote. Black Bottle is said to include every Islay malt—but much else besides.

9. I would suggest that apportioning the following percentages as a theoretical formula for the creation of flavor in malt whisky is roughly representative of the industry consensus:

Barley variety (assuming appropriate)	1%
Barley origin	3%
Malting (especially peated or not)	26%
Yeast type	2%
Water source	3%
Fermentation specifics	10%
Distilling specifics	26%
Type and quality of wood for aging	26%
Precise location of aging within Scotland	3%

10. See, for example, Charles MacLean, *Malt Whisky* (London: Mitchell Beazley, 1997), pp. 36–37 (water); pp. 38–39 (barley); and p. 60 (atmospheric conditions).

11. Charles MacLean, *Scotch Whisky: A Liquid History* (London: Cassell, 2003), pp. 23–32.

12. Notably at Kilchoman on Islay and at Daftmill in Fife.

13. Michael S. Moss and John R. Hume, *The Making of Scotch Whisky* (Edinburgh: Canongate, 2000), pp. 56–58 and p. 78ff.

14. Ibid., pp. 82–85 and p. 108ff.

15. For example, Glenrothes, a well-known Speyside malt considered to be a "top dressing" by blenders, sells just 2 percent of its annual production of five million liters of pure alcohol as a named malt whisky of single origin.

16. The concept of finishing is a slippery one. "If matured on site," says Robert Ransom of Glenfarclas, "the distillery does produce a finished but unpackaged product . . . as an ingredient for another product" (Robert Ransom, personal communication).

17. Alan D. Gray, *The Scotch Whisky Industry Review 2006* (Edinburgh and London: Charles Stanley Sutherlands, 2006), p. 70.

18. Though it is not impossible, especially when (as in 2008) world demand for Scotch is rising strongly. "Laying down stock," says Mark Reynier of Bruichladdich, "is capital intensive. But it is also an appreciating asset." Reynier also claims that historic overstocks have produced tired, over-aged whisky, and that high-quality distilling and the use of outstanding casks mean that even malt whisky can be ready sooner than the customary age statements of malt would suggest. "We have released 5- and 6-year-old whisky which has won tastings and approval ahead of much older spirits—even 30- and 35-year-old whiskies [which are] often overly woody, imbalanced and lacking vigour" (Mark Reynier, personal communication).

19. These regional names, it should be noted, will refer only to the place of distillation (a mere week or two in the life of the whisky) and do not include any requirement for the spirit to be stored in those same places (a period lasting between three and thirty or more years).

20. Two-fifths of Islay single malt is unpeated, for example, and three-fifths peated.

21. Gray, *The Scotch Whisky Industry Review 2006*, pp. 196–203.

22. Andrew Jefford, "Which Whisky to Drink on Burns Night," *Financial Times* (January 19, 2008). Global sales of Johnnie Walker in the year to June 2006 were 15.4 million cases.

23. David Williamson of SWA notes, "The diversity of the industry remains one of its defining characteristics and one of its great strengths" (David Williamson, personal communication).

24. Scotch Whisky Association news release, April 30, 2008.

25. Gray, *The Scotch Whisky Industry Review 2006*, p. 25.

26. Scotch Whisky Association, news release, June 19, 2008.

27. Brian Townsend, *Scotch Missed: The Lost Distilleries of Scotland* (Glasgow: Angels' Share, 2000), p. 84ff, p. 113ff, p. 116ff, and p. 176ff.

28. Charles MacLean, *Scotch Whisky* (London: Mitchell Beazley, rev. ed. 1998), p. 116ff.

2

Provenance and Authenticity
The Dual Myths of Scotch

Ian Buxton

Claims of provenance and authenticity have a long record in the marketing and thus, presumably, the consumption of Scotch whisky. Much play is made of the first written reference to Scotch whisky (1494)[1], and as early as 1897, Dewar's claimed its blends to be "The Whisky of his Forefathers" as a series of ancestral portraits came alive and reached out for the glass and bottle of a magnificently attired Scots gentleman. Yet this is arguably a modern industry not recognizable until the development of blending in the 1860s or even, it might reasonably be maintained, only following the industry's restructuring with the growth of the Distillers Company Limited (DCL) in response to the recessionary conditions of the early 1900s.

Today, though more than 90 percent of global Scotch whisky sales remain in blended whisky, a disproportionate amount of the industry's marketing effort and informed consumer attention is focused on single malt, which, through its emphasis on *provenance*, is seen as more *authentic*. These, it would seem, are the concerns of the twenty-first-century connoisseur consumer. In the race for the consumers' cash, appeals in this emotionally charged arena can be quite blatant. Indeed, one independent bottler of note, Douglas Laing & Co. of Glasgow, actually has a range of whiskies known as Provenance; Speyside's BenRiach proudly labels its 21-year-old single malt "Authenticus"; the Islay distillery of Ardbeg once released a limited edition bottling subtitled "Provenance" and another third party bottler, Cadenhead, offers an "Authentic Collection."

But such terms are loaded with emotion and value judgments. What does 'provenance' mean in a world of shifting corporate allegiances and ownership, and what price 'authenticity' in the light of constant evolution in distilling practice? Does *terroir* play any part in the production of whisky? Can the products of a single distillery in long-term family ownership be meaningfully distinguished from those of a conglomerate concerned with issues of portfolio management and constantly aware of shareholder pressure? How far have we moved since the "What is Whisky?" debate of 1906, and the subsequent Royal Commission? Will the new labeling regulations for Scotch whisky inform or further confuse a consumer unsure about what is meant by "blended malt"? To what extent does Scotch owe its success to the Irish rejection of blending—and should Irish whiskey (the pot still variety, at least) thus be considered the keeper of the true flame?

By examining the use of provenance and authenticity in the marketing of Scotch whisky I aim to show that these concepts have been pressed into commercial service with greater regard for their emotional appeal than strict historical accuracy, and demonstrate that, far from representing nongradational absolutes, such constructs are relative and, in many cases, rely upon interpretation and the engagement of the audience.

But first, a brief and necessarily truncated history lesson is indicated.

A Brief History

While a product resembling whisky was made in 1494 by the immortal Friar John Cor, and surely was known and enjoyed long prior to that, the Scotch whisky industry remained a parochial and fragmented one for a further three centuries. Single malt whiskies in the sense that today we understand the term were essentially the preserve of the Scots themselves and English interest (as, for example, in the exhaustive Parliamentary Commission into the distilleries in Scotland of 1798–1799) was largely concerned either with the complete suppression of distilling or, having recognized the total impracticality of such a step, "the best Mode of levying and collecting the Duties upon the Distillation of Corn Spirits in Scotland."[2]

Less than twenty-five years later, attitudes had changed. The 1822 Illicit Distillation (Scotland) Act greatly raised the penalties for illicit distilling, smuggling, or even knowingly sanctioning the same and reduced the powers of the justices of the peace.[3] But by deliberate contrast, the Excise Act of 1823 aimed to encourage the legal industry, and it was hoped that many more distilleries would be opened to trade legitimately. At first, this was vigorously resisted, especially in the Highlands of Scotland: George Smith of the Glenlivet (a location to which we will return), famously the first distillery to be licensed under the 1823 Excise Act, wrote later that he regularly carried a pair of pistols against the threat of his neighbors to "burn my new distillery to the ground, and me in the heart of it."[4]

Shortly after this, Robert Stein patented the first continuous still (itself a development of the rapidly worked shallow pot stills used by Lowland distillers such as Stein and his contemporary James Haig) and this was soon developed by Aeneas Coffey, who patented his design in 1830.

The potential of blending whisky seems first to have been fully understood by Andrew Usher, who since 1853 had sold a blended malt whisky as Usher's Old Vatted Glenlivet.

(Supporters of the currently controversial proposal promoted by the Scotch Whisky Association to create in European law a category of "blended malt" might pause to consider the claims of precedent thus established for the rival term 'vatted'.) Soon he saw the opportunity to create a more consistent and repeatable product, combining the fuller-flavored Highland malts with lighter and more economically produced grain whisky from the continuous still.

However, it took further legislation, this time the Spirits Act of 1860, to release the spirit of Victorian entrepreneurialism and create the great "whisky barons." The act allowed whiskies to be vatted before the payment of excise duty, giving freedom to experiment with more limited capital and, fortuitously, promoting the practice of aging the resultant blend with a consequent benefit to the flavor.

Several influences then came to bear, permitting Scotch to move onto a worldwide stage. Early mass tourism and the romanticized Victorian view of Scotland, pioneered by Queen Victoria and her consort Prince Albert, made Scotland (or "North Britain," as it was widely known) fashionable with the English. The development of the British Empire under Victoria, often led by Scottish regiments and followed shortly by bureaucrats and merchants, promoted the global availability of Scotch whisky, and the collapse of the French cognac industry due to the attack of the phylloxera aphid[5] created a gap in the market that was quickly exploited by a number of innovative and energetic entrepreneurial whisky blenders—Usher, Alexander Walker, John and Tommy Dewar, and James Buchanan (a group of whom the playwright Sir James Barrie memorably remarked, "There are few more impressive sights in the world than a Scotsman on the make"). Significantly, these pioneers were initially *blenders,* not distillers, though they soon moved to ensure the vertical integration of their rapidly growing businesses by acquiring the means of production.

Grain whisky, or "silent spirit" as it was known, was not universally welcomed. The great Dublin distilling firms campaigned energetically against it, to the delight of the Scotch blenders, one imagines. But even in North Britain, opinion was divided. The North of Scotland Malt Distillers Association fought a long and determined action against the incursion of grain, and Sir Walter Gilbey, proprietor of Glen Spey, Strathmill, and Knockando distilleries railed against it in a pamphlet[6] as "nearly free from taste and smell." The scandalous exposure of the fraudulent blending practices of the Pattison brothers further complicated matters.

The argument was settled, at least in a legal sense, by the 1908–1909 Royal Commission on Whiskey. In a landmark decision, it resolved that both grain and single malt spirits could be sold as whisky, clearing the way for the development of the modern industry.

Global Brands Emerge

By the early 1900s we see the emergence of the first global brands, most notably Johnnie Walker and Dewar's. And make no mistake, these were *brands*—with all the marketing paraphernalia and the same tightly focused control of their image that today characterizes the promotion of Coca-Cola, McDonald's, and, of course, Johnnie Walker, Dewar's, and a host of others.

As often as not that image was based on a fictionalized and highly romanticized view of Scotland. Promotional material from the Victorian and Edwardian eras generally features either the military, the upper classes, or, best and most potent of all, a selection of Scots worthies, resplendent in full Highland dress and possessed of magnificent facial hair! For decades afterward, Scotch whisky wrapped itself in tartan, confident of the uniquely persuasive appeal of the land of lochs, hills, and glens—an explicit use of provenance, in fact. Indeed, some industry leaders now blame the emphasis on "tartan and bagpipes marketing" for the slowdown of Scotch whisky sales in the 1990s.

Speaking in January 2008, Diageo CEO Paul Walsh said:

> I think the reason that Scotch languished as it did in the
> 1990s was that as marketeers we relied too much on
> the wonders of the product, and we communicated those
> wonders through—forgive me—bagpipes, heather, and
> tartan. Those are very important and relevant qualities,
> but in today's world they are not enough to position the
> product to a new age consumer. There comes a point that
> you are such a believer that you end up talking to your-
> self rather than ending up talking to a wider audience.[7]

But, in recommending what he termed "lifestyle-oriented"
marketing, Walsh was explicitly discussing long-standing
Diageo brands such as Johnnie Walker, J&B, and Bell's—
blended whiskies all. At Diageo's rivals, Chivas Brothers
(part of the French-owned Pernod Ricard conglomerate)
and Dewar's (now controlled by global giant Bacardi), the
approach is much the same. In promoting Chivas Regal,
the emphasis is on "living the Chivas Life" and experiencing,
albeit vicariously, a glamorous round of jet-setting, parties, and
ceaseless travel. Bright young people (they are relentlessly
and inevitably young) are seen on fabulous yachts, in fashionable clubs, and in exotic locations, enjoying Chivas Regal
with tartan, kilts, and bagpipes nowhere to be seen. This is
lifestyle marketing of blended whisky taken to the ultimate.

Dewar's is curiously schizophrenic: a high-tech Web site and
the trendy pop-up venue marketing of the Dewar's Academy
combines deliberately retro typography with images of today's
beautiful young people; radical cocktails with carefully edited
glimpses into the Dewar family heritage; and consciously funky
bar furniture with electronically generated room sets based
on a pastiche of Tommy Dewar's late Victorian "library" in
Dewar House, London—itself drawn, not from the original,
but from a faux-authentic room set in the brand heritage center at the Aberfeldy distillery (a space once a working malting
but now devoted to the creation and reworking of myth).

When we realize that the original "library," now lost, was itself not a library but an office dressed as a library, and not Victorian but built in 1908 in conscious imitation of Victorian upper-class country house style in order to reflect the prestige of the ruling classes onto the sons of a Perth grocer, the confusion only grows further. As essentially nouveau riche lower middle-class representatives of trade, John and Tommy Dewar were anxious to escape their background and ape the manners and style of their social superiors (successfully, as it happens, since both were rewarded with peerages[8]) in order to confer badly needed respectability on a drink that only a generation or two before was the preserve of the working classes.

True Believers

So where in this particular marketing mix do we find authenticity? Is the virtual environment of the Dewar's Academy authentic? Certainly, it offers an experience, and as experiential marketing pioneers James Gilmore and Joseph Pine argue, ". . . there is no such thing as an inauthentic experience—because experiences happen inside of us; they are our internal reaction to the events unfolding around us."[9] Of course, as Gilmore and Pine go on to show, the environment that stimulates the experience may be more or less artificial, more or less natural, and it is unarguably the case that the environment of the Dewar's Academy is artificial, though nonetheless stimulating for all that.

Is the recreation at Dewar's World of Whisky authentic other than in its physical dimensions? And to what extent was the original office masquerading as a library itself authentic anyway? Is this not, in fact, all theater but with a plot directed to commercial rather than artistic ends, and are we not, as audience, complicit in all of this artifice? After all, as first observed by the English poet and critic Samuel Taylor Coleridge,[10] surely all marketing seeks, like art before it, "to transfer from our inward nature a human interest and a semblance of truth sufficient to procure for these shadows of imagination that willing suspension of disbelief for the moment, which constitutes poetic faith."

A recent experiment at Stanford University Business School sheds further light on the suspension of disbelief. Professor Baba Shiv and colleagues served, on different occasions, a group of subjects various wines, telling them that one cost $45 a bottle and another $5. It was, as you may have guessed, the same wine on both occasions, and as you have by now predicted, the group reported the more "expensive" wine to taste better. But the researchers went further and, using functional magnetic resonance imaging (fMRI), investigated the deep pleasure centers of the subjects' brains to demonstrate that they really did react more positively to the perceived higher-priced wine. As they conclude, "Our results show that increasing the price of a wine increases subjective reports of flavor pleasantness as well as the neural computations of experienced utility that are made in brain areas such as the medial orbito-frontal cortex."[11] For these subjects, the lower-priced wine tasted authentically more expensive.

Apparently, then, if we believe, or even consciously elect to go along with, the illusion for a while, that is enough. So it seems that whether we judge an experience to be authentic is, in many ways, dependent upon us, i.e., it is subject relative. Thus, if we believe that something is authentic, e.g., as in the experiment above we could be told that a particular wine is "authentic," then our experience (including what happens in our brain) will *appear* authentic to us. In other words, we are apparently *unable to distinguish* between the following two scenarios: first, an experience that we take to be authentic and actually is (i.e., it actually is expensive, good-quality wine); and second, an experience that we take to be authentic but actually isn't (i.e., cheaper wine that we're merely told is expensive, good wine).

It would seem, therefore, that the commonsense belief that whether something is authentic has to do only with things outside of our perception (i.e., something is either authentic or not regardless of our perception) is a misapprehension, and that authenticity is thus a relative concept. However, if as Gilmore and Pine argue, it is impossible to have an inauthentic *experience*, we have to distinguish between experience and environment, and it follows that we may have an authentic experience in an inauthentic environment—hence we can learn about and enjoy whisky in a virtual recreation of a long-lost distiller's office. As willing participants, we enter as actors into this particular drama.

Dewar's World of Whisky, the company's brand heritage center, is an interesting representative of a wider phenomenon by which the industrial tourism of the 1970s (tours of the distillery) has evolved into the "visitor centers" of the 1990s, and the "brand homes" of the present day. These are consciously moderated spaces, subverting the iconography of the museum to strictly commercial ends. The guides work using carefully controlled scripts (with occasional visits by mystery guests to ensure that no deviation can occur); the artfully arranged and stylishly lit displays are curated to show only a sanitized official version of history, and the tour route is carefully organized to culminate in a tasting of the product that, entirely deliberately, occurs just far enough ahead of the ever-present shop that the visitor's natural inhibitions will have been temporarily lulled into abeyance.

Today, there are even VIP tours. At Macallan, Glenfiddich, Aberlour, Glengoyne, and elsewhere, an extra payment (up to £100, roughly $200, in one case) will secure you access to additional areas and levels of tasting and interaction with the distillery staff not open to the standard visitor. There are even secret areas; inner sanctums open only to a privileged few. At Glenlivet, for example, a conventional enough visitor center is open to all, but a few "Guardians of Glenlivet" can gain access to a hidden room where they can sit at Captain Smith's tasting desk and enjoy a complimentary dram or two of rarer whiskies (I do not propose to spoil their fun by revealing how to become a Guardian or the location of the door—after all, we don't want the place getting too crowded, do we?)

At Glenlivet, much is made of the claim that this is "the single malt that started it all." As far back as 1924 the company's literature laid great stress on George Smith's admittedly farsighted decision to obtain the first license for legal distilling a hundred years previously. It seems clear-cut: what whisky could be more authentic and lay a greater claim to provenance than the Glenlivet?

Can Provenance Be Rebuilt?

But what, we might inquire, does the Glenlivet that we drink today (fine whisky though it undoubtedly is) tell us about the Glenlivet produced by George Smith? In this, it represents in microcosm much of the industry and highlights the central problems of authenticity and provenance at the heart of the marketing and promotion of single malt whisky.

It must be immediately apparent to even the most casual of visitors that George Smith was not distilling on the present-day scale. In fact, some 6 million liters of alcohol can be distilled annually from the current distillery, which is shortly to be expanded with the addition of a new mash tun, six new stills, and eight new wash backs, which will roughly double production. By contrast, Smith's original distillery had a capacity in 1824 of less than 230 liters per week (somewhat less than 12,000 liters annually, assuming year-round distillation, impossible at that period). In other words, once expanded, today's Glenlivet distillery will be more than one thousand times larger than the facility Smith built.

In fact, it's not even on the same site—and Smith's 1824 distillery wasn't even the one on which he had built his initial reputation! When he resolved to give up smuggling and apply for a license, he completely rebuilt his bootleg operation. As the company's anniversary history records, "In *rebuilding* his distillery in 1824 he had used his own plans, and *in improving*

49

his plant at the same time he made wise use of such science as there then was . . . the pot-still, *vastly improved*, remains the method in The Glenlivet Distillery today."[12] [italics added].

Even since 1924, though the fundamental principles remain the same, virtually the whole technical practice of distilling has changed. To mention just a few of the major innovations, new varieties of barley are used; fermentation regimes and yeast strains have evolved; direct firing of stills and the use of the rummager have been abandoned; worm tubs have largely given way to shell and tube condensers; wood management is rigorously controlled; and dunnage warehouses have been increasingly phased out in favor of racked and even palletized storage.

I do not wish to suggest that the Glenlivet is unique in this. Virtually the same story could be told of any distillery picked at random. In line with its global success, Scotch whisky production has been expanded massively, and there have been inevitable changes in distilling practice driven both by the need for greater volumes and the inexorable pressure to reduce costs. Today, though much emphasis is laid on the traditional, hand-crafted nature of single malt whisky distilling, large distilleries are regularly controlled by a single operator seated at a computer console.

It is debatable how much all of this matters. While the loss of employment through increased automation in the distillery itself can be deplored, tourism (a marketing function) has created many new jobs with more agreeable working conditions. George Smith and his successors across the industry are still improving their plant and will continue to make use of science so long as they see a commercial return in doing so without (in their opinion) compromising the essential quality of the spirit that they rely on in the first place.

The Glenlivet, of course, no longer belongs to the Smith family; Dewar's is today owned by the Bacardi group; and Diageo's distilleries are in the hands of a global network of shareholders, many of whom will never have set foot in Scotland. Are the whiskies they distill any the less "authentic" for this?

Meet the Peat Freaks

Some purists would argue firmly that some indefinable quality has been lost. At Bruichladdich, for example, self-styled "progressive Hebridean distillers," great stress is laid on the use of original equipment and the fact that the distillery was "state-of-the-art" for 1881, when it was founded—a claim curiously at odds with the boast that Bruichladdich employs "preindustrial distilling techniques." Whatever else it might be, a state-of-the-art distillery in 1881 was certainly not pre-industrial.

Such a claim, verging on the disingenuous, serves Bruichladdich's commercial aims, of course. As a small, independently owned company with limited financial resources, it suits Bruichladdich to appeal to the romantically inclined true believers, the so-called "malt maniacs" and "peat freaks," and position themselves as renegades, even heretics, battling against an army of gray-suited corporate megalomaniacs bent on world domination and determined to impose a dull uniformity on our drinking, with bland, homogenized, chill-filtered, and colored blends.

It's a conscious appeal to the medial orbito-frontal cortex. Our pleasure centers light up at the thought of these noble campaigners, battling on our behalf against a tide of conformity—and we are consequently prepared not just to pay but to savor actively the premium prices Bruichladdich asks for its products. Be a rebel! Live a little! Drive a Harley! Drink Bruichladdich! It's almost as gratifying as giving to your favorite charity, with the added bonus of a bottle of whisky as reward for your virtue. (And, may I add, what very tasty whisky it is.)

The larger distilling companies are, of course, at pains to demonstrate how all of their technical innovation and increased efficiency have not come at the cost of any compromise on product quality. Quite the reverse, in fact. The whisky produced today is better than ever, we are assured. Closer control of the process means a tighter and more consistent specification; better wood management means no rogue casks with the consequent elimination of off flavors; and larger warehouses, many remote from the distillery itself, have no impact on maturation and final flavor.

Does Location Matter?

This is a troubled area, speaking directly to the question of provenance. Some distillers, such as Bruichladdich, passionately believe that where whisky is stored has a significant influence on its taste, citing specifically the distillery's coastal location and the reputedly high levels of airborne salt that coat the warehouse walls and windows and saturate the very air the casks breathe. So adamantly do they hold this belief that a study has been commissioned from Florida State University's Department of Chemistry to demonstrate the effect. The results are awaited with interest. Others, such as Glenfarclas, also stress the influence of locality and the traditional nature of their dunnage warehouses with their open floors, high humidity, stable temperatures, and excellent air circulation.

On the other hand, Diageo, the world's largest distiller of Scotch, prides itself on its scientific and technical expertise, and, as an industry leader, generously sets out to share at least some of its knowledge with commentators and its commercial partners round the world. One way in which this is done is through its excellent and informative Malt Advocates course, an intense weeklong immersion in the history, production, evaluation, and consumption of single malt whisky.

Part of the course, naturally, is devoted to the critically important maturation process, where students are told firmly that while warehouse location may play a part in the final character of the maturing spirit, "these effects are minor compared to the flavor contribution from other production conditions and are not normally used to shape final character."[13]

That all seems clear. All the more curious, then, that Diageo should market its Talisker single malt, in the French market at least, with the headline that *"Sur l'île de Skye, la mer frappe le Talisker de ses parfums iodés"* ("On Skye, the sea caresses Talisker with its iodine air") and goes on to inform the reader that *"L'air de la mer et une tourbe iodée donnent au Talisker son puissant caractère marin, teinté d'algues et de poivre"* ("The sea air and peaty iodine give Talisker its powerful marine character, with hints of seaweed and pepper").

The Classic Malts Web site[14] adds, "Talisker embodies all the spirit of this rocky, storm-lashed island and its strong, steadfast people." So no confusion there, then.

It's nice to think that sea air does fundamentally affect the flavor of whisky. We want to believe that lengthy maturation on this rugged island surrounded by a stormy sea and exposed constantly to its salty air is essential to the flavor of Talisker (or that the gentler Islay air breathes subtly differently on Bruichladdich in sheltered Loch Indaal [pronounced lock-ING-*doll*]). It excites our pleasure centers and allows us to rationalize in an agreeably romantic way the taste differences that really do exist between these whiskies, and, incidentally, to explain to our partner why the extra cost was worth every penny.

Could Flavors Be Authentic?

However, suppose that we wanted to exercise even greater influence on the flavor of whisky. Suppose that we wanted to add our own flavors at the bottling stage. It's a radical idea, currently outlawed by both custom and legislation. Single malt Scotch may only be made from water, yeast, and malted barley. Flavorings, such are as found in some rums and vodkas, are out.

But some are prepared to at least consider the idea. At the 2007 World Whiskies Conference in Glasgow, Dewar's global brand director Neil Boyd floated the idea that to compete with vodka and appeal to younger drinkers, consideration should be given to a category of flavored Scotch whisky. He was immediately castigated by enraged purists. But, one year on at the 2008 event, a more powerful voice was raised.

Dr. Vijay Mallya is an Indian multimillionaire. Among the many commercial interests he owns are United Spirits of India (the dominant force in India's near one-hundred-million-case whisky market) and recently purchased Scotch whisky distillers Whyte & Mackay for a reputed £595 million (approximately $1.18 billion US at the time). Coming from India, where much of the locally produced "whisky" is in fact based on molasses, the idea of a flavored whisky was not presumably as alien to him as to many in his audience. Dr. Mallya noted: "There is a trend towards different-tasting products and Scotch is losing out to categories such as vodka, which is growing at 30 per cent, and wines, which are growing at 50 per cent. I'm not suggesting radical changes but maybe natural additives could be used to make it more exciting for this young target market."[15]

There was clear and immediate opposition to the proposal, even to the suggestion that the subject could be discussed. Yet what could be more authentic? Had they chosen, Boyd and Mallya could have rooted the idea of flavored whiskies in traditional custom and practice. After all, an early distilling text gives detailed instructions making for 'Fine Usquebaugh' adding mace, cloves, cinnamon, coriander seed and several other natural additives to malt spirits.[16]

This recipe dates from 1725. Flavored whisky could, it seems, make a claim to authenticity predating Glenlivet by nearly one hundred years. Where and when does "authenticity" begin?

We find ourselves in a semantic wilderness of mirrors, with each distiller claiming to outdo the others: "My authenticity is more authentic than your authenticity" they shout, ever more stridently—marketing demonstrating an understandable preference for increased sales over intellectual coherence. For Bruichladdich, authenticity begins in 1881, for

Glenlivet 1824, while the proponents of flavored whisky could claim precedence over all, with authentic texts to grant authority.

Provenance is an equally vexed construct. Certainly there seems little point in looking to the marketing department for authoritative guidance. We grasp blindly for absolutes that simply don't exist. Distilling practice has indisputably changed, yet everything is the same—only better: 1881 is preindustrial; sea air has a minor effect, yet shapes character; told that a $5 bottle costs $45 we believe it superior and actually enjoy it more.

Much, then, comes back to Coleridge's "willing suspension of disbelief." Perhaps in considering questions of authenticity and provenance, it's a question of choosing your preferred myth and sticking to it. Possibly the Glenlivet got it right with the subtitle of its 1924 corporate history—provenance and authenticity we may reasonably conclude is "Where Romance and Business Meet."

NOTES

1. John Cor is the name of the friar who recorded the first known written reference to a batch of Scotch whisky on June 1, 1494. "To Friar John Cor, by order of the King, to make aqua vitae VIII bolls of malt," recorded in Scottish Exchequer Rolls 1494–1495, Vol X, p. 487.
2. As the committee noted, distillation in Scotland at that time took place using both malted and unmalted barley and bear (a primitive variety of barley), and occasionally when grain prices permitted, wheat. A case of sorts might therefore be made for the *authenticity* of grain whisky.
3. Justices of the peace were local magistrates, responsible for enforcing the antismuggling legislation. Being close to their immediate community and aware of its impoverished state, especially in remote rural areas, many were tolerant of or even positively sympathetic to the lawbreakers. A few magistrates were actively complicit with them.
4. This was no idle threat. As late as 1841, the original Lochnagar distillery was burned down by rival smugglers enraged by the decision of the owner, a former bootlegger, to pay the license fee and embrace legitimacy under the law.

5. Phylloxera, a type of aphid, devastated European wine production following its introduction into France on imported North American vines in the 1860s. As a result of the dramatic reduction in wine production, the availability of cognac and brandy, previously the drink of choice of the middle- and upper-class drinker, was severely restricted, and a huge sales opportunity was created for Scotch whisky. This was skillfully exploited by the makers of the new blended style.

6. Sir Walter Gilbey, *Notes on Alcohol in Brandy, Whisky and Rum* (London: Vinton & Co., 1904).

7. For a discussion, see Colin Donald, "More to Exporting than Bagpipes and Tartan," *Scotsman*, http://business.scotsman.com/business/More-to-exporting-than-bagpipes.3652292.jp (accessed June 30, 2008).

8. The peerage is a system of titles of nobility in the United Kingdom, part of the British honors system.

9. James H. Gilmore and B. Joseph Pine II, *Authenticity: What Consumers Really Want* (Boston: Harvard Business School Press, 2007).

10. Samuel Taylor Coleridge, *Biographia Literaria* (London: Rest Fenner, 1817).

11. Hilke Plassmann et al., "Marketing Actions Can Modulate Neural Representations of Experienced Utility." Unpublished manuscript available at http://w4.stern.nyu.edu/emplibrary/jobmarket_paper_plassmann_final.pdf (accessed May 30, 2008).

12. Anonymous, "Glenlivet. Where Romance and Business Meet," Glenlivet Distillery, 1924.

13. Anonymous, "Malt Advocates—Course Notes," Diageo plc., 2006.

14. See the Talisker information page at www.malts.com/en-gb/Malts/summary/Talisker.htm (accessed May 30, 2008).

15. For discussion, see Brian Ferguson, "Whisky Trade Chokes as Tycoon Targets Youth with 'Alcopops'," *Scotsman*, April 24, 2008, http://news.scotsman.com/scotland/Whisky-trade-chokes-as-tycoon.4014481.jp (accessed May 30, 2008).

16. George Smith, *The Practical Distiller* (London: Bernard Lintot, 1725).

3

The Heritage of Scotch Whisky
From Monks to Surgeon Barbers

David Wishart

When you open a single malt Scotch whisky, you not only release the spirit of the malt, you expose its soul. Malt whisky is uniquely different from practically every other potable drink. It has a heritage that hearkens down the ages. It connects you with its Scottish roots and with a history that predates most of the New World. Take great care when you choose your favorite Scotch malt whisky, for the selection makes a lifestyle statement about you. It is not just a drink; it's an icon of your taste.

Scotch whisky must by law be matured in oak casks for at least three years before it can be called 'whisky', and most malt whiskies are matured for ten or more years. The malt whisky in your glass today was hand-crafted by dedicated whisky makers in the last millennium. Scotch malt whiskies are full of diverse flavors that stand on their own, without needing to be modified by mixers or ice.

When you discover a single malt whisky that you really like, the chances are you will want to find out more about it, for example, where it's made, the people who make it, and its history. All this adds to the pleasure and appreciation of the malt. You cannot do that with drinks like vodka, gin, or rum—they are anonymous beverages, lacking any provenance, partaken for their alcoholic content, to be mixed with something like tonic water, dry ginger ale, vermouth, fruit juices, or soda.

Robert Louis Stevenson put it well in his famous poem "The Scotsman's Return from Abroad," from *Underwoods*, 1880:

> At last, across the weary faem,
> Frae far, outlandish pairts I came.
> On ilka side o' me I fand
> Fresh tokens o' my native land.
> Wi' whatna joy I hailed them a'—
> The hilltaps standin' raw by raw,
> The public house, the Hielan' birks,
> And a' the bonny U.P. kirks!
> But maistly thee, the bluid o' Scots,
> Frae Maidenkirk to John o' Grots,
> The king o' drinks, as I conceive it,
> Talisker, Isla, or Glenliviet!

This essay traces the history and romance of Scotch whisky through the ages, from the *aqua vitae* of the early monasteries, the alchemist's quest for the elixir of eternal life, and the hedonistic *uisge beatha* of remote Scottish bothies, or concealed huts, to Edinburgh's Royal Mile taverns and world-famous single malt brands such as Glenfiddich, Glenlivet, and Royal Lochnagar. The royal romance with Scotch whisky started with James IV, was rekindled by George IV, and flourished under Queen Victoria. Whisky is evoked in the poetry of Robert Burns, in the art of Sir Edwin Landseer, and in the travelogues of Robert Louis Stevenson. London society toasted with brandy in the Regency period, but when a tiny phylloxera beetle devastated cognac in 1863, the upper classes turned to whisky and the famous Scotch brands were born.

Today, the flavor of malt whisky is more diverse than ever. In this essay, we trace its unique heritage through the centuries.

Medieval Origins

To understand how the outstanding cultural diversity of Scotch whisky developed, we must go back several centuries to trace its heritage. It began as the technology of the medieval monasteries. The monks had of necessity to cultivate their own produce, and across Europe they grew vines and cereals from which they made wine and beer. European monasteries were famous for their beers, and some are still famous today.

We do not know precisely how the monks developed distillation, but it may well have been a byproduct of alchemy in the search for an elixir of eternal life. Alchemists were already distilling liquids such as urine in the fourteenth century in their quest for the Philosopher's Stone. Or, as Hieronymus Braunschweig wrote in *Liber de arte distillandi* (1500), "purifying of the grosse from the subtyll, and the subtyll from the grosse." Here Braunschweig is describing how he believes that a gross liquid such as urine could, through the process of distillation, be transformed into a subtle spirit, and, ultimately, to gold.

The technology of distillation was already available in the Middle Ages, for it had been used to make perfumes in Arabia since the eighth century. All that was needed was to adapt the process to wine or beer to refine them into potable distilled spirits, and it is probable that wine was distilled first to produce brandy.

Aqua Vitae

In the northern climates of Scotland and Ireland, it is not possible to grow vines and make wine. The technology of distillation transferred along the monastic "grapevine," but the crop did not, so the technology was adapted to another crop that grew easily in a northern climate, namely, cereals. No doubt several cereal varieties were tested until, by trial and error, it was discovered that a fine spirit could be distilled from barley beer. Crushed barley was first fermented to produce a rough barley beer that was then distilled to obtain a clear barley distillate. They called it *aqua vitae*, the "water of life," for it was generally believed to have medicinal properties. In Scotland, it was considered a tonic, a cure-all for ailments such as colds; it had a warming effect when drunk, and when applied to a wound it helped the healing process as an antiseptic due to the high alcohol content.

The first written record we have of Scotch whisky is in the accounts of King James IV of Scotland. At the age of fifteen, after his father was killed at the Battle of Sauchieburn in 1488, James had stopped at Tullibardine Brewery to collect beer on the way to his coronation at Scone Palace. It is a great heritage story for Tullibardine Distillery, which makes and sells not only its "1488" Tullibardine Whisky Ale but also a range of very fine single malt whiskies.

By 1494, James and his court were enjoying their Scottish summers at Falkland Palace, the king's holiday retreat in Fife. There they would pass the long summer days hunting in the forests for deer and wild boar and pass the evenings feasting on their kill with wine, beer, and spirits. I like to imagine that they possibly stumbled upon Lindores Abbey during a hunt and commanded the head friar to procure refreshments, whereupon the royals discovered *aqua vitae*. It is more likely that word spread to the palace, some ten miles from the abbey, that the local monks were making an interesting strong brew from their prolific barley crop. For Lindores Abbey was a very wealthy Catholic establishment, owning much land and property in the area of north Fife bordering the river Tay. The truth we shall never know, but it is a fact that James IV took to *aqua vitae* to the extent of placing orders for it—"To Friar John Cor, by order of the King, to make *aqua vitae* VIII bols of malt," as recorded in the Exchequer rolls of Scotland for 1494–1495, which are the king's accounts.

Surgeon Barbers' Monopoly

The first license for the production and sale of *aqua vitae* was granted to the Guild of Surgeon Barbers in Edinburgh by Royal Charter of James IV in 1505. In it the guild was given the exclusive monopoly to produce and sell *aqua vitae*; and for a good part of the sixteenth century, it defended its rights with frequent prosecutions for infringements, for *aqua vitae* had now been discovered by the masses and was becoming a popular national drink. Many of my Scottish physician friends bemoan the fact that if they had only maintained their monopoly to the present day, the Royal College of Surgeons, as they are now, would be extremely wealthy, to the extent that the practice of surgery would have become a gentleman's pastime.

Needless to say, the Guild of Surgeon Barbers was not the distinguished body of surgeons presiding at the Royal College today. In the sixteenth century, there were no anesthetics for use in surgery, and the only practical way to numb the pain of an amputation was to get drunk on *aqua vitae*. If a person had an accident or was injured in battle such that a limb became gangrenous, the only lifesaving treatment was to amputate the affected limb. And to assuage the pain of the surgery, the surgeon barber would offer his patient a good measure of *aqua vitae* beforehand.

Early Farm Distillation

At around this time, the Protestant Reformation, led by Henry VIII's split with Rome, attacked the ruling Catholic Church. The outcome was that almost all the Catholic properties in England and Scotland were sacked, and the monks either were killed or disappeared.

Whereas the monks were well versed in Latin, the general populace was not; and *aqua vitae*, or "water of life," translated into Gaelic, the Scots' natural language, as *uisge beatha*.

Among common folk, this became corrupted in old Scots to
uiske, eventually developing into 'whisky' or 'whiskey' in the
eighteenth century. As it had become a popular drink, whisky
production moved to the farms and stately houses that produced the barley.

In these times, whisky making was seasonal winter work,
an adjunct to the main farming activity. The farmers were
fully occupied during the spring, summer, and fall, so it was
during the quiet winter season that they converted any surplus barley into whisky. By the eighteenth century, it was
common for farms and large houses to have their own stills
of around ten gallons capacity, which could legally be used
to distill whisky for private consumption. Anything larger
had to be licensed, on payment of government taxes. Whisky
continued to grow rapidly in popularity, and the government
reacted by taxing ever-smaller stills. In 1779, the legal size
of a private unlicensed still was reduced to two gallons, and
in 1781 private unlicensed stills were prohibited altogether.
Excise officers were appointed in numbers and empowered to
confiscate and destroy any stills that were not licensed.

In the Scottish Highlands, this had the effect of driving private whisky making underground. It was then made illicitly
in secret places, such as hollowed-out banks of streams, in
bothies on remote hillsides, even in secret rooms within the
larger houses. At a croft high above the river Spey, a farmer
named John Cumming was making whisky illegally at this
time; and his wife, Helen, would fly a red flag from their barn
to warn other illegal distillers when the excisemen were in the
glen searching for illicit stills. Helen and John Cumming were
later to apply for one of the first licenses to produce whisky
in the Spey region, and their farm at Cardow (now Cardhu)
became known for, among other things, being run by Helen
Cumming, the first woman in the whisky business.

By far the most famous exciseman at this time was Scotland's
national bard, Robert Burns. While earning his living by
prosecuting illicit whisky distillers and smugglers in Dumfries,
he also wrote his famous poems and ballads, several of

which feature Scotch whisky. In 1782, he published the poem "John Barleycorn: A Ballad," in which "John Barleycorn" is his alias for barley, and whisky is its "blood." It concludes as follows:

> John Barleycorn was a hero bold,
> Of noble enterprise;
> For if you do but taste his blood,
> 'Twill make your courage rise.
>
> 'Twill make a man forget his woe;
> 'Twill heighten all his joy;
> 'Twill make the widow's heart to sing,
> Tho' the tear were in her eye.
>
> Then let us toast John Barleycorn,
> Each man a glass in hand;
> And may his great posterity
> Ne'er fail in old Scotland!

George IV Discovers Glenlivet

Back in Edinburgh, the city burghers were in a party mood as George IV had ascended to the British throne on the death of his father George III in 1821. At that time, no British monarch had stepped foot in Scotland for over 150 years. So the Scottish establishment led by Sir Walter Scott resolved to change that and invited the newly crowned King George to Edinburgh. The King accepted, landing at Leith in August 1822, whereupon he and Sir Walter toasted their health with the finest Highland whisky Scott could procure. The king loved the whisky, for it tasted unlike any he had previously tried. There followed a grand royal welcome to Edinburgh with feasts and engagements lasting many days, in the course of which the king frequently demanded his newly discovered favorite Highland whisky.

Lady Elizabeth Grant of Rothiemurchas records the events in her *Diary of a Highland Lady*: "The Lord Chamberlain was looking everywhere for pure Glenlivet whisky; the King drank nothing else. It was not to be had out of the Highlands. My father sent word to me to empty my pet bin, where was whisky long in wood, mild as milk, and the true contraband goût ["flavor"] in it." This is the first reference we have to the fact that when whisky is stored in oak casks it is mellowed, rounded out, and softened, a process we now call maturation. We can be confident that with the new king visiting Edinburgh for the first time in living memory, Scott would have procured the very best whisky he could obtain. The fact that it was contraband whisky was purely incidental. King George liked it so much that he declared that only Glenlivet should be used for the royal toast in Scotland.

Illicit Distillation at Glenlivet

This was a considerable embarrassment to the Scottish authorities because the fine Glenlivet whisky, so much appreciated by the king, was contraband Highland whisky, the illicit spirit distilled slowly and secretly by whisky smugglers in remote mountain caves to evade being taxed. There were good reasons why the whisky made at Glenlivet had the highest reputation. First, good whisky cannot be made in a hurry, and the glen's remoteness made it very difficult to police. Excise officers could be spotted miles away, allowing plenty of time to hide the product and equipment.

Second, the essential ingredients for making fine malt whisky—barley, peat, and a copious supply of fresh, clean water—were all abundant at Glenlivet. The fertile valley of the River Spey below provided good barley. The hills above were layered with peat, an unlimited supply of free fuel. And the water that flowed from the peak of Ben Rinnes down the River Livet was ideal for making whisky—cold, soft, pure melted snow. It's little wonder that Lady Grant selected whisky with the "true contraband goût" to send to Edinburgh.

Furthermore, the contraband stills used by the smugglers were of necessity small and portable, typically around two gallons' capacity. They had to be carried into the hills and needed to be concealed easily from the excisemen, so small copper stills were invariably used. In his painting *The Highland Whisky Still*, Sir Edwin Landseer captures the romance of secret illicit distillation in a bothie hidden in the hills above Glenlivet. In the detail of the painting, a smuggler's equipment is visible, which is authentic, suggesting that Landseer painted it from life, in 1829.

We now know that when whisky is distilled, the copper of the still and condenser has a catalytic reaction with the vapors to release esters and aldehydes, the fruit flavors and delicate fragrances that are characteristic of fine malt whiskies. Small pot stills provide greater exposure to copper and therefore encourage these reactions, resulting in a richly flavored spirit, brimming with floral and fruity character. By comparison, the licensed distilleries in the Lowlands and cities operated large stills that were run fast to produce spirit cheaply in bulk, much like vodka today.

The contrast between legal Lowland and contraband Highland whiskies could not have been starker, which is why Elizabeth Grant sent her best contraband Highland whisky to the king. Herein lies the distinction, which some maintain exists to this day, between the regional flavor styles of Highland and Lowland Scotch malt whiskies.

George Smith of Glenlivet

After the king's visit, new legislation was rushed through parliament in 1824 to legalize illicit whisky making by licensing small Highland stills with lower excise duties. One of the first to obtain a license was George Smith, a farmer by day and illicit whisky distiller by night. He converted his farmhouse in the Braes of Glenlivet to a legal distillery, and the first licensed Glenlivet whisky began flowing early in 1825.

When one visits Glenlivet distillery, the ruin of his farmhouse at Upper Drumin can still be seen high on the hill.

The illicit distillers were furious as they did not relish the presence of excisemen in the glen, and they did their damnedest to put Smith out of business. "I was warned before I began by my civil neighbors," Smith recalled years later, "that they meant to burn my new distillery to the ground and me in the heart of it."[1] Other early licensed distillers were driven out and their farms burned. But George Smith was made of sterner stuff. He mounted a guard on his distillery round-the-clock and carried a pair of flintlock pistols at all times to defend himself against the smugglers.

Once, when staying at an inn, he was attacked in his bedroom by a gang of smugglers led by a thug named Shaw, who threatened to kill him with a butcher's knife. Smith whipped out his guns from under the bedcovers, held one to Shaw's head, and fired the other at the fireplace. A deafening blast and a cloud of sooty embers were enough to send the gang fleeing in fear. "I let it be known everywhere that I would fight for my place to the last shot," he told a reporter for the *London Scotsman* in 1868.[2]

At other times, Smith was adept at defusing potentially dangerous encounters by subtler negotiation. In the same interview, Smith continued, "if you are in a tight place, where I have often been, try them wi' a drap o' whisky and if that does not mend matters, I dinna ken what will." Producing arguably the best malt whisky in the glen, most of Smith's opponents could be won over by a taste of his "mountain dew of Glenlivet."[3]

Queen Victoria and Royal Lochnagar

In 1848, the young Queen Victoria and Prince Albert toured Scotland looking for a suitable summer retreat, finally settling for Balmoral Castle on the banks of the River Dee, below the brooding mountain of Lochnagar. Balmoral was rebuilt to meet their requirements and became their summer residence, and so it has remained for most of the royal family that have followed.

Quite close to Balmoral was a farm licensed to produce whisky, and in 1848 it was converted to a distillery with new buildings and equipment. Located in a spectacular setting beside the River Dee, Lochnagar distillery is a Highland gem retaining a farmyard atmosphere to this day, its visitor center occupying a former Victorian barn. In 1848, the manager, John Begg, wrote to Prince Albert inviting him to sample his new whisky and was surprised when the Prince and Queen Victoria arrived without notice, together with the royal children. The Queen and Prince Albert toured the distillery and sampled their first dram, while the children played tag around the barrels, and the Queen's royal warrant was duly granted, one of the fastest on record. Royal Lochnagar whisky has been enjoyed by generations of the royal family and their Balmoral staff for over 150 years. Indeed, it was Queen Victoria's enthusiasm for whisky, following her visit to the distillery, that helped establish the international demand for Scotch in the nineteenth century.

At the start of Queen Victoria's hunts at Balmoral, each guest would be given a bottle of whisky and whatever remained at the end of the hunt was traditionally given to the stalker. Victoria also made a general order that royal coaches should always travel with a bottle of whisky under the coachman's seat for use in "emergencies," though what constituted an emergency was never defined.

William Grant of Glenfiddich

Not long after Glenlivet was licensed, John and Helen Cumming also obtained a license for Cardow farm. They were succeeded by their son Lewis in 1839, and, when Lewis died in 1872, by their daughter-in-law Elizabeth. Earning the title "Queen of the Whisky Trade" for her tough business acumen,

Elizabeth Cumming rebuilt the distillery on a new site in 1884 and extended it further in 1887 with larger stills. The three original small stills of Cardow, now surplus to requirements, were bought in 1886 by William Grant, the manager at Mortlach Distillery. Grant immediately gave his notice at Mortlach and left to set up one of the great whisky dynasties of Scotland.

In less than a year, William Grant and his sons had built their distillery, obtained a license, and the first spirit flowed on Christmas Day 1887, just in time for Queen Victoria's Jubilee. William was greatly impressed by Sir Edwin Landseer's famous painting *Monarch of the Glen*, so he named his distillery Glenfiddich, Gaelic for "valley of the deer." It was to become the most successful malt whisky of all, and William Grant & Sons was the first family whisky dynasty to be founded in Scotland.[4]

French Phylloxera Plague

The whisky industry flourished during Victoria's reign, partly due to all things Scottish becoming fashionable in royal society. It was also helped by a plague of phylloxera aphids, which from 1880 onward devastated the vineyards of France such that English brandy drinkers turned to Scotch whisky.

The quality and consistency of most whisky was unreliable, however, and it was possibly for this reason that the practice of blending was introduced. The famous whisky merchant Andrew Usher was Glenlivet's first distributor, and he introduced it to London society in 1844 as "by far the purest and finest spirit made in any part of these dominions."[5] When Usher pioneered blended whiskies in 1853, his first successful brand had Glenlivet whisky at its heart and was called Usher's Old Vatted Glenlivet. It sold well in London, at a premium to other whiskies, and was soon being exported to India, Australia, and throughout the British Empire. Charles Dickens was another convert to Glenlivet, recommending a rare old specimen of it to a friend in 1852.[6] As previously noted, Robert Louis Stevenson also included it in his famous poem "The Scotsman's Return from Abroad": "The king o' drinks, as I conceive it, Talisker, Isla, or Glenlivit [sic]."

Blended Scotch Whiskies

The delicious feature of single malt whiskies is that their flavors are so diverse. Usher had found that a blend of malt whiskies from different distilleries would deliver several raw flavors simultaneously, usually layered, in perfect harmony. His discovery led to a number of whisky blends being launched in the latter half of the nineteenth century that went on to become household names.

Some people argue that a fine blended Scotch whisky is greater than the sum of the component parts. While this may well be true, it is the component malts that deliver the flavor character, or signature, to the top blended whiskies. Whereas a blended whisky may typically contain twenty to thirty different malt and grain whiskies, several producers now identify the principal malt whisky in their blends: for example, Strathisla is the heart of Chivas Regal; Glenrothes is the "signature" malt in Cutty Sark; Famous Grouse is built upon Highland Park and Macallan; and Johnnie Walker is closely identified with Mortlach. For the first time, malt whiskies were classified by their flavor, the blender's art being to choose a malt, or to substitute one for another, according to its flavor profile and thereby maintaining the balance and consistency of the blend.

Single Malt Whiskies

For over a hundred years, blended Scotch whiskies held sway. But a blended whisky, however famous, is merely a recipe. It has no provenance and little heritage other than the originator's name or brand. Prior to the 1960s, virtually all the malt whisky produced in Scotland was used for blending. But in the 1960s, demand for Scotch whisky became buoyant again, triggering a major expansion of production. Scottish malt distillers increased their production capacity by more than 50 percent, several silent distilleries reopened, and three new distilleries were built. This massive investment doubled the output of Scotch malt whisky, and more than half of it was owned by one conglomerate.

Fearing for their independence in the face of such consolidation, the directors of Glenfiddich set stock aside for sale internationally solely as single malt whiskies. The rest of the industry watched with mild amusement, believing that the future was with blends, not with single malts. William Grant & Sons were fortunately not deterred, and Glenfiddich rapidly seized the market lead for single malts, a position it has held ever since. In 2006, Glenfiddich was designated a UK "Superbrand," the only drinks company to earn this cherished accolade. It is in recognition of having achieved the finest reputation in its field, offering consumers emotional and tangible advantages over other brands, being instantly recognizable with its stag deer emblem and distinctive triangular bottle, wholly produced and bottled at Glenfiddich, in the valley of the deer.

Today, single malt whisky is the strongest growth category for Scotch whiskies, and production cannot keep up with demand. Closed distilleries are being reopened, and new distilleries are being built. Whisky festivals flourish across Scotland and throughout the world. Every year, Scotland plays host to thousands of whisky tourists eager to follow the malt whisky trail and trace the provenance of their favorite malts. Scotland's homecoming festival has designated May 2009 to be "Whisky Month," one of its four main Scottish themes. For it is the distinctive character, provenance, and heritage that characterizes Scotch malt whiskies and differentiate them from all other drinks. They have a unique history, which echoes down the ages and can be traced back to their founding fathers, to a place, to a time, and to the dedicated people who first created them.

NOTES

1. Interview in the *London Scotsman*, 1868, cited in F. Paul Pacult, *A Double Scotch* (Hoboken, NJ: John Wiley & Sons, 2005), p. 66.
2. Ibid.
3. Ibid.
4. See discussion in David Wishart, "William Grant of Glenfiddich," *Malt Advocate* 16.2 (2007): pp. 52–57.
5. An advertisement in the *Morning Post*, an Edinburgh publication, June 14, 1844, cited in Pacult, *A Double Scotch*, p. 116.
6. Ibid., p. 119.

4

Women, Whiskey, and Libationary Liberation

Ada Brunstein

For a few days in April of 2008, whiskey was big news. A high profile woman downed a dram in Crown Point, Indiana, to the tune of husky howls and a solo "Yeah, baby" (the after-hours version of the proverbial pat on the back). The media pounced. Every major station ran clips about the woman who tossed back what many called the "shot heard 'round the world." The whiskey was Crown Royal. The woman, Hillary Clinton. The question: why was this news?

The clip, which at the time of this writing could be found on YouTube in over a dozen incarnations (one titled "Hillary Gone Wild,"[1] another "My Prez Wants to Party All the Time"[2]) prompted countless comments from viewers, bloggers, and talk show hosts. Some of the cries from those who found this event newsworthy went like this: "She's pounding it," "It's 80 proof," "This is what at like 6 in the afternoon, I wanna know how she'd be at 3 am answering that phone," "She's like taking a shot and then talking about the campaign,"[3] "She's too old to be doing this," "She's trying too hard."[4]

To my surprise, Jon Stewart jumped on the bandwagon: "Is she running for president or pledging? That's all we need, a president who gives in to peer pressure." He even started in on her choice of whiskey, asking what "this hardscrabble Archie Bunker type" was drinking.

Maureen Dowd, an unapologetic Clinton hater, invoked traditional *Wild West* lore when she called Clinton Annie Oakley in a *New York Times* article titled "Eggheads and Cheese Balls." Hillary was feigning "Main Street cred," Dowd wrote.[5] What, if anything, should we make of all this?

In this essay I will argue that the world of whiskey is still largely a man's world and that the women who have been drinking whiskey are to some degree using whiskey to acquire some of the attributes widely attributed to men. I will argue that in doing so, they are assimilating to the masculinity of whiskey culture and that this assimilation mirrors the assimilation of women into male culture at large. I will also argue that this is a transitional phase: the next one being a phase in which women develop a culture of strength and independence and whiskey on their own terms, quite apart from any of the testosterone-filled trappings of the past.

The Conference

On April 7, 2008, exactly seventy-five years after the end of prohibition, I attended the American Distilling Institute's annual Whiskey Conference in Louisville, Kentucky, the heart of bourbon country.[6] How I got there is still a bit of a head-scratcher. I'm a wine girl. Reds. Deep and velvety and infused with meaning. I've had some of the best conversations of my life over wine. Wine makes me a funner, chattier, more thoughtful version of myself. Maybe that's the wine talking; but still, I like what it's saying.

Whiskey just hurts. The handful of times I'd had whiskey, I either gave an honest reaction (gag, cough, shake—the whiskey wince, not very attractive) or I faked it, mainly because

I was trying to impress the guys who offered it to me. This was a difficult thing to admit, even to myself. I'm a grown-up, I told myself. I'm long past the point of having to fake anything for anyone. Why was I faking whiskey? It was like faking an orgasm, which no woman should have to do after college, where it's a necessary evil: he doesn't know what he's doing or he smells funny or he reminds you of someone you hate or he's the one you hate and you have no idea how you ended up naked in his bed. Maybe it was the whiskey. Sometimes you want to get it over with more quickly, but other times (you really like him but his hands are everywhere except where they should be) you know that feigned pleasure will make him happy, and you know it will make you that much more appealing. I did the same with whiskey—faked liking it to appear sexier.

It was in this disturbing realization that this essay was born: why on earth would I think faking whiskey would make me sexier? Was there any truth to that perception? If so, what sociocultural mechanisms made it true? These are the questions that led me to Kentucky, where I found myself surrounded by men, at the Maker's Mark distillery, with my fingers dipped deep into a vat of simmering wheat.

Of the 170 people at the conference, I was surprised to find only about 10 women, and of the ones I spoke to, not one liked whiskey. I met a self-proclaimed "vodka girl" and a "beer girl." Others preferred wine like me. The women were there to learn about the business. In that sense, they were carrying on a long tradition of women who made whiskey, without necessarily drinking it.

When it came to drinking whiskey, women have traditionally been tainted. In the 1930 movie *Anna Christie*, Greta Garbo played a hard-bitten woman with a sordid past. Garbo's first spoken words on the big screen were: "Gimme a whiskey—ginger ale on the side. And don't be stingy, baby." In *Some Like It Hot*, Sugar Kane (Marilyn Monroe) is a bourbon-drinking runaway with a nasty habit of falling for womanizing saxophone players. In the original

Stepford Wives (1975), it's the libertine women Bobby and Joanna who "break into Walter's scotch" before they, too, are replaced with domestic drones. This wasn't Sinatra, whiskey glass hanging like a jewel from his hand, with nothing to prove or hide. Whiskey-drinking women were misbehavin' women.

A New Era?

But things have changed . . . or have they? Hillary's swillin' incident, the fact that it was an incident at all, would seem to suggest not. How many U.S. presidents have shot a stiff whiskey in the Oval Office without as much as a passing mention? Men drink it in greater numbers than women, marketing campaigns mainly ignore the women's market, and sexism lingers in some ads.[7] Most images that the spirit conjures are infused with masculinity, creating a sort of tension between whiskey and femininity. And most of the women I spoke to seemed to play deliberately on that tension between femininity and whiskey as the tipple with all the testosterone.

In Louisville, Kentucky, where women are surrounded by bourbon lore and distillers, I found a bistro review in a local magazine with a distinctively feminine voice. The magazine was called *Underwired*, and the article went like this:

> The thought of us girls going out for bourbon made us all feel somewhat strong. I know for me, it conjures up images of powerful CEO's [*sic*] enjoying an after-hour cocktail. It then dawns on me that the images I am envisioning are male, and I realize how wrong that is. I should admit though, I did have some small reservations around the idea . . . wondering if I would actually be able to handle my liquor. Blame it on early sips from my father's locked cabinet as a teenager for ruining my ability to acquire taste and appreciation for it.[8]

This brief and not so well-written passage highlights the key dynamics surrounding whiskey and women: that whiskey is associated with strength, that strength is associated with powerful positions, that strength and powerful positions (such as CEO) have masculine associations, that it's wrong for women to appeal to and enjoy masculine associations, that whiskey poses a physical challenge ("wondering if I would actually be able to handle my liquor"), and, finally, a not uncommon reference to sneaking sips from her father's locked cabinet.

Whether or not any of the above statements is true is beside the point. What's important is whether people believe them, and I think they do.

In the remainder of the essay, I will take those perceptions and show how together they sum up women's roles in whiskey culture, and by association how they sum up the still progressing integration of women into men's roles in American culture at large. Let's take each of those one by one, but in a slightly different order.

First, let's talk about the strength associated with whiskey. In order to appreciate whiskey, you have to be able to handle the kick in the mouth. Only after you get past the tongue-lashing can you start to savor the drink. Whiskey is a "considered" drink. A deliberate choice, compared to the frivolity of ordering a Cosmo, for example. You need a reason to keep at it. Because whiskey is challenging, there's a perception that if you can take the hit, then you're tough (and by extension if you're a wimp, then you can't take it).

An extreme example appears in Carrie Underwood's 2008 Grammy-winning song "Before He Cheats." The song's narrator takes a stab at the woman her boyfriend cheats with by citing her inability to drink whiskey among the many signs of her weakness. It's a mark of strength for the woman who can shoot whiskey (the scorned woman, in this case) and a deficiency on the part of the woman who orders a fruity drink instead. And while the fruity drink drinker got the guy, the whiskey drinker is the one who comes out triumphant. She launches an all-out assault on his car, shattering headlights, slashing tires, and doing unspeakable things to his leather seats. The whiskey-drinking woman is not to be trifled with.

Outside the exaggerated world of stardom, if a woman can take a confident yet understated swig, as if it's nothing at all, and if she can convey the slightest hint that she relishes it—with the corner of her mouth turned up—she's an instant bombshell.

This brings us to the second perception about whiskey. Men and women both describe whiskey-drinking women as sexy, tough, and independent. And women are conscious of this image. "Have you noticed that men are very into Laphroaig? It is like a code word to use on them," says one Bostonian writer who preferred not to be named.

Men like whiskey-drinking women for the same reason they like Angelina Jolie. She rides motorcycles, she flies planes, she could tear you to shreds if she wanted to, but lucky for you she doesn't want to. Anything you can do she can do better. It's not that she's one of the boys—it's that she can pulverize the boys without sacrificing her sex appeal. In fact, her sex appeal comes from that very point—that someone who *looks* like a woman can put a man in his place. The ultimate dominatrix in her myriad incarnations. Whiskey has a similar effect. It helps women who may not be able to leap tall buildings in a single bound appear as if they could, and somehow this translates into sex appeal.

But what exactly is the essence of that appeal? In some ways it's a rebellion against the ultrafeminine, which has gone out of vogue because it represents tradition, docility: the good girl. Somewhere along the way, misbehaving became sexy. Maybe it's because in recent decades women have had to break with tradition (with traditional roles) to have a voice: to vote, to enter the work force, to have the chance to climb through the ranks. The traditional, dare I say docile and obedient, woman carries with her the tightly pulled corset strings of the presuffragette era. The rebel, the rule breaker, is appealing because she is the one who achieves.

These images of feminine toughness are not entirely new. In *Well-Behaved Women Seldom Make History*,[9] Harvard historian Laurel Thatcher Ulrich writes about the myth of the Amazon. Ulrich coined the slogan "well-behaved women seldom make history," which first appeared in a 1976 scholarly paper by Ulrich about funeral sermons for Puritan women. The slogan was catapulted to the public eye (and to T-shirts and bumper stickers) in 1995 by a writer who happened to read the paper and liked the line. In 2007, a MacArthur Fellowship and a Pulitzer Prize later, Ulrich published a book by the same name that tells the story of history-making women, who you might've guessed didn't exactly play by the rules.

In the book, Ulrich reintroduces us to the Amazons, the belligerent race of women who have morphed into countless incarnations throughout the ages. Her claim is that "An Amazon is more than a female soldier. She is an object of fantasy, longing, inspiration, and fear."[10] Wonder Woman, she says, was an instantiation of an Amazon, and her creator, William Moulton Marston, wrote,

> Wonder Woman is psychological propaganda for the new type of woman who should, I believe, rule the world. . . . What woman lacks is the dominance or self-assertive power to put over and enforce her love desire. I have given Wonder Woman this dominant force but have kept her loving, tender, maternal and feminine in every other way.[11]

It is Ulrich's account of 1970s history professor Abby Kleinbaum that may help explain how this power translates to sex appeal:

> Kleinbaum argued that in Western literature the Amazon was "an image of a superlative female that men constructed to flatter themselves." Winning an Amazon, through love or war, made a man a hero. If a woman was an exemplary warrior, then the skills of the man who defeated her appeared all the greater. If she was

both beautiful and resistant to male advances, then the man who won her heart and bed was irresistible. Kleinbaum's argument recalls Virginia Woolf's observation in *A Room of One's Own*, "Women have served all these centuries as looking-glasses possessing the magic and delicious power of reflecting the figure of man at twice its natural size."[12]

So, too, with whiskey, perhaps. Might the appeal of the whiskey-drinking woman be born of the same appeal of the woman warrior, of Wonder Woman? Might the whiskey-drinking woman conjure up a modern Amazon?

But whiskey isn't just sexual currency, it's power currency. It's a communication tool. That's the third whiskey feature we'll talk about. Women use whiskey as a tool with which to communicate with men on their terms. Sometimes they're communicating power, other times they're communicating camaraderie.

Was Hillary consciously using whiskey to communicate that she was one of the guys? Maybe. Was her whiskey shot interpreted that way by an overwhelming majority? I think it was.

At the Whiskey Conference I heard a story about a woman who at thirty was the vice president of a bank, traditionally a man's role, and a much older man at that. The woman grew up drinking Scotch, her father raised her on it, I was told. I wondered what that meant. A thimbleful every day since she was five? Apparently this VP is fond of deliberately ordering Scotch when she takes businessmen out for lunch. This is a sentiment I heard echoed many times over—that whiskey makes women feel more powerful in contexts that are still dominated by men. In the case of this VP, the woman was using whiskey to put herself on the same playing field as her male colleagues. In this sense, whiskey was a tool for communicating power in a situation where she might have feared her gender might be inaccurately perceived as a weakness.

Nina,[13] a Bostonian neuroscientist (who proposed to her boyfriend, so we already know she's a convention breaker), had similar experiences at conferences.[14] Like many women, Nina is well aware that her whiskey drinking gets a reaction. "If you're in a guy bar and everyone is ordering PBRs and you order a Jack Daniel's, the bartender looks at you differently. You get this tough girl image even if you're the biggest softie ever." And here's where it gets even more interesting; "it can be useful in some situations," she says.

How? At her first conference in a field dominated by men, a faculty member brought a bottle of Scotch. It was generous and collegiate, she says, but it was also a way for him to break the ice. It was very effective, she adds. So she thought she'd do the same. "It worked like a charm," she says. "Apart from a major paper, it was the best thing I could've done. By the end of the night I was at a picnic table surrounded by ten people (mostly men) and had the best conversations about gossipy neuroscience politics stuff that maybe you only get to hear when you're drinking, but a lot of it was also creative brainstorming. Their inner playful scientist was coming out. I wouldn't have seen that side of them otherwise." That night she established both professional and personal relationships that have remained with her.

Let me pause here and say that I'm not suggesting women who drink whiskey don't appreciate it for its taste, its nuance, its myriad flavors and textures. That would be inaccurate, and it would undermine the sensory experience that these women are having and in some cases their years of acquiring in-depth knowledge of whiskey. What I'm suggesting is that initially women seem often to be drawn to whiskey—and get past whiskey's kick—in order to connect in various ways with men. And here's the rub: this isn't necessarily different from the way in which *men* come to whiskey. But what is commonplace is that both men and women bond with men over whiskey. Neither sex tends to begin to drink it in order to bond with women, and many of those who have been drinking it for extended periods of time mainly talk about drinking it with men, not women.[15]

An Immigration of Sorts

Because whiskey is hard on the palate, it has to be worth the effort. So what's the gain? What's in it for us? I learned to like coffee because of the caffeine. Wine was a challenge for my sweet tooth at first, but there was a social reward long before I learned to love it for itself.

Whiskey, too, has its rewards. As mentioned above, for many it offers a way to connect with the world of men, at least at the beginning. For others it's cultural. My mother, who grew up in Russia, liked whiskey long before she ever tasted it. Hard liquor was part of the culture, and the pleasant associations were ingrained in her mind before she took her first sip.

This sentiment was echoed by some of the women I spoke to. When they recall their earliest experiences with whiskey, they were conscious of the image that went with it—cool, strong, independent—long before they started drinking it. They often chose whiskey in a deliberate effort to acquire that image. One woman asked her friend (also a woman) to teach her how to drink whiskey because she wanted the image that went with it—a sort of rite of passage, like asking a friend to show you how to put on eyeliner.

I won't pretend that some men don't also learn to love whiskey for the image that goes with it. But the question is what's the purpose of that acquisition? And why does whiskey achieve it? Rarely is its purpose to project strength or *cool* to women, and whiskey achieves it because of its long-standing association with men, who until recent history were the one and only gender to embody strength and independence as a group.

If it's true that women who drink whiskey acquire traditionally masculine attributes and do so to be part of male culture, then maybe we can look at the gradual emergence of women in whiskey culture as a sort of immigration.[16] Women have been assimilating into what has been a dominant culture, using the characteristics normally attributed to that culture.

In a 2006 *Wall Street Journal* article titled "He Drinks, She Drinks,"[17] Eric Felten inadvertently reveals exactly this phenomenon, though instead of relying on adjectives like 'tough' and 'independent', Felten uses 'serious'. He writes about the freedom offered to women to choose "to indulge in the saccharine offerings designed with them in mind, or opt for more serious drinks, all without reproach." He goes on to write that "women who buck convention and drink gin martinis or Scotch on the rocks raise no eyebrows—instead, they are rightly applauded for the sophistication of their choices. But for guys, the choice [of indulging in saccharine offerings] brings no small risk of social stigma. If men think that they're being judged by the drinks they order, they're right."

While the general message of Felten's article is one of libationary liberation and equality—that women and men should be able to drink what they want without stigma—implicit in his choice of language is that women should be praised for drinking what were previously thought to be men's drinks. The indulgences of the dominant culture are good, while those of the minority culture carry negative stigmas.

The Boston-based publication *stuff@night* published an article by Sara Faith Alterman called "For the Boys (and Girls): An Ode to Bourbon" (note the parenthetical caveat). The author opens as follows:

> I'm told that I'm kind of a dude. Not between the legs, but between the ears. I've always been more comfortable running with the boys, playing a game of pool in my sweats on a Friday night in lieu of getting my boobs all gussied up for an evening of pink martinis and eyelash batting. I'm lewd, I'm crude, I swear too much, I call my friends by their last names, I have absolutely no clue how to put on eyeliner. Guys in emo bands know more about makeup than I do.
>
> Most important (at least for the sake of this column), I drink like a dude. This doesn't mean that I drink like a frat boy—funnel in my left hand, limp junk in my

right—or spend the night pounding beers in an effort to see who can be the first to boot and rally. Rather, this proclamation refers to my whistle-wetter of choice: bourbon. I like it neat, I like it sweet, and I like it quietly, without a big fuss over the fact that I'm passing on the strawberry-mango caipirinhas.[18]

Here, too, we see a woman who associates her whiskey drinking with masculine characteristics.

Nina, the neuroscientist, offers an apt metaphor. "It's like the shoulder pads of the eighties," she says. It was a women's fashion designed to imitate a masculine feature: broad shoulders.

In fashion, in sex, in the business world, women have to some degree integrated themselves by adopting men's attitudes and behavior, not because that's what they set out to do, but because such is the nature of assimilation into a dominant culture. Shoulder pads were designed to mimic physical features, but there are more subtle examples of the same phenomenon as well. In her book *Female Chauvinist Pigs*,[19] Ariel Levy argues that feminism has swung the sexuality pendulum so far that not only are women sexually liberated, but they are actually treating female sexuality the way men have—by objectifying other women and themselves. Whiskey mirrors these trends. As women have entered the world of men, they have taken on the characteristics of the previously dominant male culture. As women entered the world of whiskey, they latched onto male images and characteristics.

It may be worth pausing to ask, why is it that the drinks that women drink cause embarrassment while the drinks that men drink are reason for praise? It's no more or less arbitrary than the fact that men who sew or knit or vacuum are being feminized (a bad thing) and women who ride motorcycles are sexy. So, add a little testosterone to the girlie girl, and she rises in everyone's estimation. Add a little estrogen to the man's man, and he should crawl under a shawl of shame. (With this formula, women are left teetering between masculine and feminine images, juggling them according to context. Recall that Hillary Clinton was not only criticized for her whiskey shot, but the *Washington Post* also ran an entire story about her cleavage.[20])

In part, the whiskey industry is at fault. It hasn't done much to create images of whiskey-drinking women that people like Nina could embrace. But in part it's something else. In his *Wall Street Journal* article,[21] Felten says, "The recent revival of interest in classic cocktails presents a long-overdue opportunity to break out of the tyranny of the girly, giving men the freedom to order mixed drinks without shame and women the chance to order drinks worthy of grown-ups."

Lauren Clark, an avid whiskey drinker and whiskey writer, agrees with Felten. In her blog, drinkboston.com, she echoes Felten's sentiment about the tyranny of the girlie:

> Yes, we are all under the well-manicured thumb of the collective Cosmo drinker. But classic cocktails will set us free! Gender stereotypes at the bar will be crushed![22]

Perhaps it's time we women break through the comfort zones of our drink choices.

We might hope that the next phase both in whiskey culture and beyond will be the evolution of a woman's culture that is independent of male images. Maybe we can envision a whiskey market that includes women and a whiskey culture that nurtures the interest that women have, without stigmatizing either the women who do drink it or the women who don't (after all, isn't *choice* the hallmark of women's independence?).

It's up to interested women, then, to develop a whiskey culture of our own. And in fact this movement is already starting.

Woman's Spirit

May 8–13, 2008, was World Cocktail Week, a festival created by the Museum of the American Cocktail in New Orleans. The Boston branch of a group called LUPEC organized a charity event to benefit the museum at the Green Street Grill in Cambridge, Massachusetts. LUPEC[23] stands for Ladies United for the Preservation of Endangered Cocktails. Its mission: "dismantling the patriarchy one drink at a time."

The guest bartenders revived four classic cocktails, including Remember the Maine. According to LUPEC's Web site the drink is:

good rye or bourbon, sweet vermouth, cherry brandy, absinthe or Pernod, [and was] described in Charles H. Baker Jr.'s *The Gentleman's Companion,* published in 1939. "Stir briskly in clock wise fashion—this makes it sea-going, presumably!" wrote Baker.

Misty Kalkofen, Green Street Grill bar manager and LUPEC Boston founder, hosted the event along with LUPEC blogger Lauren Clark. The bartenders, some donning classic thirties bar attire, chatted with the patrons about the history of the drinks and the recipes.

The LUPEC women are the closest I've come to a whiskey culture that nurtures the particular interests of women. LUPEC is not just about the drinks. It's about the history of cocktails and of women. It's about charity, about empowerment. It's about the "strong spirited woman—our grandmothers," one member tells me.

If the LUPEC "broads" (as they sometimes call themselves) had a logo, it might be the image embroidered on the black cardigan donned by one of its members who goes by Bourbon Belle: a skull embedded in a butterfly. "Feminine with an edge" she calls it.

These women have come a long way since their first whiskey, and while, like others, their first drinks may have had roots in the images described above (the toughness, the independence, and the coolness that whiskey evokes), they have since developed their own whiskey culture. They discuss whiskey the way a historian might discuss the rise of Western culture, or philosophers might debate moral relativism. They know their stuff. They've thought about it. They've discussed it over Manhattans at their monthly gatherings. They research historical figures and give each other minipresentations about them. They host events with titles like Drinkin' Dames in Classic Cinema. They blog about everything from the bar scene to the role of the pimento in cocktails. In other words, they are creating a world of images surrounding whiskey that brings with it a distinct character and history, one that offers women something new.

Rhiannon Walsh, whose father trained her nose, grew up in Wales and Ireland with a father who was a whiskey enthusiast and a grandmother who was an herbalist. Rhiannon has been written up in *Entrepreneur Magazine* as well as in Britain's *Whisky Magazine* and is now president of CelticMalts[24] in the United States.

Her story is an unusual one. Her grandmother taught her how to distill when she was a child. Though her grandmother distilled flowers and herbs, Rhiannon says, "distilling is distilling,"[25] whether it's grain, flower, fruits, brandy. Rhiannon took the combination of her distilling skills and her highly trained nose into the whiskey business.

In 1999, Rhiannon started the Whiskeys of the World Expo (the largest spirit expo of its kind in North America, she says). That first year only 3 percent of the attendants were women. In the years to come, she made a deliberate effort to connect with women. She e-mailed, she networked, she did what she could to reach this underrepresented part of the market. This year, nine years later, women made up 47 percent of the attendants.

"There hasn't been a lack of interest," Rhiannon says, "there just hasn't been anyone paying attention to developing the interest women have." Until ten to fifteen years ago, dark spirits in particular were thought of as things women wouldn't touch. They weren't classy enough, she says. But now women have more disposable income, they're more educated, and the prejudice against dark spirits has fallen away.

Rhiannon has also observed that women articulate their whiskey experiences differently from men, and she encourages that. They make association to all kinds of things in their own life and are less inhibited to come up with terms for things, she says. Men stick to language they've seen in magazines—preapproved terms. "I don't care if it tastes like cat piss, just tell me what it tastes like," she says. "That's what you want when they develop nose vocabulary." Through Rhiannon's efforts, as well as LUPEC's, maybe women who find themselves interested in whiskey can indulge in the spirit that indulges their femininity as well.

Nina, the neuroscientist (who is not a member of LUPEC), offered a characterization of the whiskey woman that has the same spirit. "It's the woman who doesn't need to be drunk to dance. Or she'll go to a Japanese restaurant and order the fermented soy beans that everyone says is gross, but she wants to try it. Or she'll cut off all her hair and not mourn the loss." These are images a girl can latch on to without appealing to the boys.

These women all agree that the whiskey industry isn't offering enough of the kinds of images they can relate to: sophisticated women looking smart holding whiskey; urban career women relaxing at the end of the day with a glass in their hands. "A thirty- to thirty-five-year-old woman should feel comfortable with the image," says Nina, "it should evoke Jackie O."

Final Thoughts

Perhaps it's been the case that whiskey-drinking women have been misbehavin' women. And perhaps that spirit of misbehavior was important because the toughness and independence that came with it were inextricably linked to memorable achievement. As Laurel Ulrich told us, well-behaved women seldom make history. But maybe it's time to change what it means to behave.

The good girl, the traditional woman, has gone out of style. The rebel has gotten the spotlight. In many ways that's great. But I think this rebel revelry is a transitional phase. Why should it be the rebel, the atypical woman, who is independent and strong and successful? Why is it that only the woman who deviates from the norm earns those adjectives? Why shouldn't the average woman embody those qualities? By characterizing the history-making woman as the rebel, the deviant, we're suggesting she's still not the norm. By characterizing the whiskey-drinking woman as particularly strong or independent, we're accurately reflecting that she's still not the norm. Until she is, we have a way to go.

NOTES

1. No author, "Hillary Gone Wild," YouTube, www.youtube.com/watch?v=i1vdwAOthGA&NR=1 (accessed June 30, 2008).
2. No author, "My Prez Wants to Party All the Time," YouTube, www.youtube.com/watch?v=cBDsXDD_dd0&feature=related (accessed June 30, 2008).
3. Fox News commentary, "Hillary Takes a Shot, Has a Beer, & Fox News Makes Up Story," YouTube, www.youtube.com/watch?v=9AMDz8vDslc&feature=related (accessed June 30, 2008).
4. Fox News internal poll at the end of commentary, "Hillary Takes a Shot, Has a Beer, & Fox News Makes Up Story," YouTube, www.youtube.com/watch?v=9AMDz8vDslc&feature=related (accessed June 30, 2008).
5. Maureen Dowd, "Eggheads and Cheese Balls," *New York Times* (April 16, 2008), www.nytimes.com/2008/04/16/opinion/16dowd.html?_r=1&scp=1&sq=eggheads%20and%20cheeseballs&st=cse&oref=slogin (accessed June 30, 2008).
6. For information about the American Distilling Institute, see its Web site, www.distilling.com (accessed June 30, 2008).
7. Clontarf's new whiskey ads show two women kissing over the slogan "Kiss me, I'm Irish." See Clontarf's Web site, www.clontarfwhiskey.com (accessed June 30, 2008). Canadian Club's new "Damn Right Your Dad Drank It," advertising campaign is also typical of this focus on male drinkers with ads titled "Your Dad Was Not a Metrosexual," "Your Mom Was Not Your Dad's First," and "Your Dad Had Groupies." See the Canadian Club Web site, www.canadianclubwhisky.com (accessed June 30, 2008).

8. Laura Grinstead, "Dish," *Underwired,* April 2008.
9. Laurel Thatcher Ulrich, *Well-Behaved Women Seldom Make History* (New York: Knopf, 2007).
10. Ibid., p. 50.
11. Ibid., p. 58.
12. Ibid., p. 52.
13. The source preferred not to be named. "Nina" is an alias.
14. Nina, personal communication.
15. It is always difficult to make such generalizations, and they are generalizations—patterns rather than rules. But this phenomenon was so widespread among the people I spoke with that I feel comfortable with the generalization.
16. Richard A. Grucza, an epidemiologist at Washington University School of Medicine, came to a similar conclusion. "We can think of U.S. culture as having been traditionally dominated by white men," added Grucza. "As women have 'immigrated' into this culture, they have become 'acculturated' with regard to alcohol use." See Richard A. Grucza, "Alcoholism Is Not Just a 'Man's Disease' Anymore," Press Release, Eurekalert, May 4, 2008, www.eurekalert.org/emb_releases/2008-05/ace-ain042808.php (accessed June 30, 2008).
17. Eric Felten, "He Drinks, She Drinks," *Wall Street Journal,* October 21, 2006, http://online.wsj.com/article/SB116138159885699385.html?mod=googlenews_wsj (accessed June 30, 2008).
18. Sara Faith Alterman, "For the Boys (and Girls): An Ode to Bourbon," *stuff@night,* May 19, 2008, http://stuffatnight.com/boston/liquid/archive/2008/05/19/for-the-boys-and-girls-an-ode-to-bourbon.aspx (accessed June 30, 2008).
19. Ariel Levy, *Female Chauvinist Pigs: Women and the Rise of Raunch Culture* (New York: Simon and Schuster, 2006).
20. Robin Givhan, "Hillary Clinton's Tentative Dip into New Neckline Territory," *Washington Post,* July 20, 2007, www.washingtonpost.com/wp-dyn/content/article/2007/07/19/AR2007071902668.html (accessed June 30, 2008).
21. Felten, "He Drinks, She Drinks."
22. Lauren Clark, "Ladies, Lads, Liquor," drinkboston, http://drinkboston.com/2008/03/22/ladies-lads-liquor/ (accessed June 30, 2008).
23. See LUPEC Web site, http://lupecboston.com/ (accessed June 30, 2008).
24. For more information, see the Celtic Malts' Web site, www.celticmalts.com (accessed June 30, 2008).
25. Personal communication with the author.

5

The Manhattan and You
Thinking about a Classic Whiskey Cocktail

Hans Allhoff

Men who pursue a multitude of women fit neatly into two categories. Some seek their own subjective and unchanging dream of a woman in all women. Others are prompted by desire to possess the endless variety of the objective female world.

—*Milan Kundera,* The Unbearable Lightness of Being

This essay is devoted to a whiskey cocktail that I love and that I believe any whiskey drinker *ought to love*: the Manhattan. I'll confess at the outset that I've got way more to say about the Manhattan than I do about philosophy. Indeed, when Fritz and Marcus told me they were doing a book on whiskey and philosophy, I told them that I wanted to write on the Manhattan; I had no idea then, nor even when I started writing, what the philosophical hook would be.

I'm grateful to Kundera, then, for giving me the needed hook. What I want to do in this essay is talk about the

Manhattan in the same way that Kundera dichotomizes womanizers. Better put, I want to talk about *approaches* to the Manhattan that track the womanizer's approaches to women, as Kundera spells those out.

It's first important to recognize that Kundera isn't talking about all men and their attitudes toward women. He's talking about a particular subset of men—those who pursue a multitude of women—and *their* attitudes. Similarly, I have in mind a particular subset of whiskey drinkers, namely those who love the stuff and are prone if not to obsession at least to connoisseurship (the kind of drinker, I imagine, who would pick up a book like *Whiskey & Philosophy* in the first place and take the time to read an essay on the Manhattan). This isn't meant to be condescending toward those barflies who like to chase a shot of Maker's Mark with a beer. I don't think there's anything wrong with that. I just think that, whatever there might be to say about that approach (and for it), it doesn't demonstrate an approach to whiskey that parallels one of the womanizer's two approaches to women. What, then, are the approaches to the Manhattan that do?

Kundera called the obsession of men who "seek their own subjective and unchanging dream of a woman in all women" *lyrical*. What they crave in women is their ideal, and naturally they're easily let down. But it's all right: "The disappointment that propels them from woman to woman gives their inconsistency a kind of romantic excuse, so that many sentimental women are touched by their unbridled philandering."[1]

To be precise, there are actually two subspecies of Manhattan drinkers whose obsession is lyrical. One, whose ideal Manhattan is admittedly *subjective,* is more closely aligned with the lyrical womanizer. These are folks who only drink a Manhattan a certain way, albeit *their* way. We will meet two such drinkers in a bit (look out for Bookie Bob), but because they're in between the dichotomy I want to explore, they're not essential to it.

We see the other lyrical approach to the Manhattan in those whose ideal is admittedly *objective*; they are, in common usage, your typical cocktail purists. They're committed to the classics almost as a matter of duty; they're *classics* for a reason, after all. What they're committed to, more specifically and more philosophically, is a Platonic form of the Manhattan (more on Platonic forms later). As a result, they're inclined to not look kindly on deviations from or variations of it. They drink in pursuit of an ideal and most likely are too often frustrated. This frustration, in turn, propels them from drink to drink, hopefully over many months and not in the course of a night.

The obsession of men who "desire to possess the endless variety of the objective female world" Kundera called epic. This man "projects no subjective ideal on women, and since everything interests him, nothing can disappoint him."[2] The Manhattan drinker whose approach to the cocktail is epic is your antipurist. He may acknowledge that there's a classic way to make a Manhattan, perhaps even that there is a Platonic form of the drink, but this is of no normative consequence as far as his drinking it goes. Since he doesn't impose any normative ideal on the Manhattan, he's not easily disappointed. (Clearly *some* women disappoint the epic womanizer, just as *some* Manhattans will gag the epic consumer of them.) But neither is he easily impressed; without some operative ideal, how could he be? It's endless variety he's seeking, assuming some baseline threshold has been satisfied.

It's these two approaches to the Manhattan that I want to explore in this essay: the objective lyrical drinker and the epic drinker. What can be said for them, and what can be said against them? But first, the most important few sentences of this essay: What we're talking about here, at the end of the analysis, is just a drink, albeit a drink worth getting to know better and learning to enjoy (responsibly). The fact that J. P. Morgan, himself, drank one on Wall Street every day when trading ended can't make it more than that. Nor can the best ingredients, nor can the best bartender. Nor, probably, can philosophy, though philosophical reflection will likely enhance the experience and certainly add some perspective.

"A Manhattan? I'm Sorry, What's in That?"

A Manhattan is a cocktail, served in a cocktail glass, that's a mixture of whiskey, sweet vermouth, and bitters. I'll say more about each of these ingredients in a moment. Too typically, a Manhattan will come garnished with a maraschino cherry—and may well lack the bitters. It should come with brandied cherries on a cocktail pick. To make the drink, first dash your bitters into a mixing glass full of ice, and then add two ounces of whiskey to one ounce of sweet vermouth.[3] Stir the mixture, and then strain it into a chilled cocktail glass.[4] Add the cherry or cherries.

Where does this recipe come from? The Manhattan is thought to have originated in the mid- to late 1800s. One story, probably not true, has it that the Manhattan was invented at New York City's Manhattan Club in 1874 at a party thrown by Winston Churchill's mother in honor of Samuel Tilden, then the governor of New York and later the Democratic candidate for the presidency. In Harry Craddock's classic compendium of cocktail recipes, first published in 1930, there are actually four different Manhattan recipes listed. It's Manhattan (No. 2) that's probably the closest to the Manhattan that's become the standard: "Dash of Angostura bitters, ⅔ Canadian Club Whisky, ⅓ Ballor Italian Vermouth."[5] (Canadian Club has a lot of rye in it, the more traditional Manhattan whiskey, which may explain Craddock's choice.)

What's whiskey, what's sweet vermouth, and what are bitters? Whiskey is a distilled grain spirit (like gin and vodka) that's aged (unlike gin and vodka) in an oak barrel. So, like Scotch? Sure, but not as far as Manhattans are concerned. Scotch is primarily distilled from barley.[6] Manhattans, on the other hand, are made with either bourbon whiskey, distilled predominantly from corn, or, more classically, a spicier, more robust whiskey distilled from rye.[7] I don't want to get too into labels here, but bourbon standards may include Wild Turkey,

Maker's Mark, and Bulleit (which has a lot of rye in it).[8] (Before I met rye, I preferred Maker's, if only because there was something alliteratively cool about asking for a Maker's Manhattan.) You can always class it up a notch, of course, with a more expensive bourbon like Basil Hayden's. Beyond those labels and their peers, you're getting into well-aged and small-batch bourbons that are, arguably, better had by themselves, or neat. As for ryes, Jim Beam makes one, as does Wild Turkey, but more commonly you'll find Manhattans made with Rittenhouse or Old Overholt. For a pricier alternative, there's Sazerac Rye and Old Potrero Rye. It's really up to you, your palate, and your wallet. The good news is that as with a lot of cocktails, you're not necessarily getting a better drink just because you buy the good stuff.

Vermouth is where Manhattans get interesting—and good. Vermouth is fortified wine (wine to which alcohol has been added) flavored with aromatic herbs and spices.[9] Sweet vermouth, typically called Italian vermouth (in contrast to the dry French vermouth used in a martini), is really where the balancing act in making a decent Manhattan begins.[10] Standbys include Martini & Rossi and Noilly Prat. If you want to get a little more serious, Carpano makes two great vermouths: Punt E Mes and Antica Formula. There's also Vya from California, which is quite good, though almost a different sort of thing altogether.

Bitters are made from herbs and roots dissolved in alcohol. A long time ago, they were thought to have medicinal and digestive purposes. Today, they add depth and complexity to cocktails. Bitters may not be the most important Manhattan ingredient in terms of overall taste, but they may well be the linchpin of the drink. Without bitters, say bartenders Jeff Hollinger and Rob Schwartz, "the Manhattan lacks the characteristically herbaceous flavor that makes it one of the most popular cocktails mixed today."[11] Angostura bitters are the most common bitters used in a Manhattan, but it's not an affront to the drink to use orange bitters instead. What I don't recommend are Peychaud's bitters, which brings anise into the flavor profile of the cocktail; do keep some

Peychaud's around for a Sazerac, however, another classic whiskey cocktail.[12] Bitters are measured in dashes, meaning they're strong; a dash too few or a dash too many can make for a Manhattan that a Manhattan lover might hate.

"Perfect I Can Do. Perfection I Can't."

The lyrical womanizers, we've seen, "seek their own subjective and unchanging dream of a woman in all women." So it is with the lyrical Manhattan drinkers but with an important difference. There's nothing *subjective,* they'll say, about their dream drink. Rather, they see the Manhattan as a classic cocktail; as drinkers, they believe it's their duty to replicate it, get it right, and drink it as it was meant to be drunk. Replicate what, though; get what right? That's precisely Kundera's point, and it's a point I want to urge: "[S]ince an ideal is by definition something that can never be found, they are disappointed again and again."[13] Bartenders can certainly make a great Manhattan, but the lyrical drinker won't, indeed can't, be thoroughly satisfied.

What's driving this attitude (mistakenly, in my view) is some imagined ideal, an ideal I want to suggest that we might think of as the Platonic form of the cocktail. Let me introduce Plato's theory of forms, then, in as few words as possible. (It's at this point, when I have to get serious, that it may appear to the reader that I know more about drinking than I do about philosophy.) As Plato understood them, forms are what answer the question "What is that?" with "It's a Manhattan." When discussing the forms, Socrates says the following to an interlocutor in *The Republic*:

> Let us take any common instance; there are beds and tables in the world—plenty of them, are there not. . . . But there are only two ideas or forms of them—one the idea of a bed, the other of a table. . . . And the maker of either of them makes a bed or he makes a table for our use, in accordance with the idea.[14]

So, particular instances of tables and chairs (i.e., individual tables and chairs) share the same form. Likewise, we can say that particular Manhattans share the same form. It's a *form* that makes a certain drink a *Manhattan* (that lends it its Manhattan-ness) and not a gin and tonic or a Budweiser. That is, to be a Manhattan is to possess certain properties that themselves are necessary and sufficient to compose the form of Manhattans. Take one of those properties away, or add a property to them, and then the debate begins on whether we still have a Manhattan and not some modified version of one (or some other drink entirely). Just think of a form as providing both the necessary and sufficient characteristics that a thing must have to be the thing that it is.

Forms are real under Plato's theory of forms—indeed, they're reality at its highest—but they're not real in the everyday sense of the way we use the term 'real'.[15] They're not of the material world; that is, we are unable to apprehend them with our senses.[16] They are, however, the basis of reality; they're what make everything what it is.[17] What does this mean? It means that you can't walk into a bar and ask for the form of a Manhattan. What you can do is order a Manhattan, and whether you're served one will depend on whether the drink you're served *corresponds* to the form of the Manhattan. How "real" a Manhattan you'll enjoy will depend on how well aligned this correspondence is. So, if a Manhattan is made with whiskey, vermouth, and bitters, and a certain dive bar doesn't have bitters but mixes whiskey and vermouth quite competently, we might say that they serve passable Manhattans. If they also don't have vermouth, it's probably safe to say they can't serve a Manhattan at all.

This is where the idea of a cocktail purist comes in. Purists are people who adhere, almost as a matter of principle, to certain ways of doing or having things. We might speak of a jazz purist, for example, who insists on listening to jazz either live or on vinyl. She may also hate avant-garde and free jazz. A bicycle purist would not be caught dead riding the kind of bike that Lance Armstrong rode to seven Tour de

France victories; it's too easy to ride, built of too many things that aren't necessary. He'd rather be on the kind of bike you see people riding around the streets of Amsterdam, even if there's much that might be wrong with it. The brakes may be sticky. The rotational weight of the wheels may be too high. Its geometry may make for an uncomfortable or inefficient ride.

What unites all of these purists is that they're anti-innovation, antimodification, and antiadaptation, among a lot of other things. On the positive side, they're essentialists, meaning they believe in more or less rigid categories (think strict constructionism of Plato's theory of the forms) to distinguish between what's authentic and what's an impostor. It is, for sure, some cocktail purist who came up with 'mocktail' to describe a lot of what young people these days drink (in Buddha-themed lounges, of course).

The problem with all of this is that the Platonic form of the Manhattan can't be described with sufficient specificity to be of any great guidance. There may be certain threshold requirements that, if met, elevate a Manhattan to a higher level, but there simply isn't one *single* way of making the drink that outdoes all others. The ideal—rye whiskey, sweet vermouth, and bitters, garnished with a brandied cherry or three—isn't particular enough. This is because that ideal, that is, the form of a Manhattan, doesn't touch on a lot of those *negotiables* (and various combinations of them) that make the drink good, great, or perhaps gross.

Let's take two drinks to illustrate this point. The first is what, short on supplies, I might make at home: Maker's, Cinzano Rosso, and Angostura bitters garnished with a maraschino cherry. There's absolutely no doubt that that's a Manhattan and that it'll taste delightful. The second is the Manhattan at Absinthe Brasserie and Bar in San Francisco: two ounces of Maker's, one ounce of Carpano Antica Formula, a dash each of Angostura and orange bitters, three brandied cherries, *and* an orange twist for garnish.[18] Both of those drinks, as far as the form is concerned, are Manhattans, but neither can be said to be beyond improvement. Perhaps the most that can be said of each, assuming they're made properly, is that they're very good considering what they are.

The lyrical Manhattan drinker, like Kundera's lyrical womanizer, may well be easily and often disappointed. And maybe that's even a bit harsh; perhaps it's better to say that he'll always want more. What, then, is the upside? A lyrical drinker may feel like he has no choice; there's no other way to judge anything than with reference to its possible perfection. The true reward, I suspect, comes with drinking a cocktail that's over a century old, and drinking it as people did more than a century ago. There's something about that communion with past drinkers, and communion with present drinkers also in communion with the past, who "get it." This is a drink with a history, a story, and a style; that's what it means to be a classic cocktail.

> Whereas a martini is celebratory and chrome-plated, a Manhattan is nostalgic, like a black-and-white movie. It is cocktail noir: sip one long enough and its rich, dark retrospection will evoke double-breasted suits and Bakelite telephones with Butterfield 8 exchanges (the Lady in Red is optional).[19]

To order one is to appear the informed, seasoned, and mature drinker. What's lost, of course, is variety and differentiation, both of which may well make for a damn good drink.

"Delightful. We Do a Wonderful Manhattan Here."

The epic drinker is above all of this. This isn't to say he's not committed to a Platonic form of the Manhattan—whiskey, vermouth, and bitters garnished with a cherry—but rather to say that he understands that the form sets a threshold above which there's a lot of drinking to be done. Like Kundera's epic womanizer, then, the epic drinker *can* be disappointed; just because he imposes no subjective ideal on the Manhattan doesn't mean that he'll drink anything. To the extent that the epic drinker is impressed and pleasured by the drink, however, it's a purely subjective reaction. It has nothing to do, no offense to the lyrical connoisseur, with the idea that he's perfected the drink, or achieved some imagined ideal. He likes the classics, but he doesn't think being classic gives them any kind of normative authority. This is why he's fine with riffs and innovations.

Consider, for example, the New York City bartender Yvan Lemoine's Smoked Manhattan.[20] Lemoine begins by making a Manhattan as we know it: he pours bourbon, sweet vermouth, and bitters into an empty mixing glass. Then he rests a strainer on top of the mixing glass, and he places a wood chip on top of the strainer. Using a kitchen torch, Lemoine ignites the wood chip and covers the glass and strainer with a metal shaker for forty-five seconds. The wood chip then goes into the mixing glass with ice, and it's chilled for about thirty seconds before it's strained into a cocktail glass. Arguably, this is no riff on the Manhattan at all but rather the addition of something that's implicit in the whiskey for which the Manhattan calls, namely, the smokiness that comes from the spirit being aged in charred oak barrels. Another bartender, or mixologist if you prefer, who goes to this kind of length is Scott Beattie of Cyrus, a restaurant in Healdsburg, California. Beattie makes a Manhattan, like the rest of us, with whiskey, sweet vermouth, and bitters, but he uses a bourbon whiskey that he infuses with vanilla bean and citrus (lemon and orange) zests.[21]

Lemoine and Beattie, arguably, deliver a Manhattan that's an enhanced version of what the Platonic form allows, and it's a version the lyrical drinker may find offensive. But perhaps not. The lyrical drinker may like a vermouth that has hints of vanilla; if that's the case, Beattie's Manhattan might really please him. Ditto for Lemoine. Different wood chips will add a different flavor profile to the drink, and some may not tweak what we expect a Manhattan to taste like but rather make it taste *more* like we expect it to.

But what happens when we add, or take away, an ingredient that's essential? At San Francisco's Cantina, Duggan McDonnell makes a Pomegranate Manhattan with Woodford Reserve bourbon, pomegranate molasses, Cynar, and house-made "Casablanca" bitters (which includes cinnamon, saffron, and some other North African flavors).[22] There's some deviation there, on two counts. Most obviously, the pomegranate molasses is an alien addition to the Manhattan; the recipe neither calls for it nor anything like it for which it's a substitute. Cynar is an artichoke-based bitter aperitif from Italy; in other Manhattan variations, Cynar is a substitute for more traditional bitters. The cocktail may well have the flavor profile of a Manhattan, but will it please the lyrical drinker? Probably not; it's a *Pomegranate* Manhattan, which, like a *Perfect* Manhattan, deviates in a meaningful way from the form of a Manhattan as he understands and appreciates it. You can't have a Manhattan without sweet vermouth. Plain and simple. A Manhattan at Perbacco, also in San Francisco, is made with a splash of Cynar *and* Carpano Antica Formula vermouth. The lyrical consumer may still have a problem with that; the recipe calls for more traditional bitters, Angostura or orange.

The epic drinker, to experience "the endless variety" of Manhattans out there, may well be pleased by all of this. And, just as important, it's not that the epic drinker craves this kind of bold experimentation and variety; it's more that he's fine with it. Each drink, he thinks, has something new and different to offer him. And the variations need not be dramatic. Thus, when the cocktail critic for the *San Francisco Chronicle*, Gary Regan, devoted an entire column to the Manhattan—"the true sovereign of the V-shaped glass"—he gave up his preferred recipe:

> I typically make my Manhattans with two parts spicy bourbon—think Wild Turkey, Buffalo Trace, Evan

Williams Black Label and Bulleit—one part Noilly Prat sweet vermouth, and too much Angostura bitters for most people's palates. About six dashes, if you please.[23]

Just a matter of months later, however, Regan was raving about a very special Manhattan at the Windmill Lounge in Dallas, Texas, named after a regular named Bookie Bob:

"Bookie Bob's Manhattans are not for the faint of heart—they call for Booker's barrel-proof bourbon, sweet and dry vermouths, a dash of bitters and a secret ingredient: black cherries marinated in Luxardo maraschino liqueur."[24]

Regan has all the tolerance, and enthusiasm, of an epic drinker. (While Bookie Bob is that drinker who straddles the operative dichotomy in this essay; as a subjective lyrical consumer, he has an ideal, but it's not one that he thinks is normative.)

Kundera thought that an epic womanizer could not be disappointed: "since everything interests him, nothing can disappoint him." Extending this analogy to epic drinkers isn't a perfect fit. As we've seen, the epic drinker, interested as he is in variety, won't drink just anything. (Although, query whether the epic womanizer is satisfied with just any woman who will crawl into bed with him.) He's more open, however, to experimenting with different whiskies, different bitter components, and perhaps even substitutes for vermouth. Though he may prefer one preparation of the Manhattan to another, he's not wedded to that preparation as a normative commitment. What he loses out on is *consistency* and the self-confidence that comes with having *a* drink that is his own. The epic drinker, like the epic womanizer, is a tourist. The latter has no woman to call his own. The former has no Manhattan.

"Care for Another?"

I am entirely open to the charge that all I've done is dress up, in so many words, two very basic approaches to imbibing. You can either be committed to the classic construction of a cocktail and hold every one you have up to that normative ideal, or else you can be open to variety, to experimentation, to deconstruction. You can be either a lyrical drinker or an epic one. This dichotomy tracks more than just two prevailing approaches to drinking among *serious* drinkers, however. More broadly, it tracks a divide in cocktail culture that, certainly since the mid-1990s, has really taken off and gone stratospheric. Describe the trend as you will, but the fact that bartenders can now go by mixologist, spirit savant, and liquid engineer says it all. There's probably no better time to be a drinker in America's history than right now. The question, now that we're taking cocktails seriously once again, is how to drink them.

In the Manhattan I think this is all apparent on a micro level. With the Manhattan we have a cocktail that in David Embury's classic 1948 book *The Fine Art of Mixing Drinks* is listed as one of the six basic drinks. It's a cocktail that most importantly has endured and that we can pursue lyrically or epically today. Each approach has something to recommend it, as I've tried to convey. It is Craddock, though, who imparts the most important words of wisdom.

If everyone knew a little about the absorbing subject of absorbing alcohol there would be even less Prohibition in the United States than there is now. The great mistake is that everyone knows either too little or too much. Those who know too little either do not admit their lack of knowledge and make an enemy of alcohol by abusing it, or are so terrified of it that they regard it as being something supernatural and satanic and utterly anathema. Those who know too much about it become intolerant of every form of liquid which does not happen to be the one concerning which they consider themselves to be an expert.[25]

The Manhattan, in other words, is a drink. Get to know it, and get to know it well. But don't abuse it, and don't develop a taste for the Manhattan to the exclusion of the other wonderful libations that are out there, classics or riffs thereon.

NOTES

The chapter epigraph is taken from Milan Kundera, *The Unbearable Lightness of Being* (New York: Harper & Row, 1984), p. 194.

1. Ibid., p. 195.
2. Ibid.
3. You're welcome to make a bigger Manhattan, but I'd recommend finishing this one and just making a second instead. Drinks like the Manhattan and martini can go warm and flat on you, and you don't want that.
4. I've learned to stir a cocktail like the Manhattan, or the martini, by making forty rounds in the mixing glass with a cocktail spoon. One reason for this is that when you're dealing with a cocktail made only of spirits, you want to minimize dilution; shaking a drink with ice dilutes it a bit more than stirring it carefully does. The other reason has to do with presentation. A shaken drink has a cloudiness to it as a result of the shaking adding air bubbles. Presentation obviously matters when it comes to food; why shouldn't it matter, too, when it comes to drink?
5. Harry Craddock, *The Savoy Cocktail Book* (New York: Simon and Schuster, 1934), pp. 100–101. Manhattan (No. 1) calls for two dashes of either curacao or maraschino and a quarter of a slice of lemon. Also, whereas the other Manhattan recipes are provided in parts whiskey to vermouth, Manhattan (No. 1) calls for "1 Pony Rye Whisky" and "1 Wineglass Vermouth (Mixed)." Craddock also offers a "Sweet" Manhattan that has more Italian vermouth and less whiskey (and no bitters) (and is stirred) as well as a "Dry" Manhattan that has equal parts French and Italian vermouth to equal part whiskey (and no bitters) (and is also stirred). Manhattan nos. 1 and 2 are to be shaken.
6. There is a variant of the Manhattan made with Scotch, but it's called a Rob Roy. The Irish whiskey variant is called a Paddy.

7. In *The Art of the Bar: Cocktails Inspired by the Classics*, Jeff Hollinger and Rob Schwartz tell us that bourbon began to replace rye in the Manhattan after Prohibition, when rye was harder to find. Acknowledging that other bartenders will argue the point, they believe that either spirit will work in a Manhattan. See Jeff Hollinger and Rob Schwartz, *The Art of the Bar: Cocktails Inspired by the Classics* (San Francisco: Chronicle Books, 2006), p. 22. *Esquire* writer David Wondrich is one who will argue, "No amount of fiddling with the vermouth can save this drink if you've got bourbon in the foundations; it's just too sticky-sweet." See his *Esquire* Manhattan recipe, www.esquire.com/drinks/manhattan-drink-recipe (accessed June 22, 2008).

8. A bartender friend (who really knows what he's doing) once told me he likes making Manhattans with Old Crow, which you'll find on the lowest shelf of your corner liquor store. So don't feel obliged to ask for what's behind the counter.

9. Gary Regan, in a great article on the Manhattan, lists the following: hyssop, coriander, juniper, cloves, chamomile, orange peel, rose petals, calamus root, elderflowers, gentian, ginger, allspice, and horehound. See Gary Regan, "The Manhattan project: A Bartender Spills His Secrets on the King of Cocktails," *San Francisco Chronicle*, September 21, 2007, www.sfgate.com/cgi-bin/article.cgi?f=/c/a/2007/09/21/WI1ORSF9C.DTL (accessed June 30, 2008).

10. This is the proper place to mention the so-called Perfect Manhattan, which calls for equal parts sweet and dry vermouth and is typically garnished with a lemon twist.

11. Hollinger and Schwartz, *The Art of the Bar*, p. 22.

12. For a discussion and recipe for the Sazerac, see Hollinger and Schwartz, *The Art of the Bar*, pp. 16–17.

13. Kundera, *The Unbearable Lightness of Being*, p. 201.

14. Plato, *The Republic*, Book X, 596b, trans. Benjamin Jowett, The Internet Classic Archive, http://classics.mit.edu/Plato/republic.html (accessed July 21, 2008).

15. In *The Republic*, Socrates speaks of someone who "recognizes the existence of absolute beauty and is able to distinguish the idea from the objects which participate in the idea, neither putting the objects in the place of the idea nor the idea in the place of the objects." In other words, there's a distinction between the form—a higher reality—and things that exist and are of that form—the reality that our senses apprehend. See Plato, *The Republic*, Book V, 476c.

16. See discussion in Plato, *Symposium*, trans. Alexander Nehamas and Paul Woodruff (Indianapolis, IN: Hackett Publishing, 1989).

Here Plato, through a participant in the conversation, speaks of "the Beautiful itself, absolute, pure, unmixed, not polluted by human flesh or colors or other great nonsense of mortality, but . . . the divine Beauty itself in its one form" (211E–212A).

17. See discussion in Plato, *Phaedo*, trans. G.M.A. Grube (Indianapolis, IN: Hackett Publishing, 1977). Here Plato notes that "it is through Beauty that beautiful things are made beautiful. . . . It is through Bigness that big things are big and the bigger are bigger" (100e).

18. Absinthe is one of the best bars in San Francisco—as well an excellent restaurant—and among the first to offer a superb cocktail program.

19. Thomas Vinciguerra, "I'll Take Manhattan (Brooklyn, Too)," *New York Times*, October 21, 1998, http://query.nytimes.com/gst/fullpage.html?res=9401E4DC173DF932A15753C1A96E958260 (accessed June 30, 2008).

20. See Gary Regan, "Updated Classic Cocktails," Cocktail Guru, www.thecocktailguru.com/press/2006/wine_enthusiast_february .PDF (accessed June 22, 2008).

21. Ibid.

22. Gary Regan, "The Manhattan Project." The recipe also appears on Cantina's Web site. For details, see www.cantinasf.com/menu .html (accessed June 22, 2008).

23. Regan, "The Manhattan Project."

24. Gary Regan, "The Cocktailian: A Texas barkeep takes on the Manhattan," *San Francisco Chronicle*, April 11, 2008, www .sfgate.com/cgi-bin/article.cgi?file=/chronicle/archive/2008/04/11/WINLVTBUV.DTL&type=wine (accessed June 30, 2008).

25. Craddock, *The Savoy Cocktail Book*, p. 8.

UNIT II

The Beauty and Experience of Whiskey

6

Whiskey, Whisky, Wild Living, and the Hedonistic Paradox

Robert Arp

One of my high school friends named Jim died of an alcohol overdose in college; he liked his Jack Daniel's too much and, in fact, that's what killed him in this case. Jim's death made me think of the kind of life he'd led. He was always living in the moment, a pleasure seeker with the motto "If it feels good, do it twice." And he loved Lynyrd Skynyrd, which included their song, "Whiskey Rock A-Roller," from the *Nuthin' Fancy* album.

I've got another friend named Dan who is also a big fan of whiskey—make that *whisky*. You see, Dan knows the difference between what he calls "low-grade whiskey, with an 'e' " from places like Ireland and the United States, and "high-grade whisky, without an 'e' " from places like Scotland and Canada.[1] Dan's particular poison is Canadian Club (and I suspect he's an alcoholic). I told Dan about my high school friend Jim dying of an overdose of JD, and we got into a discussion about whiskey, whisky, wild living, and what is known as *the hedonistic paradox*, namely, the idea that whenever pleasure itself is sought, one ultimately finds pain.

Not only did Dan say that he knows the difference between whiskey and whisky, but he also thinks that he could never succumb to the hedonistic paradox because "his tastes are too refined *merely* to drink his whisky without an 'e.'" He "makes love" to his CC. (Interestingly enough, Dan is also a Skynyrd fan! Given his "refined" tastes, you'd think that Southern rock was beneath him.)

All of these things—namely, thinking about the death of Jim from a whiskey overdose, Jim's wild lifestyle, my conversation with Dan about "making love" to his CC, whiskey, whisky, and pleasure seeking—form the bases for this chapter. First, I'll discuss the distinction between bodily pleasure and mental pleasure, introducing two forms of metaphysical dualism. Next, I'll discuss pleasure seeking and the hedonistic paradox. Then, we'll see if someone with more refined tastes, like my friend Dan, can avoid the results of the paradox. I'll offer some possible solutions for people who would like to seek some form of pleasure while trying to avoid the hedonistic paradox. In the end, however, we'll see that it's most likely the case that whiskey drinkers and whisky drinkers alike cannot avoid the results of the paradox if the pleasure associated with drinking is the *only* goal they're seeking.

Snortin' Whiskey and Savoring Whiskey

There's *drinking* whisk(e)y, and then there's *savoring* whisk(e)y (either kind of whisk(e)y, because it doesn't make a difference here). Let's say that the whiskey drinker is someone who drinks whiskey to satisfy a *bodily* need, whether this need be simple thirst or an addiction (as is hinted at in the Pat Travers song titled "Snortin' Whiskey"). Here, the bodily need is associated with basic physiological desires as one might have for caffeine, nicotine, sex, other drugs like alcohol, cocaine, crack, heroine, or, of course, rock 'n' roll! Think of the wasted, low-life dregs at the local biker bar gulping down Jack Daniel's and Busch beer while some lousy garage band plays out of tune on stage in the dimly lit corner of the bar.

On the other hand, the whiskey savorer drinks whiskey knowing that a bodily pleasure will be fulfilled *but* with the added benefit of a *mental recognition* of that fulfillment. Here, it's not just a non-conscious, animalistic bodily need that is being fulfilled (although it may be); there is also the conscious, *experiential awareness* of the fact that the bodily need is being met, fulfilled, or satiated. Think of the more sophisticated gentry at the downtown jazz club sipping on their Cutty Sarks and apple martinis—while Medeski Martin and Wood play on stage in a less dimly lit corner of the club—who sit back and "take in" and relish all of the wonderful tastes, sights, and sounds of the entire jazz club experience.

Thus, whereas the whiskey-drinking, wasted, low-life dreg fulfills a bodily need that is non-conscious and physiological (even animalistic; after all, the bar is just like a watering hole), the whiskey-savoring, sophisticated, gentrified person fulfills a mental need that is conscious and experiential (and probably reserved only for humans).

Now, to buy this distinction between whiskey drinking and whiskey savoring, you must hold to some sort of *metaphysical dualism*. *Metaphysics* is the area of philosophy that investigates the nature and principles of things that exist. Metaphysicians want to know what really exists in reality (Is it all material stuff, immaterial stuff, or some combination?); what kinds of things make up reality (Does some god or gods exist? Do I exist? Do minds? Souls? True freedom?); and how things are related to one another (Is what I perceive *really* reality? Are there real causes? Events?). The English word 'dualism' comes from the Greek word *duo* meaning "two." According to metaphysical dualism (in the metaphysical subdiscipline of philosophy of mind), a person is made up of two fundamental things: a material body and an immaterial mind/soul/spirit. Let's now consider two versions of metaphysical dualism, *substance dualism* and *property dualism*.

According to substance dualism, a person is made up of two wholly distinct *substances*, an immaterial mind and a material body, that can exist apart from one another. Those who believe in the immortality of the soul are substance dualists because they think that the death of the body does not mean the death of the soul. The soul lives on as a separate substantial thing after the death of the body, which is another distinct, separate substantial thing. A lot of people on the planet are substance dualists of one sort or another, probably because of their religious upbringing.[2] Think of the cartoons where a character gets killed and his/her body stays flat on the ground while the soul/mind/spirit/immaterial substantial part leaves the body and ascends into a heavenly world—this is straightforward mind-body substance dualism.

Contemporary discussions of religious and nonreligious forms of substance dualism in Western history usually trace their roots back to the famous Modern philosopher, René Descartes (1596–1650), but forms of substance dualism can be found in the history of Western philosophy in the twentieth century and back through Thomas Aquinas (1225–1274) to St. Augustine (354–430), Plotinus (204–270), Aristotle (384–322 BCE), and Plato (ca. 428–348 BCE).[3] In fact, the cartoon character rendition of the soul leaving the body is very close to what people have actually believed in most Western societies throughout the history of Western civilization. The histories of Eastern and Middle Eastern philosophy are also peppered with beliefs in various forms of substance dualism.[4]

According to property dualism, a person is one substance that is made up of two wholly distinct properties: an immaterial mental property (the mind and mental states capable of savoring whiskey) and a material bodily property (the brain and neurophysiological states capable of drinking whiskey). On this view, the mind and brain are distinct properties of some one person, similar to the way that "roundness" and "blackness" are distinct properties found in the period at the end of this sentence. Just as we can distinguish the property of roundness from the property of blackness in some one period, so, too, can we distinguish an immaterial mental property from a material bodily property in some one person. However, just as the roundness and blackness of that particular period can exist only while that particular period exists, so, too, according to property dualists the mental and bodily properties of a person can exist only while that person is alive. So when we delete the period, the properties of roundness and blackness in that particular period cease to exist along with the period. Likewise, when a person dies, both that person's body and mind cease to exist. Such a view of mind in relation to body seems to be consistent with scientific data, and is appealing to those who do not believe in the immortality of the soul.[5]

In either form of dualism, the body, in some form, seems to be necessary in order to maintain a person's existence as the individual makes his/her way around in this world. At the same time, in both substance dualism and property dualism, a distinction can be made between characteristics or properties of one's bodily life, and characteristics or properties of one's mental life. In other words, both substance dualists and property dualists think that there is something about the mental realm that makes it distinct from the bodily realm; again, either in *substance* or in *property*.

Satisfying Pigs or Dissatisfying Socrates

The famous moral philosopher John Stuart Mill (1806–1873) was a property dualist (at least) who would likely agree with my whiskey-drinking versus whiskey-savoring distinction. In his famous work titled *Utilitarianism*, he distinguishes between lower pleasures/pains and higher pleasures/pains.[6] There are those "lower" pleasures/pains that are most appropriately understood as *feelings associated with a body*. Examples of these pleasures and pains would be aches, pains, and butterflies in the stomach, as well as euphoric surges, adrenaline rushes, thirsts, and other physiological urges. Normally, when we think of pleasure and pain, we think of them in this bodily way, associated with the neurophysiological processes of a living animal with an intact nervous system. This is probably what my high school friend, Jim, was after in his rock-a-rollin' pursuits, with JD, sex, and Skynyrd shows.

Then there are "higher" pleasures and pains, understood as *qualitative experiences associated with a mind*. Examples of these would include the pleasure of discovering the solution to a complex math problem, the pain of having made an immoral decision that cannot be undone, the joy of knowing one is loved by a friend, and the savoring of a single malt, lowland whisky from the Auchentoshan Distillery in Scotland. Here, the pleasures and pains are less bodily and more mental, and have names like *joy, contentment, satisfaction, regret*, and *sorrow*. This is probably more of what my (somewhat elitist) friend Dan was getting at when he said that he "makes love" to his CC; he relishes, cherishes, and savors his whisky, and *he knows that* he relishes, cherishes, and savors his whiskey.

Dan actually thinks that his taste for whisky puts him in a better place than those "tasteless brutes who drink that caramel-colored water" known as whiskey with an 'e.' In other words, as a *whisky* drinker and savorer, his tastes are qualitatively, *objectively* better than some poor *whiskey* drinker and savorer (if you could even savor that crap). When asked what grounds he has for his claim of superiority, he will note that (1) he doesn't just drink whisky, he savors it, and (2) he has experienced both "*piss*key" (as he calls it) and whisky, and he knows better.

Interestingly enough, Mill actually would agree with Dan's reasons. In *Utilitarianism*, he claims that "it is better to be a human dissatisfied than a pig satisfied; better to be Socrates dissatisfied than a fool satisfied."[7] His arguments surrounding this claim have to do with what we spoke about already, namely, the intuition that pleasures of the mind are qualitatively better than pleasures of the body and, hence, pleasures of the mind should be pursued. We're humans, after all, with the gift of conscious experience, and not merely animals.

But Mill also notes that it is the person who has experienced both kinds of pleasures and consistently goes for the pleasures of the mind that gives us a clear reason for going for the pleasures of the mind. If you've seen gay Paris, you wouldn't want to go back to the farm, anyway. According to Mill, take an honest look at the people who have experienced higher and lower pleasures, and you will see that, on the whole, they prefer higher pleasures.

However, this argument has failed to persuade lots of people. Who's to say what pleasures are better than others, especially since pleasures and pains seem to be so much a matter of personal, subjective taste? Further, I'm my own person with my own uniqueness, and I don't care what most people think and prefer. Someone might say this: "I don't care if you've been to Paris and the farm, I still find the pleasures of the farm much more gratifying, and much more fulfilling, than the damn city, even though I've never been to the city! I prefer the farm!" Or, more damaging to Mill's argument, someone may say something like this: "I've been to Paris and the farm myself just like you, Mr. Mill, and I still prefer the farm!" There are lots of sophisticated, gentrified folk who really dig Jack Daniel's.

Mill also gives a kind of "pleasure metric" such that there are better and worse pleasures of the mind as well as better and worse pleasures of the body. And, this pleasure metric is based on and justified by the person who has experienced any and all forms of bodily and mental pleasure. Think about it again: once you've eaten filet mignon, experienced valet parking, and vacationed in Palm Springs or Malibu, who in their right mind would ever go back to burgers, self-parking, and the Jersey Shore? Now, apply this kind of thinking to any and all pleasures of the body and mind. Is the argument persuasive? That's for you to decide.

The following represents my rendition of a classification of Millian pleasures:

Higher Pleasure of the Mind
Example: philosophical contemplation, Mill's Socrates satisfied

Lower Pleasure of the Mind
Example: Dan's *savoring* whisky, Mill's fool's *mind* satisfied?

Higher Pleasure of the Body
Example: Dan's *drinking* whisky, eating filet mignon

Lower Pleasure of the Body
Example: Dan's drinkin' *piss*key, Mill's pig satisfied, Mill's fool's *body* satisfied?

Whiskey Rockin' and Rollin' and Rockin' and Rollin' and Rockin' . . .

Of course, not everyone who drinks whiskey is a rock-a-roller type like my dead friend Jim (God rest his soul). Yet, there are people, like Jim, who can't stop drinking whiskey, or snorting cocaine,[8] smoking crack, eating fatty foods, having casual sex, and/or engaging in other bodily pursuits. Such pleasure seekers must confront the *hedonistic paradox*.[9] The basic idea behind the hedonistic paradox is that whenever pleasure itself is the object sought, either it is not found or it is found. If pleasure is not found, the result is the pain associated with not finding the pleasure one seeks. Think of the junkie who is jonesing for the next fix, when he or she is suffering the pain associated with *not having* that fix. I recall Dennis Hopper's drunk character from the movie *Hoosiers* (1986) and James Franco's strung-out character from the movie *City by the Sea* (2002) both acting this way as they yearned, and almost writhed, for that next taste.

On the other hand, if pleasure is found, especially on a consistent basis, the result is still pain. The pain results from either finding pains that are *mistaken for* pleasures in the long or short term, or from the boredom of always getting the pleasures one wants. Regarding mistaken pleasures, think of the junkie who contracts HIV from a fix or the sex addict who impregnates his one-night stand. Concerning the issue of boredom, consider the Paris Hiltons of the world or those who "suffer" from the effects of the Don Juan syndrome by being "so, like, totally bored with, like, having everything you want, like, whenever you, like, want it . . ."

Either way, whether pleasure is found or not, the result *paradoxically* is still pain. The hedonistic paradox is *hedonistic* because of the focus on the pleasure being sought (*hedon* is Greek for 'pleasure'). It is a paradox in the sense of an *ironic riddle* because one consistently finds the exact opposite (pain) of what one set out to find in the beginning (pleasure). Other riddling paradoxes might be (1) why it is that certain things that taste and feel so good to us turn out to be really bad for us, like sugary or fatty foods, or (2) why it is that the drunk is the only one who survives the car accident that he himself caused, while everyone else dies. I'm sure more ironic riddling paradoxes can be thought of.

Is there any way out of the hedonistic paradox for someone who wants to continue pursuing pleasure for the sake of pleasure itself? People may not fall victim to the hedonistic paradox for a couple of reasons. One of the problems with pursuing pleasure is the boredom associated with always getting what one wants. A central question that needs to be answered is whether there could be innumerable pleasures to be had at one's disposal. Put another way, given the number of possible activities imaginable, and the pleasures associated with those activities, is it possible to exhaust all of those activities, gain the pleasures, and become bored with the pleasures attained? If there could be innumerable pleasures out there to be had, then it seems like it would not be possible to achieve all of those pleasures; in which case, boredom would never ensue. There's a gazillion different ways to brew and age whiskeys and whiskies, right? Could we ever really get tired of the variety of tastes?

Further, the distinction between lower bodily pleasures and higher mental pleasures may help us out here. Within the bodily realm, there seem to be a variety of different pleasures associated with a variety of different bodily activities. In fact, any pleasure or pain is only a pleasure or pain as it is associated with some form of bodily or mental activity for a human. There are no lower or higher pleasures or pains without bodily or mental activities. This being the case, pleasure is aligned with activities that run the gamut from hurting us in the short term and hurting us in the long term, to helping us in the short term and helping us in the long term. For example, there is a difference between the pleasure had from smoking crack and the pleasures had from pursuing a variety of extreme sports. All things considered, the likelihood of the crack harming you regardless of the precautions you take is much higher than consciously and cautiously pursuing an extreme sport.

Is it possible to pursue pleasure and avoid the paradox? It is easy to see how a life of pursuing lower bodily pleasures leads one into the pains of either not finding what one seeks, mistaking pain for pleasure, or even boredom. But could one fall victim to the hedonistic paradox in the pursuit of higher mental pleasures? Consider the distinction between pleasures that result from *ongoing activities* and pleasures that result from *the knowledge of being in certain completed states*. Think about solving a complex math problem, being honored for an achievement, or being loved by a friend. These are not ongoing activities but completed states of being, in which one has knowledge of these states. The knowledge of these states brings with it a sustaining, almost satiating, form of mental pleasure.

Aristotle has something like this in mind when he investigates various forms of pleasure in his famous work in moral philosophy titled *Nicomachean Ethics*.[10] It may be that bodily pleasures are more the result of ongoing activities, while mental pleasures are more the result of being in a certain state. With this distinction in mind, we may be better able to understand how hard core mathematicians, overachievers, true friends, and whisky savorers achieve satisfaction, contentment, or joy associated with these states. If math equations don't do it for you, think of some tough project, assignment, or task that you have completed and are happy about having completed. Or, think of the runner who trained all of her life for, and actually finished, the big marathon, the father of three who finally got his MBA through night school, or the hero who saved the child from drowning. Now think of these folks reflecting upon their accomplishments with joy. Such joys would seem to be of the kind that, when reflected upon, last a lifetime. A stronger case might be made for one falling victim to the hedonistic paradox in the *pursuit* of either the solution to a math equation, a lasting friendship, a marathon race, or an MBA *prior to* achieving a completed state in that one may never find what one seeks. However, once in a certain completed state it would seem that the pleasure is continuous with the knowledge of the completed state. The same could go for the savoring of a decent drink, or the *afterglow* of Dan's having made love to his CC.

What Would Whisky-Drinking and Whisky-Savoring Dan (and Mill) Do?

If a person engages in physical pleasure seeking for the sake of that pleasure seeking, then we can see how such a lifestyle would lead to a kind of hollowed-out existence, not unlike that of a junkie. A junkie gets to the point where he or she physically must have the drug in order to survive, at least in the short term. Most junkies choose, at first, to use drugs and can change their ways. Maybe junkies and whiskey rock-a-roller types we see featured on VH1's *Behind the Music* should be pitied. But even those members of our community who cannot control themselves, like certain pedophiles, must regulate their desires or have their desires and actions regulated for them.

Can one be said to have skirted the hedonistic paradox altogether, either by pursuing higher mental pleasures or by engaging in activities for the sake of the activities themselves, rather than for the pleasure to be gained from the activities? People have varying degrees of desires for different kinds of things. Consequently, certain people will fall victim to the hedonistic paradox. If one's focus is consistently the pursuit of bodily pleasure itself, then we can see how pain will result. More banal people could live lives that are both blessed and cursed. They could be *blessed* in that they indulge in their every physical desire; yet, this is the very thing that, ultimately, becomes *cursed* for them.

One need not be that experienced in life to see that the *sole* pursuit of pleasure offers little blessings, especially the sole pursuit of bodily pleasure. Many of the wisest of the wise sages in Western and Eastern philosophy talk about how, for most people, bodily pleasures lose their luster the older we get in life.[11] Whisky-savoring Dan and Mill are probably right about a lot of pleasures in that we should seek pleasures of the mind and look to the experienced person for a justification for this kind of pursuit. Notice that I said "a lot of pleasures"; it may be that there is no objective way to decide varying degrees of importance for some pleasures. For example, I consider myself a fairly sophisticated, worldly person, and I'd take Skynyrd and a Polish sausage with mustard and onions over an operatic aria and escargot any day.

When all is said and done, there is wisdom in Mill's claim that happiness in life is attained by *not* making pleasure one's focus: "Those only are happy who have their minds fixed on some object other than their own pleasure. . . . Aiming thus at something else, they find happiness along the way. . . . Ask yourself if you are happy, and you cease to be so."[12]

NOTES

1. No offense, whiskey drinkers. See Dave Broom, *Whiskey: A Connoisseur's Guide* (London: Carleton Books, 1998); and Charles MacLean, *Scotch Whisky: A Liquid History* (New York: Cassell Illustrated, 2005).
2. For corroboration of this claim, see, for example, the articles in John Morgan and Pittu Laungani, eds., *Death and Bereavement around the World* (Amityville, NY: Baywood Publishing, 2005). See the articles in the other books in this series, too.
3. See Gordon Baker and Katherine Morris, *Descartes' Dualism* (London: Routledge, 1996); and John Foster, *The Immaterial Self: A Defence of the Cartesian Dualist Conception of the Mind* (London: Routledge, 1991). Also see Descartes, *Discourse on Method and Meditations on First Philosophy*, trans. Donald Cress (Indianapolis, IN: Hackett Publishing, 1998); Thomas Aquinas, *The Soul: A Translation of St. Thomas Aquinas' De Anima*, trans. John Patrick (New York: B. Herder Book, 1949); Augustine, *St. Augustine's Confessions*, trans. Henry Chadwick (Oxford: Oxford University Press, 1991); *Plotinus, Plotinus: The Enneads*, trans. Stephen MacKenna (Burdett, NY: Larson Publications, 1992); Aristotle, *Aristotle's De Anima*, trans. Hugh Lawson-Tancred (New York: Penguin Books, 1986); Plato, "The Republic" and "Phaedo" in *The Complete Works of Plato*, ed. John Cooper (Indianapolis, IN: Hackett Publishing, 1997).
4. See, for example, Stephen Knapp, *The Universal Path to Enlightenment: The Eastern Answers to the Mysteries of Life* (New York: World Relief Press, 1992); the papers in Glenda Abramson and Hilary Kilpatrick, eds., *Religious Perspectives in Modern Muslim and Jewish Literatures* (London: Routledge, 1995); and S. H. Hook, *Middle Eastern Mythology: From the Assyrians to the Hebrews* (London: Penguin Books, 1963).
5. See the sections on substance dualism and property dualism in K. T. Maslin, *An Introduction to the Philosophy of Mind* (Oxford: Polity Press, 2000); also John Heil, *Philosophy of Mind: A Contemporary Introduction* (London: Routledge, 1998); George Graham, *Philosophy of Mind: An Introduction* (London: Blackwell, 1998); Jaegwon Kim, *Philosophy of Mind* (Boulder, CO: Westview Press, 1998); and E. J. Lowe, *An Introduction to the Philosophy of Mind* (Cambridge: Cambridge University Press, 2000).
6. John Stuart Mill, *Utilitarianism* (Indianapolis, IN: Hackett Publishing, 2002).

7. Ibid., p. 260.
8. Probably to emphasize the wild and carefree rock and roll lifestyle, Pat Travers' song "Snortin' Whiskey" repeats this line numerous times: "been snortin' whiskey and drinkin' cocaine."
9. The term first was introduced by Henry Sidgwick, *The Methods of Ethics* (London: Macmillan, 1874); also see Fred Feldman, "Hedonism," in *Encyclopedia of Ethics*, eds. Lawrence Becker and Charlotte Becker (London: Routledge, 2001), pp. 100–113.
10. Aristotle, *Nicomachean Ethics*, trans. W. D. Ross (Oxford: Clarendon Press, 1908), Book X.
11. See, for example, the discussion of pleasure in Book 1 of Plato's *Republic*; also *Confucius: The Analects*, trans. D. C. Lau (Hong Kong: University of Hong Kong Press, 1979); the four stages of life for the Buddhist, as in Thubten Chodron, *Buddhism for Beginners* (Ithaca, NY: Snow Lion Publications, 2001).
12. John Stuart Mill, "Autobiography," in *The Harvard Classics*, ed. Charles Eliot Norton (New York: P. F. Collier & Son, 1909), vol. 25, p. 94.

7

What to Drink?
Why We Choose the Bourbons We Do

Mark H. Waymack

As someone who has written on whiskeys, I frequently get asked what the best whiskey is. And I have consistently (for consistency is philosophically prized) regarded this as a misguided question. The misguidedness, so to speak, stems from a couple of directions. First, I enjoy a wide variety of whiskeys, not just one. Which particular one I might reach for depends upon my mood, the time of day, the weather. Second, as we all should know, what suits my particular tastes may not suit someone else's palate. And third, to speak of one whiskey being "the best" would seem to presuppose some sort of Platonic form of whiskey[1] that defines whiskey and by which all imperfect particular whiskeys in this world are measured. But I do not subscribe to such Platonic metaphysics, at least not without a few whiskeys under my belt.

Having cleverly deflected this first misguided question, I might slip into thinking that I have escaped unscathed and can go back to enjoying a drink. But no. The questioner, particularly the questioner of a philosophical bent, might pursue the matter further, being not so easily shaken off. "Well," he may continue, "at least tell me why you choose the whiskeys you do choose, even if it's not just one all the time." This seems like perhaps a more fruitful question to pose, though it might simply be that the mellowing effects of that first shot are coursing their way through my internal organs, taking a bit off of that acerbic edge. But still, posed as such it is a question about my particular biography, so to speak, and while certain literary authors and politicians seem to feel that the rest of the world must find their peculiar autobiography of utmost fascination, I can't help but feel that the rest of the world isn't really compellingly fascinated by my own idiosyncratic personal tastes. But surely the question can be generalized a bit into a more engaging philosophical type of question: Why do we, in fact, choose the kinds of whiskeys that we do? What makes a whiskey choice worthy in our eyes, as consumers? And for the sake of making this a slightly more manageable question, I shall arbitrarily narrow it down to why do we pick the bourbons that we pick? (Though much of what emerges here should be applicable to Scotch, rye, etc.)

We are embarked, therefore, on a project in that much neglected field of applied aesthetics, the neglected stepsister to that burgeoning field known as applied ethics. My aim here, then, is to offer a sketch of key ways in which we find a whiskey to be appealing. And just as philosophers working in the trenches of applied ethics generally dance away from the challenge of being committed to any particular theoretical moral philosophy, so I shall beg the indulgence of the reader that I might avoid having to choose any one particular theory of aesthetics, but shall instead from time to time borrow a nugget from here and another from there.

Well, enough folderol. By now that shot you have been drinking as you read this essay should be exerting its effects— clearing out the cobwebs and sharpening your philosophically critical eye.

Receptivity

First, you, the imbiber, must be open to enjoying bourbon. This is both a physiological and psychological point. Some humans, for example, are tone-deaf; some are color-blind. The pleasures that most of us can enjoy by listening to an excellent performance of music are simply not accessible to the tone-deaf person. And a color-blind person simply cannot have the same vibrant perceptual experience touring the Van Gogh Museum in Amsterdam as someone with "normal" vision. Similarly, if someone has been cheated of the physical perceptual structures that make enjoying bourbon possible, then he or she will not be drawn to bourbon, at least not for any aesthetic reasons.

There is also a psychological point here. Some individuals, for particular biographical reasons, will be psychologically averse to bourbon. They may have very unpleasant memories associated with bourbon. (One of the few occasions in life when I got thoroughly inebriated was in my first year of college. In a lovelorn moment, I drowned my sorrows in most of a bottle of cream sherry. The resultant experience, as a whole, was so awful that even to this day, some thirty years later, I still cannot enjoy a cream sherry.) If this sort of thing is the case for an individual, then his or her perceptual experience of bourbon is simply not going to be typical, and other reasons that we explore here will have little relevance or play. Much more about this later.

Quality in Manufacturing

Second, the whiskey should taste good. Said as such, this would appear not to be very helpful or informative. In particular, the wording would seem to blatantly import the very sort of normative/evaluative term 'good' that we are trying to explain. But perhaps I can explain what I have in mind. The late Booker Noe, a grandson of Jim Beam and longtime master distiller for the Jim Beam Distillery, once shared a story with me about a batch of bourbon gone wrong. The grist had cooked and the mash had fermented; but a key part of the column still had broken. In an effort to avoid losing the mash, they pumped it into a holding tank and left it to sit for several extra days until the still could be repaired. But during those extra days of sitting, the mash, as might be expected, began to be populated by unwelcome organisms, including, apparently, *Acetobacter* as well as other wild yeasts and bacteria. So by the time it was pumped to the still, the mash had begun to turn to vinegar. Try as they might, the distillers could not strip the extra acids out of the distilled spirit. And the resulting distillate was very unpleasant to drink, causing a "hot" and "sour" taste and feel in the mouth. At the minimum, then, for a whiskey to be choice worthy, it has to be free of such blatant flaws. (Though I confess to keeping samples of such stuff around as a tool to educate drinkers to potential flaws in whiskeys. But those samples can be called "desirable" only in a nonstandard sense.)

Taste Profile

Third, taste (and here I include not only what happens on the tongue, but also what happens in the nose and mouth) must play a role. Taste, of course, is an (the) obvious reason we might prefer one whiskey to another. And there appears to be a significant degree of subjective variation here.

There are, of course, certain components that seem to form a sort of Wittgensteinean family resemblance for bourbon. The high percentage of corn in the mash bill (somewhere between 51% and about 90%), yields a distinctive flavor profile, a certain corn sweetness. Malted barley, familiar to Scotch whisky drinkers and vitally important for the enzymatic conversion of the starches to fermentable sugars, adds a malty body to the flavor. And while some mash bills (Maker's Mark and Old Fitzgerald, for example) use wheat, most add in a small percentage of rye. The rye adds a certain reedy depth and texture, while wheat produces a lighter, smoother whiskey. By law, of course, bourbon must be aged in new charred white oak barrels. The char of the barrel yields caramelized oak sugars and vanillin from the lignins, and, in some cases, a light hint of smoke from the char. How long the whiskey rests in the barrel and under what storage conditions makes very noticeable differences, as by some biochemical alchemy, harsh, higher alcohols and "fusel oils" dissipate while the whiskey works with the char of the barrel.

All of this is probably well known to the serious imbiber. And the serious, attentive taster will look for, notice, and cherish such differences. Some folks' taste runs toward sweeter bourbons. Buffalo Trace, Elmer T. Lee, and so on are likely to appeal to such a taste preference, and such a taster will tend to see those sweeter whiskeys as somehow better, preferable. Some imbibers' preferences run in a drier direction, and they may prefer Knob Creek or Wild Turkey, to offer two examples.

Beyond sweetness, there is a question of wood: the longer the whiskey is in the barrel, the greater the influence of the wood. Some people seem to find "woodiness" a desirable characteristic, and it is particularly sought after in the Japanese markets. However, my own view is that after twelve years or so, for bourbon, the wood tends to begin to intrude upon the bourbon character of the whiskey. Less than four years, the wood generally has not had a chance to do its job. So, a measure of caramel, vanillin, oak tannins, and so on is good, but one can get too much of a good thing.

Another taste aspect to consider is complexity. Some bourbons emphasize a clean, clear flavor. Maker's Mark, for example, prides itself on consistently leaving all the rough edges behind. They use wheat, rather than rye; and purportedly use higher-quality, longer-aged wood for making the barrels in order to avoid any "green oak" flavoring. Maker's Mark shoots for a reliably round, clear, soft, slightly sweet bourbon. A different example of heading toward simplicity might be

Wild Turkey's Kentucky Spirit or Russell's Reserve. Single barrel products, each bottle voices a certain clarity of nature; it is like listening to the chime of a single bell. Whereas Wild Turkey Rare Breed, even though it comes from the same distillery, being a marrying of at least three different barrel ages, presents layers of complexity. This is more like listening to a clarion of many bells in harmony than a single, clear, pure sound.

I cannot say that complexity per se is better than simplicity, or that sweetness is better than dryness, or that light and clear is better than heavy and reedy. Not only will different people have somewhat different preferences, to some degree, as I noted above, most of us are going to prefer different versions at different times and under different circumstances. Hence, in reaching for or asking for a particular bourbon, much should depend upon matching our taste preferences of that moment with the variety of bourbons available. This requires self-knowledge as well as knowledge of what's in those various bottles.

The Psychology of Taste and the Association of Ideas

All of this is well and good, and, I suspect, it is not at all surprising. But this cannot be the whole story. There are, perhaps, nine or so major bourbon distillers in the United States; yet a walk through a liquor store can reveal shelf after shelf of different bourbons. If there are hundreds upon hundreds of different "brands" of bourbon (but only nine producers), where do they all come from? And the answer is that the major distillers bottle their whiskey under numerous labels. Jim Beam may hold the rights to four or five dozen different labels. Heaven Hill must hold the rights to more than three hundred bourbon labels. Dozens of labels adorn the bourbon that comes from the distillery near Frankfort, Kentucky, which now operates under the name of Buffalo Trace. What gives?

Well, to some extent different bottles of whiskey from the very same distillery can taste quite different. Even if it all comes from the very same run off the still, different ages in the wood and different bottling proofs can produce different tastes. As just one example, every whiskey that comes out of the Wild Turkey plant (actually known as Boulevard Distilling Company), bears the Wild Turkey name; but even so, there are about ten different Wild Turkey whiskeys. Wild Turkey 101 at four or five years will be distinguishable from Wild Turkey at twelve years, at least to someone with some experience who pays attention.

However, consider that there are several distilleries that actively bottle under multiple labels. Go into a well-stocked liquor store and I guarantee you that you will find dozens upon dozens of bottles of bourbon with labels bearing the names of distilleries that exist only on paper. Yet there are only about nine major (physical) bourbon distilleries. A quick review by anyone in the know reveals that the physical distillery legally known as Sazerac Company, Inc., in Frankfort, Kentucky, actively puts out bourbons under a minimum of twelve different brand labels, with multiple varieties of several of those labels. These include Buffalo Trace, Blanton's, Elmer T. Lee, Ancient Age, Eagle Rare, Old Weller, to name just a few. They legally own, last I was informed, more than two hundred labels. Heaven Hill, in Bardstown, owns several hundreds of labels as well. It actively bottles at least two dozen of those labels. And Kentucky Bourbon Distillers, Ltd., whose mailing address is the still site of Heaven Hill that burned several years ago and is undergoing reconstruction (Heaven Hill now actually distills at a facility in Louisville that used to be owned by Old Fitzgerald before it was owned by United Distillers), sells under at least another dozen labels. Jim Beam Brands must actively use two to three dozen labels. It defies the imagination that a single distillery could produce dozens upon dozens of labels that are readily distinguishable by taste. Indeed, blind tasting experiments suggest that some true experts can tell the difference between some of the major producers—for example, they can distinguish between Wild Turkey and Buffalo Trace, between Jim Beam's Knob Creek and Maker's Mark, between Very Old Barton and Old Forester. But even experts can stumble in blind tastings of premium bourbons, and when we confront the realm of mass market bourbons, it is a foolhardy person who believes he can reliably discriminate and identify various bourbons in a blind tasting.

Despite not being able to tell the difference in blind tastings, your average consumer, however, still voices distinct preferences for and loyalty to certain labels. And because of these consumer preferences, distilleries are willing to continue bottling what is virtually the same bourbon under dozens of different labels. So what gives?

Well, psycho-physiological research has repeatedly demonstrated that to no small degree what we taste is conditioned by what we *expect* to taste. You can easily do this at home. Purchase a variety of bottled sparkling waters. Have a group of friends over for a tasting. When the labels are on the bottles, tasters typically have a marked preference for (and give higher scores to) well-known brand names of water: Perrier reliably beats the local grocery store label. But make the test blind, and nearly no one can tell any difference. So, the label changes what we taste.

Good sense would suggest that the same is true for our typical bourbon drinker. When the labels are in sight, the drinker will express a preference for the bourbon that he ahead of time thinks he will like most.

Now, what leads us to prefer one label over another (before the whiskey is even on our lips)? For many people, I suspect, it is nothing more or less than habit. For many of us, however, it is something much more than that: it is, I put to you, a story, an association of ideas in our minds related and called forward in a Humean fashion; that is, related to the philosophy of David Hume.

Imagine we are at a bar. I can see ten or twelve bottles of bourbon behind the bar. Which will I choose? Suppose my glance falls upon a bottle of Booker's. That label, at least for my mind, has a host of associated memories. In Hume's language, there are numerous conjunctions of ideas between that label and various past experiences for me.[2] Seeing the label, my mind pulls those other ideas forward. I can recall sitting in Booker's kitchen, drinking—of course—Booker's. I am reminded of playing the washtub bass while Booker played the jug along with a country band in Booker's backyard at a party. These pleasant memories come rushing forward, and I am inclined to ask for some Booker's Bourbon. Or perhaps my gaze focuses on the Maker's Mark bottle. Associated ideas, memories of dinner on a warm summer night at the house of Bill Samuels (president of Maker's Mark), come to the fore. A delightful tour of the Maker's Mark distillery crowds into my consciousness—the peculiar walnut bung stoppers, the cute red shutters on the black warehouses, the intoxicating aroma of a warehouse on a warm summer day. Or I see the Wild Turkey and think of the huge favor Jimmy Russell did for me by sending some Wild Turkey representatives to help conduct a bourbon tasting for some eighty Mexican academics who were visiting my department.

Yes, I do flatter myself that I have developed a more discriminating palate with regard to whisk(e)y than most people (though by no means all). But I am not so foolish as to deny that a significant measure of what I taste when I choose and enjoy a bourbon is my history with that label. Fond memories (and habit) reinforce preferences, while unpleasant memories (remember my history with cream sherry!) create self-fulfilling bad expectations.

However, as *philosophers*, what are we to think of this? After all, one generally does not choose the career of an academic philosopher for the big bucks that it dangles before us. We chose to be philosophers because of our commitment to the life of *reason*. And if we are truly to be rational in these matters, shouldn't we work at excluding these arbitrary, external, emotive factors from our taste assessments and focus our attention on the brute reality of the taste itself?

I have to agree that in some contexts such an attempt would seem to be appropriate. For example, in writing our book on bourbon,[3] Jim Harris and I visited all the fully operating bourbon distilleries. These visits, typically several days for each facility, produced a collection of "factual" information: historical dates, volume of annual production, mash bill, how many days a fermentation would run, some technical details of distillation (proof off the still, use of the "thumper," copper versus stainless), warehouse practices (aging patterns, open rick or palletized, rotated or not rotated), and so on. But we also inevitably collected innumerable emotive and affective impressions. Many people we met were quite pleasant to be with. A few were truly wonderful personalities. And a very few were a bit unpleasant to be with. A couple of distilleries we found to be architecturally pleasing and/or in beautiful natural surroundings. Maker's Mark, for example, has gone out of its way to maintain a visually beautiful facility. The relatively new "boutique" facility of Labrot & Graham, owned by Brown-Forman, is a visual delight; whereas Brown-Forman's main plant, the Old Forester facility in Louisville, is an "unquaint" brick behemoth in an urban industrial zone. (Not surprisingly, Brown-Forman assiduously steers whiskey tourists to the Labrot & Graham facility, near Versailles, Kentucky, and away from the Louisville plant.)

Now, most of the reading audience for our bourbon book *The Book of Classic American Whiskeys* have had none of these affective experiences that Jim and I share. Hence, when that reader approaches a glass of Wild Turkey, for example, there will be no memory of sharing a sip in delightful conversation with Jimmy and Jolene Russell at a Bourbon Ball in Bardstown. Master Distiller Jerry Dalton is a devotee of Taoist philosophy,[4] so it is impossible for Jim and me to drink his whiskeys without thinking back to long conversations about Taoism with him, but those memories are not available to the average reader.

This creates the challenge that if what we write about the taste of such particular whiskeys is deeply influenced by these peculiar past associated experiences, then we run the danger that what we write in aesthetic terms about particular whiskeys will not resonate with the reader. Our descriptions may fall flat or, worse yet, be regarded as inaccurate.

I believe the whiskey writer has two distinct but not mutually exclusive avenues to pursue. The first, perhaps not surprisingly, is to try very consciously to minimize the effect of such mental associations upon the taste experience. One easy way of doing this, of course, is to conduct blind tastings. In addition to the tastings being blind, we may also do the tasting with one another, comparing our present experience: Did you notice a slight touch of sour orange at the back of the mouth? I think this is sweeter than the last whiskey—do you agree? Do you get the whiff of toffee up front? Such deliberate, close analysis can help us focus more on the present experience by itself and less with those potentially associated ideas. The end result can be a description that is both more toward the "objective" end of the scale as well as being described in adjectives that carry more public meaning to the general reader.

The second strategy for writing about taste is not to ignore the association of ideas that become part of our tasting experience. Rather, we try to write in such a way that we communicate some of those associated ideas to the reader. To the degree that we are successful in that attempt, the reader can begin to share some of those associated ideas in a Humean "sympathetic" fashion. That is to say, the reader, through descriptions and accounts offered by the writer, gains complex ideas that he or she may not have directly experienced before. By communicating in writing some aspects of our past experiences—of personalities associated with bourbons, of picturesque locals, and so on—the reader will acquire a resembling idea, though of course distinctly fainter and far less vivid, to borrow Hume's language.[5]

In each of these ways, the idiosyncrasies that differentiate us, the writers and the readers, from each other become, to some extent, minimized. We have, so to speak, succeeded in adopting a more general point of view. And it is this general point of view that, for Hume, makes both ethics and aesthetics feasible.

But we have strayed, somewhat, from our thread of analysis. Our fourth reason for selecting a particular bourbon, then, is its association with past experiences. We are more inclined to choose bourbons with which we have enjoyable past experiences, and we are more likely to eschew those with which we have unpleasant past experiences. Furthermore, while, as philosophers, we might be inclined to celebrate our nature as *rational* creatures, I have no doubt that empirical research would demonstrate that this element of past experiences that become associated with the present label has a disproportionately large influence on our choice of what to drink. Distillers, or at least their successful marketers, clearly understand this. Hence they take great pains to invest each label with something of a story. The story that any particular label presents acts as a prompt in our brain, a prompt that recalls the romantic/romanticized image of a quaint distillery in the wooded hills of Kentucky, the image of the camaraderie of drinking this whiskey with a group of close "buddies," the image of the practically wise, long-experienced master distiller who reverently shepherds the craft production of each single barrel. That there does not exist such a particular small distillery in a beautiful setting, that these are not our friends (maybe we don't even have any drinking friends!), that the master distiller of a modern, high-volume distillery cannot possibly lovingly caress or even visit every single barrel of whiskey produced is somewhat beside the point. For the generally uncritical consumer, such images delivered by marketing and now associated in the mind with that particular whiskey are relatively effective in their purpose: they get us to look through the sea of bourbon labels and then to reach for *that particular bottle.* And not only do those images in our memory help prompt us to choose that bottle, they also help us actually enjoy the whiskey therein. The presence of those images in our minds *changes what we taste.*

My point is something like this: although Aristotle characterizes us as the rational animal, and René Descartes or Immanuel Kant might emphasize our rational nature, the reasons that we pick one whiskey rather than another have only very partially to do with "the taste itself," if such a thing could actually be totally isolated by itself. As in so many other areas of our modern life, the person who says to us that he selects his bourbon based totally upon its objective taste qualities is, I suggest to you, engaging in an act of self-deception. Instead, Hume's philosophy of the association of ideas gives a far more insightful and plausible account of what goes on when we select and drink a whiskey. Deeply important in our making a selection and then experiencing the whiskey is the story that our minds will associate with that particular label, the story of how it was made, the story of where it was made, the story of what happened in the past when drinking it and with whom we drank it. And these stories are effective in their influence upon us whether they are "truths" or "fictions," though if we detect the fiction we may be adversely put off.

Does this detract from the joy of drinking fine bourbon? I certainly think not. Nothing I have argued suggests that we will actually choose and enjoy (chemically) bad bourbon. Nothing I have said rejects the idea that the serious, determined, and talented taster cannot learn to discriminate among several different bottlings of bourbon. Rather, think of what I am arguing as simply explaining some not purely "rational" ways in which Hume's principles of the association of ideas are at work in our minds, not detracting from but contributing to the richness of our aesthetic experiences. Accumulating good, enjoyable associated memories can, thus, make good bourbon taste even better.

NOTES

1. For a discussion of Platonic forms as they relate to the Manhattan, see Hans Allhoff's essay "The Manhattan and You: Thinking about a Classic Whiskey Cocktail," pp. 90–105 (this volume).

2. See, for example, David Hume, "Of the Association of Ideas," in *An Enquiry Concerning Human Understanding*, ed. Tom L. Beauchamp (Oxford: Oxford University Press, [1748] 1999), Section 3.
3. M. H. Waymack and J. F. Harris, *The Book of Classic American Whiskeys* (Chicago: Open Court Publishing, 1995).
4. See Dalton's essay "Heisenberg's Spirits: Tasting Is More Uncertain than It Seems," pp. 195–207 (this volume).
5. See, once again, Hume, *An Enquiry Concerning Human Understanding*, Section 3.

8

The Phenomenology of Spirits
How Do Whiskeys Win Prizes?

*Douglas Burnham and
Ole Martin Skilleås*

The title of this essay is a joking reference to German philosopher G. W. F. Hegel's famous *Phenomenology of Spirit* of 1807. However, to be perfectly honest, if we are making use of any philosophical 'phenomenology' in this essay, it is not Hegel's, but Edmund Husserl's. Phenomenology is an area of philosophy concerned with, among other things, the analysis of the relationship between a whole and its parts. For us here, the issue is how a thing (like a whiskey) comes to be perceived as a whole instead of as a set of discrete elements (this buttery flavor, that scent of peat, and so on). Perceiving a whiskey as a whole is important because we don't drink buttery flavors, and we don't award Single Malt of the Year prizes to the best peat smell.

Now, there are many projects in which we can be engaged when tasting whiskey, from evaluating a new release from a classic distillery, playing what amounts to a party game of blind tasting a whiskey and trying to work out the origin, all the way to getting blind drunk. Our question in this essay is whether it is even possible to have as a project the *aesthetic* evaluation of whiskey. Here, we argue that it is indeed possible; moreover, such evaluations are both more common and more important than is generally realized. An aesthetic evaluation is that particular type of judgment most familiarly used to evaluate *art*. (Note that we are not claiming that whiskey is or should be considered art.) The issue of how perception as a whole happens is interesting to us because it is an important part of forming aesthetic judgments. The aesthetic evaluation of something is an evaluation of it as a *meaningful whole*.

In order to answer this question, we are going to start by looking at how experienced professional tasters of whiskey describe their experiences. What types of language are used, and what types avoided? The majority of experienced tasters refuse to offer such aesthetically evaluative judgments, seeing them as merely subjective chat, not serious, objective, and neutral attention to the whiskey. In order to show that aesthetic evaluations are indeed possible, we need to answer this charge of mere subjectivity. To this end, we shall discuss what it means to be an experienced taster—and, no, it doesn't mean a heavy drinker!—and how this experience makes specifically *aesthetic* evaluations possible.

Types of Whiskey Rhetoric

As in the world of wine, there are two broad schools of thought concerning the appropriate mode of writing and speaking about whiskeys. The first school, let us call it the descriptive school, tries to build up an image of a whiskey's taste through an accumulation of straightforward flavor or aroma identifications. So, one encounters terms like 'butter', 'toast', 'dried apples', 'heather', and so forth. This school has its mavericks, to be sure, who search beyond the ordinary for more precise aroma identifications such as 'carbolic soap', 'pink elastoplast', 'Werther's Originals', or 'sprout water'. Descriptive terms, whether ordinary or esoteric, are frequently found modified by quantitative adjectives such as 'hint of', 'strong', 'soft', 'trace', and so forth. Moreover, the description is given a time dimension, as the description moves from initial aromas through to initial flavors toward aftertastes: flavor or aroma elements can 'emerge', 'develop', 'last', or 'fade'. Clearly, the point and the virtue of this whole approach is to give the reader as clear a picture as possible of what a whiskey tastes like, and to do so in terms that avoid interpretation or opinion. The reader can then decide whether or not this particular whiskey is something that he would like, if the new description is relevantly similar to a description of something he already knows and enjoys. This notion of "relevantly similar" is closely related to the idea of *typicality*. There are well-known, broad types of whiskey, generally tied to traditions of making and/or to geography. So, in helpful tasting notes one will often see a sentence like "If you like highland malts such as A or B, then you will probably also like X." X may not be a highland malt at all (it may have been distilled halfway across the world from Scotland), but it is relevantly similar.

The second school, that is, the evaluative school, uses the same descriptive terms but freely also uses *evaluative* terms. (For our purposes, aesthetic terms are a subtype of evaluative terms.) In general, evaluative terms are indicators of the following: first, whether particular elements of the whiskey, or relationships between elements, or for that matter the whole, are a good thing or not; and second, why they are a good thing. So, for example, the 'butter' element could be 'blatant', 'abrasive', 'sickly', 'weak'; or, alternatively, 'bold', 'smooth', 'pleasant', 'rich'. As soon as one reads the former terms, one knows the tasting notes are not going to be positive; the latter terms signal a whiskey that has been evaluated as enjoyable and is recommended. The evaluative terms also explain the evaluation: the element that is 'blatant' lacks subtlety, presumably; whereas the element that is 'bold' may be strong, but this is somehow in balance or harmony with the rest. Many of these terms come from cognate areas of discourse, particularly food writing. They are relatively straightforward descriptions of our immediate positive or negative physiological responses to flavors or odors. Let us therefore call this type of evaluative term 'physiological.' Now that we are discussing evaluative terms it is easy to see that what is really going on in either evaluation or description is *judgment*. By 'judgment' we mean the act by which a person decides or affirms that one thing is something else—in this case, that a whiskey is and should be described as buttery or that it is and should be evaluated as blatant.

The controversy over the use of evaluative terms (and thus evaluative judgments) is pretty obvious. On the one hand, whether a particular flavor or odor element is 'weak' seems subjective. By 'subjective' we mean that the evaluation of the flavor or odor is not *in* the whiskey *per se,* but rather should be understood as 'in' the person who is tasting, that is, as dependent upon the particular way in which his or her body is reacting to something. Calling evaluative terms of this type 'physiological' draws our attention to this fact. By 'objective', on the other hand, we mean that a particular quality is actually in the whiskey, and moreover that the evidence for its presence is publicly available. The chemical correlate of the butter scent could presumably be identified in the laboratory, quite independently of anyone's nose or palate. The butter scent, and its intensity, may be an objective fact about the whiskey; the *evaluation* of it is not. Of course, there is an age-old problem with such a claim to objectivity: tastes and smells are examples of archetypal Lockean secondary qualities.[1] By 'secondary quality', John Locke meant (in contemporary terms) that a smell exists only as the interaction of some airborne chemical with the membranes of the nasal cavity, together with the brain's response to the resulting nervous stimulus. Considered as a secondary quality, a smell can never exist separately from a person and her nose in the way that, say, a measure of alcohol strength can. Nevertheless, we are still able to distinguish meaningfully between qualities that are really in the whiskey (such as those with a chemical correlate like a butter scent) and those that are not (such as the evaluation of it as weak or as a pleasing hint).

This all seems very well, but if all we have to go on is the straightforward descriptions of elements, how are we to recommend (or not) a whiskey? In particular, how are we to judge contests or annual prizes? *Whisky Magazine*'s annual awards are admirable in that they reproduce the tasting notes of their panel.[2] Some on the review panels for these awards appear to belong resolutely to the descriptive school, and the reader is left to wonder why this smoky malt with hints of heather and peppermint won first prize while another whiskey with a similar description (perhaps even a different run from the same distillery) does not even receive an honorable mention. Those who use evaluative terms can, at least, offer an explanation for these judgments. Moreover, physiological evaluation may not be as subjective as it first seems. Above, we defined 'subjective' in terms of the individual way that a body responds to a stimulus; however, what if individuals are not so variable as such a view seems to presume? The response may be physiological in nature, but human physiology doesn't vary that much. Thus, the experienced taster's palate serves as a kind of objective laboratory where certain responses can be observed under controlled conditions. On these grounds, the second school, then, also claims something *akin* to objectivity for judgments.

Not all evaluative terms, though, are like those discussed above. By 'aesthetic terms' we mean evaluative terms that do not relate so obviously to our immediate physiological responses. In whiskey writing, one sometimes finds terms like 'balance', 'harmony', 'complexity', 'subtlety', and even 'imaginativeness', or 'originality'. Such terms also are rarely if ever used with respect to a single flavor element. A butter flavor, considered on its own, might be 'sickly' or even 'faint' but could not be 'subtle'. Its subtlety is determined with respect to the other flavor elements around it, and perhaps even with respect to the whole set of sense impressions. Aesthetic terms are thus always evaluative judgments of complex relationships. They thus always indicate a sense of the quality of the whiskey being *greater than* the sum of its parts, because it is about the way that these parts relate to one another across the whole experience.

Some of the physiological evaluative terms seem to be surreptitiously aesthetically evaluative. Above, we explained the difference between 'blatant' and 'bold' by referring to the concepts of 'subtlety' and 'balance.' This was, of course, deliberately sly on our part, but it does show how thin the line can be between types of evaluative terms. The descriptive school of thought will use this observation to illustrate the slippery slope that comes with deviation from the straight and narrow of mere description. Here, though, we argue that this shows that reference to the whole (and not just to individual parts) is more significant and indeed more common than it might seem.

However, showing that the critical rhetoric employed by at least some experienced whiskey tasters includes aesthetic evaluation terms does not necessarily mean that it is *entitled* to do so. These terms may be used illegitimately, of course, as an elegant mask to cover individual prejudice. The charge of mere subjectivity seems to have more merit in this case, since we have left behind the physiological evaluative judgments that seemed defensible above. If the charge of mere subjectivity held up, this would mean that the aesthetic judgment is merely the personal opinion of the taster and has no validity beyond that. However, the inner logic of an aesthetic judgment contains some claim to normativity. That is, the person making the judgment sees himself or herself as making a judgment *on behalf of others* and thus expects others to agree with the judgment or at least to respect it as an informed decision. After all, a prize competition judge is not working on his own behalf but is a kind of representative of the whiskey-drinking community. Aesthetic judgments, then, *claim* a validity beyond personal, subjective preferences, but are they *entitled* to that validity?

To answer that question, we need to explore how such judgments are formed. There are two topics here. First is the question of what exactly is being asserted about a whiskey in an aesthetic judgment. We'll address this question in the section titled "Aesthetic Attributes." Second, is the kinds of knowledge or competencies that go into making an experienced taster genuinely experienced. We'll discuss this under the heading of "Funding."

Aesthetic Attributes

Above we saw that descriptive terms claim to refer to objectively present flavor and odor elements in the whiskey; and physiologically evaluative terms claim to refer to no less than real responses in the palate of the taster. What, though, do aesthetic terms refer to? In "Aesthetic Concepts," Frank Sibley points out that concepts such as 'balanced', 'elegant', 'harmonious', 'complex', 'unified', and so on are referring to what are called emergent properties. This means that the use of aesthetic terms such as these is not entailed by the application of objective criteria.[3] Aesthetic terms rest upon aesthetic judgments, which by their very nature are singular. By this it is meant that if one artist paints a picture that is judged aesthetically successful, and then she (or someone else) paints something very similar (same technique, subject, composition, and so on), then the second painting *might or might not* be judged to be aesthetically successful. This anomaly arises because of the attempt to reduce the first painting's aesthetic success to objective and descriptive criteria. Aesthetic success simply cannot be determined by ticking off a series of elements or qualities on a predetermined checklist.

We saw the same thing apparently happening in the case of whiskey. A reviewer of the descriptive school could identify the same flavor and odor elements in one Kentucky whiskey as in another but judge the first a winner and the other a disappointment. Indeed, the second could even be an *exemplary* whiskey of this type, exhibiting all the qualities that one would expect in a quality Kentucky product—yet despite this typicality be aesthetically uninteresting. This lack of necessary entailment between elements and whole is what is meant

143

here by a singular judgment and an emergent quality. However, and this is significant, what emerges in the judgment is a *quality*: something is *perceived* as balanced, unified, or complex. The experienced taster encounters the whiskey as having the quality of being balanced, and it has this quality in a way not entirely dissimilar to the way it has the quality of buttery. The whiskey itself (that is, the Kentucky whiskey) is balanced. It is a quality, however, of the whole and not of one element or a subset of elements.

The descriptive school, as we know, will latch onto the lack of objective criteria in order to reinforce its claim that the aesthetic judgment (and indeed all evaluative judgments) lacks objectivity. We noted that such qualities are *perceived as* if they were objective, but that they are not objective in the sense of not being entailed by the analysis of other objective qualities. Maybe the problem we are having is that we are seeing objectivity and subjectivity *as the only two alternatives*. Our preferred third alternative is, not surprisingly, intersubjectivity. With conceptual and practical tools developed and honed in a kind of triangulation—with yourself, the whiskey, and others as the three corners—you are well placed to develop the ability to taste and judge on behalf of others. In order to pursue this further, we need to explore the phenomenon of funding.

Funding

By 'funding' we mean the kinds of knowledge of whiskey and competencies in tasting it that an experienced taster brings to the challenge of judgment. The project of judging could be a descriptive one (e.g., a blind taste challenge to identify the maker) or an evaluative one (e.g., judging a whiskey competition). The metaphor here is with 'fund' as a preexisting pool of resources that can be put to work on this or that project.[4] Briefly, we claim that funding can be broken down into three categories. First, there is cultural funding, representing everything that can feasibly be called knowledge of whiskey insofar as this knowledge might be useful in tasting. This would include knowledge of raw materials, the distillation and aging processes, and the many subtle variations on these. It would also include regional, national, or other types and their distinctive descriptions, as well as legal or conventional rules such as strength, bottle or glass size and shape, and so forth. Second, we have practical funding, which relates to all the various competencies that enable an experienced taster to put the first type of funding to work. That some measure of experience is required is particularly obvious in the case of whiskey, where to the uninitiated the first and overwhelming sensation will be the penetrative burning of the alcohol; the alcohol doesn't go away, rather we learn to sense *past* it. It turns out that the capacity to make subtle distinctions among flavor or odor elements is subject to training and the acquisition of a shared descriptive language. To be sure, the physiology of our palate and brain are natural, but in order to be sufficiently sensitive and discriminate they must be subjected to guided training. By 'guided' we mean that one acquires this skill, a type of knowing-how, by being instructed on what to look for by a taster more experienced than ourselves. Thus, an experienced taster is not someone who has simply drunk a lot, any more than a good music critic is merely someone who listens to the radio all day.

The third type of funding we call aesthetic. Aesthetic judgments are singular, as we saw above, and this means they are not entailed by objective criteria. But this does not mean that aesthetic judgments are naive or untrained. There will always be cases of savants who can leap to reliable aesthetic judgments without much training (Mozarts of whiskey, so to speak)—people who know what they like and whose likes are surprisingly in agreement with the sophisticated, educated palates of experienced tasters. Nevertheless, this is an exception. Experienced tasters—including those who are not in the public eye but who work for distilleries or distributors—are hardworking professionals who spend a great deal of time tasting, traveling, conversing, reading, and writing about whiskey.

They belong to a *community* of whiskey tasters, and this is the important point.

These three types of funding are all at work in what we call an aesthetic practice. The formation of judgments is typically not something that just happens to me, or that comes out of the blue, but is rather something that I set out to do. It is an organized activity—a practice—that involves certain rituals, conventions, and languages. As we said at the start of this essay, there are a number of different projects we can take up in relation to drinking whiskey; in many of these, serious tasting is simply irrelevant or even ruled out. Indeed, there are several possible *tasting* practices and attitudes; an aesthetic evaluation is one, a supermarket buyer looking for particular consumer-friendly elements would be another. The procedures for blind-testing whiskeys, such as a standardization of glasses and temperature, tasting note forms, and forbidding (or perhaps encouraging) conversation among tasters are all examples of components within such practices. So, too, though on a broader stage, are the various schools of whiskey tasting and writing, and the professional community aspect of tasting described above. Tasting as a practice involves as its centerpiece and raison d'etre a certain attitude or comportment toward the whiskey. In tasting practices of the types we are discussing here, a conscious attitude toward the whiskey and more generally toward the task is taken up. It is such an attitude that permits a taster of the descriptive school to observe *relevant* aspects of the whiskey; and tasters of the evaluative school to serve as *representatives* of the whiskey community and not just blithely repeat their individual prejudices. Likewise, through a distinctive aesthetic practice and attitude, aesthetic attributes come to be perceived.

The three types of funding are, not surprisingly, interrelated. Someone hopeless at tasting whiskey seriously (however frequent a drinker!) could have acquired cultural funding on his own, to be sure. He would know in a theoretical sense how Lowland malts are characterized but couldn't recognize one blind if it leaped from the glass and bit him on the nose. Otherwise, however, each of the three types of funding entails the others. The capacity for forming aesthetic judgments is arrived at through the same types of training practices as the other two types of funding; that is to say, it is arrived at intersubjectively through guided tasting and conversation with others. By 'intersubjectivity' we mean that funding and practices are achieved, directly or indirectly, through our interactions with other people—as guides, companions, reviewers, and so on. Within the framework of an intersubjective practice, judgments are normative, defensible, and public. We have, for example, a language to use to give and explain our judgments about a whiskey being balanced. And within the practice, not only do others understand that language, they also share the conditions needed to make it meaningful (that is, within the tasting attitude they can look to their own experience of the whiskey for verification). This intersubjectivity is something we consider very important here because it begins to provide a third mode of judgment that is neither subjective nor objective. Debates about whether evaluative judgments of whiskey are subjective go around and around—and always will until we realize that the terms of the debate have to be rethought, from the ground up.

Having suggested the role of funding, practices, and intersubjectivity for whiskey tasting in general, we are emboldened to put forward two additional claims: first, that whiskey tasting can be an aesthetic practice. And second (this we hope will raise a few eyebrows!), that other tasting practices (those of the descriptive and physiologically evaluative schools of whiskey writing) are implicitly also aesthetic practices. Since if the second can be defended, the first follows, we will focus on making a plausible case that more familiar types of judgment are in fact implicitly aesthetic.

Ubiquitous Aesthetics

In fact, this argument was already introduced briefly in the section on the discourses of whiskey above. There, we pointed out that many of the judgments that initially appear to be physiologically evaluative were, surreptitiously, aesthetic. For example, compare the judgments "X exhibits a nasty scent of cheap cologne" with "The scent of cologne in Y is finely balanced against honeysuckle." The particular scent elements described here are not significant. Rather, what is important is that while the negative judgment appears physiological in nature, the positive judgment involves one (or perhaps two) physiological responses that have been *mediated*. For it is not inconceivable that the scent of cologne is (at the level of pure and isolated description) the *same* in both X and Y, that is, it is caused by the same chemical makeup. In that case, the second judgment is positive, and the scent is therefore not "nasty" and "cheap," because the experience is mediated by something other than a straightforward physiological response. A sense of balance is doing the mediating here, and we claim it must be understood as an aesthetic quality.

That this is an aesthetic judgment is evident from three observations. First, and most obviously, 'balance' is not a straightforwardly descriptive term: there is no obvious chemical correlate for it in the way demanded by the objectivity to which the descriptive school appeals. Second, balance is not an immediate, physiological response. To be sure, this is not obvious: after all, does one not sense *immediately* (as opposed to mediately) with the eye the balance or harmony in a painting or sculpture? Certainly, and this is what we meant above in saying that aesthetic qualities present themselves as qualities in much the same sense as any other "real" element. However, in the case of an aesthetic quality, this sensing that appears unmediated is a *trained* sense. I require funding (as described above) to make any subtle observations about whiskeys. Such funding must be all the more required to sense as a quality something that is *not there* (in a straightforward physiological or chemical sense), or rather is there only within an aesthetic practice. Funding and especially the know-how that puts cultural funding to work in the act of tasting is trained through conscious reflection and by many intermediaries (repeated tastings and comparisons, talking with others, reading, and writing). The experienced taster has been guided through many intermediaries. Being experienced means, among other things, to have internalized reflection so that it *seems* immediate.

The third feature of such a judgment that marks it out as aesthetic is that it is not merely a comment on preexisting physiological responses and taste elements, but that (as we noted above) it *changes* those responses. What, in other practices of judgment, we might have to judge as the *same* cologne scent is here "nasty" but there "in balance."

We are back to the issue raised at the beginning of this essay: perception as a whole. To perceive something as a whole means that the elements that make it up are insufficient in themselves to determine the whole. Thus, aesthetic judgments are not reached by adding up across lists of objective criteria; no compilation of descriptive terms necessitates an aesthetic judgment. However, perceiving as a whole *also* means that the individual elements are in some way determined from the perspective of the whole. In our examples above, the cologne and honeysuckle scents become relevant (they are noticed and worth writing down in the tasting notes) and valued (they are not "nasty") because balance is perceived as a quality, and it is these elements that are in balance. In short, they emerge as the elements one needs to notice about this whiskey precisely because of the aesthetic judgment of the whiskey as a whole. An analogous phenomenon happens in making judgments of type (e.g., this is a typical Speyside): "Speyside" serves as a template indicating signature elements and relationships among them. Judgments can proceed from the whole (the template) down to the elements; thus it becomes possible to fool even an experienced taster by giving him or her a sample of A but claiming it to be Z.

The reader will notice that this third feature is also an argument to the effect that even the descriptive school of whiskey writing and judging may implicitly involve aesthetic judgments. In this way, we provide a provisional solution as to how the descriptive school is able to reach a judgment of quality or value, as in the case of several of the panelists on *Whiskey Magazine*'s annual awards. The judgment of quality is a hidden aesthetic judgment on the whiskey as a whole. The descriptions that are provided are an indication of the relevant elements within that whole, the elements that in some aesthetic configuration make it a prizewinner; however, the account of how and why they are relevant (these parts are the implicit aesthetic account) is left out, in the interests of objectivity.

This essay began by analyzing the rhetoric typical of whiskey reviews. We distinguished three schools of whiskey writing by experienced tasters: the descriptive, the physiologically evaluative, and the aesthetically evaluative. The question then arose of how worthwhile were the latter two (and especially the third) in view of the fact that on the surface they seemed to be nothing other than the private opinions of the tasters. How could such private opinions be of value to others?

In order to address this issue, we first looked at what exactly is being asserted in an aesthetically evaluative judgment. We saw that such judgments are characterized by being singular or emergent; we described this by saying that the judgment refers to the object (the whiskey tasted) as a whole. Then we looked at what it means to talk about an experienced taster. Two key ideas emerged here: first, that the type of validity attained through experience is intersubjective; and second, that whiskey tasting needs to be considered a practice, not an isolated or uninformed event. We concluded with some arguments, which could not be more than suggestive, to the effect that both the descriptive and the physiologically evaluative schools implicitly depend upon aesthetic judgments. This, in turn, is evidence that aesthetic judgments are of no lesser worth than the other two types of judgment.

NOTES

1. John Locke, *An Essay Concerning Human Understanding* (Oxford: Oxford University Press, 1960), Book II, chapter 8.
2. See the *Whisky Magazine* home page, www.whiskymag.com (accessed June 4, 2008).

3. Frank Sibley, "Aesthetic Concepts," in *Approach to Aesthetics: Collected Papers on Philosophical Aesthetics*, eds. John Benson, Betty Redfern, and Jeremy Roxbee Cox (Oxford: Oxford University Press, 2001), pp. 1–23.

4. For a more sustained treatment of the different types of funding we have identified, please see our essay "You'll Never Drink Alone," in *Wine & Philosophy*, ed. Fritz Allhoff (Malden, MA: Blackwell, 2007).

9

The Ideal Scotch
Lessons from Hegel

Thom Brooks

How can we judge which Scotch is best? There seems no shortage of advice. Books abound, not least is Michael Jackson's outstanding *Malt Whisky Companion*, with scores of various whiskies on a scale from 1 to 100.[1] With so many experts to advise us on which drink is better than others, perhaps we should do no more than follow their advice? Yet, while experts may agree most of the time, they regularly disagree, too. It is then important for us to have some helpful insight that will give ourselves the ability to judge among different varieties of Scotch, especially where consistent advice is absent.[2]

This essay will recommend a new approach to addressing this problem. This approach originates with the work of the great nineteenth-century philosopher G. W. F. Hegel. We often find that any search for the 'truth' about a subject contains many factors. For example, if we tried to more fully understand an ordinary object, such as the mug on the desk in front of me, we would note a variety of factors. These factors would include its size, color, shape, and so on. Some factors would be more important than others. Thus, the mug in front of me is what it is in virtue of its shape: its color does not have any effect on whether it is a mug. Nevertheless, even less important factors are far from irrelevant: in this case, the color of my mug may distinguish it from others and more clearly mark this object out as mine.[3] The key in all of this is that we must have a method to organize best all relevant factors. Hegel offers a method by which we can organize factors in terms of their importance and effect on other factors that, in his view, allows us best to gain knowledge of an object of study.

The appreciation of Scotch is an experience admitting of several factors, namely, its "notes." These notes are not musical, but related to the sensation of taste. A Scotch's note may be smoke or mint, peat or fruit, spice or grass. And so on. What I will do here is outline a Hegelian approach that we can apply to judging which Scotch is best. I will first say a few words about Hegel's method and then move to a discussion of its application with Scotch. I will conclude by stating, in Hegelian terms, which kinds of Scotch are better than others. Our project is then to identify the ideal Scotch.

The Logic of Hegel

Hegel develops a philosophy that seeks to organize all human knowledge into a coherent system. This system is built upon what he calls his "logic." The character of Hegel's logic and its importance for his philosophical system has attracted much debate among scholars.[4] For our purposes, we need not enter into these debates. Instead, we need only to identify some key features of Hegel's approach that we may then apply to judging which Scotch is best.

The first feature of Hegel's approach is that it attempts to discern a rational order in the world.[5] For Hegel, philosophy is simply "a thinking consideration of objects."[6] When we focus our attention on an object, we attempt to discern certain features of this object. For example, when we focus our attention on a glass of Scotch, we may quickly discover various aspects of it. It may be dark brown or yellowish. Perhaps it is noticeably smoky or subtly fruity. We become more greatly aware of a Scotch's distinguishing features when we divert our full attention to the study of these features. The more features we can identify, the more developed our grasp of the object before us. Therefore, we best experience a glass of Scotch when we are able to identify all the different notes contained within it. If we fail to identify all notes, then we fail to properly comprehend our glass of Scotch.

A further feature of Hegel's approach is that our philosophical thinking consideration of an object should take a particular form.[7] This form is a coherent system where each feature of an object is comprehended in its relation to all other features in a particular way.[8] An example may help make this clear. Let us again focus on a glass of Scotch. Suppose the Scotch contains several notes such as lemongrass, a minty freshness, and a hint of peat. Our careful attention to identifying the different notes of our Scotch will help us understand and experience these notes. This is only one part of a larger task. For the problem then becomes how is it that we can judge that this glass with these particular qualities is better than another glass of Scotch that had, say, three different qualities. What is at issue for us is not simply the *identification* of a Scotch's notes, but the grasp of the *relation* of these notes to one another.

Hegel's approach leads to an identification of "the best" as "the ideal." The ideal is achieved when we identify all important features and comprehend them in their full unity. Therefore, an object that had fewer distinguishing features than another would be inferior to another object that was more multidimensional. Moreover, an object that has several features all jumbled together would be inferior to another that was rationally ordered. As a result, one Scotch may be superior to another if it were the most complex and possessed more features. In addition, a Scotch that carefully balanced the most features in a coherent way, allowing each feature to be easily distinguishable, would be better than one that performed this task less well. Thus, the *ideal* Scotch is one that best brings together the most features.

Of course, there is much more that could be said about Hegel's approach as outlined in his logic. Again, this logic is the focus of heated philosophical debates. However, my focus is limited solely to demonstrating a new way of thinking about Scotch and judging which is better than another. This new way of thinking derives from certain features found in Hegel's many and complex writings broadly construed, although I direct readers in the notes to further readings by Hegel and his commentators if they wish to pursue a more detailed study of Hegel's logic.[9] However, this more ambitious and scholarly task is not necessary here.

The Logic of the Ideal Scotch

We have now developed a general picture of Hegel's approach. How might we apply it to the judging of Scotch?

Scotch has various flavor components that appear in varying degrees in different bottles. Some of these traditional components are the following: smoke, mint, fruit, spice, peat/earth, and oak. Scotch from Islay, for example, is often big on smoke and peat, whereas Highlands Scotch has less of these components and more fruit and spice. These components should be fairly self-explanatory: a Scotch that is smoky, minty, fruity, or spicy will be just this. Moreover, the composition of a Scotch may take different shapes. Therefore, a Scotch that is noticeably spicy may be very different from another Scotch that has different spices. Likewise, a fruity Scotch may differ from others in which fruit flavors are found.

Perhaps less straightforward are the components of peat and earth and the cask. By peat and earth, I refer to a Scotch that has a recognizably earthy flavor whether the note is peat, grass, a faint taste of iron, and so on. These are more subtle flavors to pick out from a glass of Scotch than other more visible notes, such as smoke or mint. Most subtle of all I refer to as simply the cask. This component is the most subtle because it is the least overpowering of all components. The component of cask simply refers to notes that come to the Scotch by its cask. Therefore, those Scotches that have a recognizable taste of oak or sherry flavor would fall under this component.

Now that we are armed with these components, how do they relate to Hegel's approach? We will address this question now. Let us first consider a glass of Scotch that has just one category. Could this Scotch be the best we might choose? Following Hegel's approach, it is not. This is because such a Scotch is one-dimensional: it is either all smoky or all minty. There is very little to it. We may continue to enjoy the experience of drinking this Scotch, and this is not to be denied; however, we can say with some assurance that while a Scotch with just one category may be enjoyable it is also very limited in terms of what a Scotch may be. A glass of Scotch that has more than one component of notes is multidimensional and more developed in its complexity. Following Hegel's approach, a multidimensional Scotch is better than a one-dimensional Scotch because of the complexity and robustness of the former over the latter.

Is this, then, all there is to the application of Hegel's approach? Do we simply count how many different components of notes are present in our glass in order to decide which Scotch is best? Not quite. On this view, it is true that the *best* Scotch is one that contains all components as it will be the *most complex* and multidimensional. However, the best Scotch is not a simple collection or even a collision of flavors but a rational ordering of flavors. It is then incumbent upon us to see if we can work out a rational ordering of the components. I believe that we can.

The most basic and lowest component is *smoke*. Why? The reason is because the category of smoke can easily overwhelm and overpower all other categories. A very smoky Scotch may make all traces of mint or peat unnoticeable. If the best glass of Scotch is one that contains all components, then it should include smoke. However, smoke in the ideal glass should not be overpowering, drowning out the possibility of enjoying further, higher categories of notes in a Scotch.

A higher component is *mint*. Not unlike smoke, a strong minty flavor can easily disguise and render invisible all other components with the exception of smoke. Of all the components, a strong presence of mint in a Scotch is most likely to be detected in all but the smokiest of Scotches, but such a glass would remain limited and foreclose the possibility of enjoying other components. Therefore, the ideal glass of Scotch is one that contains smoke and mint, but these components are carefully weighed against each other. It is necessary for them to be present, but not so strong that they disguise other components if we are to enjoy all components in the best possible glass.

A higher component still is *fruit*. A fruity Scotch is one that may contain flavors such as black currant, cherry, melon, or other fruits. Fruit is a more subtle component. Let me explain why this is the case. A very fruity Scotch is never as overpowering as a very smoky or very minty Scotch. For our glass to contain recognizably the taste of fruit, it cannot be too smoky or minty. Fruit is a more subtle component precisely because it can be easily overpowered by the components of smoke and mint. These more basic components must be kept within limits in order for the fruit component to become readily identifiable in each glass of Scotch.

Moreover, that it is the case that, say, smoke can more easily overpower fruit is true and verifiable in our experience of enjoying Scotch. In other words, we can look to our own experiences in drinking Scotch in order to verify this ordering of Scotch components. It takes little imagination to see that a Scotch's smoke is far more likely to overpower the taste of fruit when we reflect on our past and present experiences with Scotch. However, I am suggesting that a Scotch whose component of fruit overpowers its component of smoke is hard to imagine: I have never known of a Scotch with such characteristics.

Even higher components are, first, *spice* and, second, *peat and earth*. A spicy Scotch can never overpower a fruity Scotch, but it can hide the presence of peat and earth. The latter, peat and earth, is a far more subtle component less readily identified than all lower components. Peat and earth notes, such as grass or iron, are light and often pleasing. Yet in order to enjoy them, the Scotch must be well balanced so that all its components can be in harmony.

This brings us to the highest component, *the cask*. A Scotch often picks up flavor from its cask, whether it be oak laden, a cask formerly used to make sherry, or something else. Even the "strongest" Scotches from, say, a sherry cask are far less strong in character than all other components. As the highest component, the cask is also the easiest to overpower. Moreover, as the highest component, its presence is not only the sign of a well-balanced, multidimensional Scotch, but it brings to our attention something else about the Scotch that is important. This importance is not the brute fact that our glass of Scotch comes from *a* cask, but *a particular* cask and one that has influenced the flavors of our Scotch. In all other cases, we take for granted that our Scotch comes to us originally from a cask. Yet, with this highest component, we recognize that its cask is of importance and its flavor adds a further dimension to the experience of enjoying this Scotch.

When we bring these categories together, we can now clearly see how Hegel's approach may help us identify the ideal Scotch. Scotch may be composed of six different components of notes. A Scotch that possesses all six components is superior to one that has fewer components, all things considered.

But this is not the end of the story. For Hegel, it is also important to identify not only all relevant features but also to see them as part of a larger system. We now see how this can be done. Some categories easily overpower others. These overpowering components are lower than more subtle, higher components. This is because our possibility of experiencing the fruity or peaty flavour of a Scotch depends upon the restraint of other flavors, such as smoke or mint. It is perhaps easiest to locate some kinds of components than others. Here again, the lower components are those easiest to identify. Thus, we may readily notice the smoky smell of our Scotch before we can pick out the butterscotch weaved within it. The combination of these lower with higher components must be balanced appropriately, and when this is achieved we find a harmony of different components that all have the freedom to contribute to its enjoyment.

This broadly construed Hegelian approach to experiencing the joy of drinking Scotch offers us a new and perhaps instructive method of identifying which Scotch may be better than another.

Before turning to my conclusion, I should first address two issues that I have not yet raised. The first is that some may object to the fact that I have nowhere factored what is consumed *with* the Scotch—and that this should be a relevant factor. Therefore, it is not only the case that some Scotches may be more complex and balanced than others but also that some best accompany a particular meal or the smoking of a fine cigar. I have not addressed this here because I do not think it changes the picture I have presented. Perhaps one Scotch may be more pleasing with one meal or cigar than another. It remains the case on my analysis that the best Scotch precisely is the most complex and balanced. I fail to see why such a Scotch could not equally be the best accompaniment for a meal. Besides, I believe it may be easier to identify the best *ideal* of Scotch rather than what one person with his or her particular tastes would enjoy now with a specific meal.

The second issue that I have left to the side concerns location. Some may object to my analysis because it lacks any discussion of *where* a Scotch is from. I do not deny that different regions produce different varieties of Scotch. Nor do I deny that perhaps some are better than others from different locations. My argument is *not* that whether one location produces a better Scotch because it is produced in one place rather than another *as such*. Rather, my argument is that whether one area can produce a superior Scotch can be determined by the use of the categorical analysis offered here.

I do not then claim that the Hegelian approach offered here is the only way or even the best way of judging whether one Scotch is better than another. Instead, I believe that this approach has something new and attractive, an original perspective to consider the quality of Scotch in a way that we may not have done before. It is in its originality that I believe that the Hegelian approach has its promise. Whether the approach is convincing must be borne out of comparing this ideal of Scotch with those that fall short. My own experience is that this ideal helps identify why I find some Scotches far better than others, and I believe this experience is shared by others rendering it credible and compelling.

The Ideal Scotch

Hegel often spoke of ideals. For example, when he speaks about the state, he will refer to it as the *ideal* of the state.[10] Hegel's purpose is to provide us with a method by which we can identify the best state and use this to measure the quality of existing states. We can do the same with Scotch. In other words, we can identify the best, or "ideal," Scotch: this is a Scotch that contains all categories of notes in a particular ordering so we can clearly distinguish smoke, mint, fruit, spice, peat and earth, and the flavor from the original cask. We can then use this ideal picture of Scotch to judge how close (or far) other Scotches come to it. Therefore, we can now say with confidence that on this view a smoky or minty Scotch may be enjoyable to drink, but it remains inferior in complexity and the full ideal of what a Scotch can be and, thus, less good than a Scotch that is more complex and multidimensional.

Hegel may not have written about Scotch, but he does highlight an approach that makes for a new and interesting guide for judging which Scotch is best. For example, there are many excellent varieties of Scotch, one of which is Macallan, which regularly scores very high (often in the 90s out of 100) in expert assessments.[11] I would not argue that Macallan is the best Scotch, but it is well worth noticing that this brand of Scotch may often have just a hint of smoke, mint, fruit, and spice, with grassy or lemongrass overtones and a rich sherry flavor from the cask: Macallan is then a high-scoring Scotch that *also* harmonizes all categories of notes not unlike the way presented above. This Scotch then both regularly scores highly in expert assessments *and* clearly satisfies a Hegelian-inspired approach for identifying which Scotch is best. Hegel's Scotch is *the best* Scotch.[12]

NOTES

1. See Michael Jackson, *Malt Whisky Companion* (London: Dorling Kindersley, 1999).
2. My discussion focuses on Scotch, although the following analysis is applicable to all kinds of whiskey whether or not it is Scotch. 'Scotch' specifically refers to whisky produced in Scotland.
3. In fact, the mug in question is different than most: it is a University of Sheffield mug purchased shortly after I received my Ph.D. there.
4. For example, see the discussion in Thom Brooks, *Hegel's Political Philosophy: A Systematic Reading of the Philosophy of Right* (Edinburgh: Edinburgh University Press, 2007).
5. We need only understand 'rational' here as that which is intelligible to those with the ability to reason.
6. G. W. F. Hegel, *The Encyclopaedia Logic: Part 1 of the Encyclopaedia of Philosophical Sciences with the Zusatze* (Indianapolis, IN: Hackett Publishing, 1991), p. 25, §2.
7. Ibid., p. 33, §9.
8. Ibid., p. 39, §14 Remark.
9. See G. W. F. Hegel, *Science of Logic* (Amherst: New York, 1999) for Hegel's most complete discussion of logic. The best commentary on any part of Hegel's logic to my knowledge is Stephen Houlgate ed., *The Opening of Hegel's Logic: From Being to Infinity* (West Lafayette, IN: Purdue University Press, 2006). I would also recommend Justus Hartnack, *An Introduction to Hegel's Logic* (Indianapolis, IN: Hackett Publishing, 1998).
10. See G. W. F. Hegel, *Elements of the Philosophy of Right*, ed. A. W. Wood (Cambridge: Cambridge University Press, 1992) and Brooks, Hegel's Political Philosophy.
11. See Jackson, *Malt Whisky Companion*, pp. 257–267.
12. I must sincerely thank Marcus Adams and Fritz Allhoff for their most helpful comments on previous drafts.

Where the Fiddich Meets the Spey

My Religious Experience

Harvey Siegel

I grew up just outside Boston in a large extended Jewish family; there were always weddings and bar mitzvahs to attend. At these events, whiskey was omnipresent. I remember tasting Seven and Sevens (Seagram's Seven and 7Up) and other whiskey concoctions, rye (especially Canadian Club), bourbon, schnapps, and so on, slipped surreptitiously to me at family affairs many times by an older brother or sister, uncle or aunt, or cousin. But the favorite potion of my family during my formative years was Scotch—as I now know but didn't then—blended whiskies. Cutty Sark, Chivas Regal, and especially Dewars were the drinks of choice. And while I tried many other types of liquor in my teens, Scotch was my touchstone. I didn't drink often or a lot. But those family affairs at which liquor flowed just kept on occurring.

It was therefore somewhat disturbing to realize when I went away to college that I didn't actually like the taste of Scotch very much. It was harsh, sharp, and bitter. For a while I didn't drink any. But after some months, I began to miss it. Whether this was caused by early training, family loyalty, masculine insecurity, lack of imagination, or something else, I cannot say. But I started drinking Scotch again. At first I drank it mixed but not in the 7Up of my youth. I took to Rusty Nails, a mixed drink consisting of Scotch and Drambuie, a Scotch-based liqueur. The sweetness of the Drambuie rendered the harshness of the Scotch tolerable, at least for a time. After a while, though, that sweetness became far too cloying, and I began to alter the mix: more Scotch, less Drambuie. Eventually, I abandoned the latter altogether and simply drank blended Scotch—usually Dewar's, as my older brother did—on ice. At this point I still had not tasted a single malt.

My first taste of a single malt came as a revelation. I believe it occurred during graduate school. I do not remember the circumstances, or the malt. What I do remember was the stunning realization that Scotch didn't have to be so harsh; that it could be smooth and remarkably flavorful. The course of my future drinking was set! I didn't become obsessed with it until later—at the time, I still had my course work, dissertation, and career to obsess about—but I began, slowly and intermittently, to explore the world of single malt.

Early Research

My studies had not progressed too far. By the time I arrived in Yorkshire (where I spent several months while on sabbatical in 1990–1991) I had done some preliminary exploration, and had discovered the glory of the "big" Speyside malts—my favorite at the time was the Macallan 12 year old—but I was still relatively ignorant, albeit enthusiastic. Then came Yorkshire and my malt-tasting adventures with my brother-in-law Steve.

Steve had an excellent palate and an incredible (to me) knowledge of beer; I delighted in his enthusiastic and revealing descriptions of the tastes and qualities of many of England's most famous pints. But his knowledge of single malt was considerably less extensive. Once our mutual interest in malt was discovered, our explorations began in earnest.

A particular gap in both Steve's and my knowledge of malt was Islay. I'm not sure I had even heard of Islay or its malts much before that point. Steve knew of them, but hadn't tasted any. So it was with considerable anticipation that we bought a bottle of (standard, distillery-bottled 16 year old) Lagavulin (pronounced *la-ga-VOO-lin*). I will never forget the day we tasted it. Steve's eyes glazed over, and his face took on a dazed, goofy, amazed, and euphoric—postorgasmic, even—expression. After what seemed like forever, he finally spluttered, "What a product!" We spent the remainder of the afternoon trying to put into words the many shocking but wonderful flavors we discovered—tar, iodine, salt, smoke, and so on—and began to plan our future studies.

There were no specialist shops in our area, but it took Steve little time to discover that a new Tesco superstore on the outskirts of York, about an hour away, had a large selection. So began a series of memorable afternoon drives. Armed with the first edition of Michael Jackson's *Malt Whisky Companion*—now referred to by us all simply as the "Bible"—we'd drive to York, spend an hour or more in the whisky aisle debating our next purchase, and drive home for a tasting. These events added considerably to my familiarity with a widening range of malts, as did our frequent visits to local pubs to sample hitherto untasted drams. (A particularly vivid memory is that of my first taste of Cragganmore, a wonderfully dry and somewhat atypical Speyside, in the Cow and Calf Hotel bar on Ilkley Moor.) But the best was yet to come.

After eight wonderful months in Yorkshire, it was nearly time to return to Miami for the beginning of the fall semester. Before going home, my wife and I had planned a final two-week holiday in Scotland. My wife Bern's father had emigrated from there to England, but she hadn't visited since her childhood; I was drooling over the prospect of more malt experiences. We had agreed that the first week would be Bern's and would center on Edinburgh, Glasgow, and matters cultural; and the second, mine, and would focus on malt.

We borrowed Steve's car, bid a fond farewell to Yorkshire, and headed north.

Tasting and Learning in the Home of Single Malt

We were ambling one day around the center of Edinburgh, as tourists do, when we stumbled upon a shop with whisky bottles in the window. Peering inside, I saw a large chalkboard with names—some of which I recognized as single malt distilleries—neatly listed alphabetically in capital letters with additional information whose meaning was not immediately apparent. I had hit pay dirt: this was Cadenhead! Cadenhead (I soon learned) is the oldest and one of the greatest independent bottlers of single malt. That is, it selects and buys casks from working distilleries seeking, for whatever reason, to offload casks taking up space in their warehouses. Cadenhead, like other independent bottlers, buys the casks and then bottles and sells the malt directly. (So these are one-off malts: once the cask is empty, that particular whisky is gone forever.) Because Cadenhead sells whisky as single malt, it chooses only those casks that its deem worthy of that status; its reputation rests mainly on the quality of the whisky it selects. In the shop were dozens of these malts, which were sold in full- (70 cl, the equivalent of 700 ml), half-, and quarter-bottles. Though none were cheap, many were reasonably priced. The older and rarer malts were, understandably, beyond my price range. Nevertheless, the range of available bottles was overwhelming, and it took some time to take in the gold mine I had stumbled into. I quietly studied the chalkboard, little by little deciphering its comments on each malt (year, region, style, type of cask, and so on), and explored the shelves, while the young man behind the counter dealt with other customers.

Eventually, the other customers departed with their purchases, and the young man asked if he could help. I clumsily explained my delight at being there, and my enthusiasm for but relative ignorance of malt. He was quite chatty and seemed not to mind explaining all matters relating to malt: how it's made, how the regions differ in character, and so on. Although by now I was no longer a rookie, this conversation proved to be as enlightening as it was entertaining.

After talking for more than an hour, the time to buy something came. My advisor suggested I try a quite unusual 24 year old Scapa, an Island malt distilled in Orkney. He described its aroma and flavor, but what clinched the deal was his claim that one could detect traces of bitter chocolate in its taste. Bitter chocolate in a malt! Since I already had a well-established love of bitter chocolate, and the thought of these two passions combining in a single taste experience had not before occurred to me, I couldn't resist the temptation. However, this particular malt was both rare and pricy. I bought a quarter-bottle, the most expensive bottle I thought I could get away with, and resolved to have it as my "home bottle" the following week when we went north to whisky country.

Driving through Speyside, the major whisky-producing region of Scotland, was a treat but also something of a schlep; by the time we arrived at our rented flat outside Elgin, unpacked, and made dinner, we were exhausted. But I had one more task to complete: the Scapa! With great anticipation, I found a suitable glass and water, read about the whisky in the Bible—which had long since become my faithful companion, and in which I had scribbled all my tasting notes from the previous months—and poured a dram.

What a disappointment: the stuff tasted awful! Well, not awful, but much rougher and less flavorful than I had antici-pated. Worst of all, I could detect no chocolate whatsoever. How could this be? For a few minutes I stewed in my chair and fretted. After a while it occurred to me to add more water; this helped quite a bit in enhancing the flavors— "opening them up," as I had learned to say—and in reducing the harshness I first encountered. I reread the Bible entry on Scapa, and began to feel a bit better when I was able to identify some of the characteristics Michael Jackson identified: sea salt, grasses ("new-mown hay"), an oily body, and a dry finish. I also thought I could taste something like cereal, but found no mention of it in Jackson's tasting notes. But I still could not detect chocolate. So chocolate and malt was not to be: a scam, no doubt, to take in the gullible American tourist. Well, it wasn't the first time I had been taken in by clever but deceptive advertising. Still, I was mightily disappointed. Exhausted, I comforted myself with thoughts of the coming days of exploration, and went to bed.

The next day we began "my" week. Even though I was still disappointed by the lack of bitter chocolate in the Scapa, I was excited as we began to plan the week's outings. Distilleries were everywhere, and we visited one or two every day—Glen Grant, Aberlour, Cragganmore, the Macallan, Glenfarclas, Linkwood, and Edradour stand out in my memory. Also noteworthy was a visit to Dallas Dhu—a favorite malt of mine, now—which was no longer a working distillery but had become a sort of distillery museum where one could walk about at leisure and explore the production equipment and soak in the environment. We took a couple of tours; some distilleries then had well-organized tours, others not (although even the ones that were officially closed to the public, like Edradour and Aberlour, were staffed by quite friendly folks who were happy to talk for a few minutes in the offices). But our main activity was simply exploring the countryside, eating in pubs, and sampling whatever looked interesting behind the bar. Since I was the one doing the malt exploring, Bern and I exchanged roles for the week: she served as designated driver. I must say that she and Madeleine (our then almost two-year-old daughter) were quite tolerant of my obsession.

Having sampled quite a bit during our first day out, and still harboring some lingering resentment at the absence of chocolate in the Scapa, I didn't have any malt that evening. That would not, as events transpired, happen again.

On Monday we drove to the small town of Elgin. There we discovered Gordon and MacPhail's amazing store. G & M has for many years been the leading (along with Cadenhead)

independent bottlers of single malts. For over a century it has bought casks, stored them, and, when in its judgment they're ready, bottled the contents. Its range is extraordinary—it is hard to find a distillery that has not contributed to G & M, and it has different "expressions" of the malts of many of those distilleries. Half of the store—really a small supermarket— is devoted to its whiskies, which stretch, aisle after aisle, from floor to ceiling. It took some time just to get an overall impression of the selection, so vast was the range of malts on offer. I slowly perused the aisles—I must have been there for two hours, Bern and Madeleine having long since aban- doned me to explore other parts of the town—delighting in the discovery of malts from distilleries I'd never heard of, many of which had long since been mothballed (taken out of production) or permanently closed. With the Bible as my guide, I read about as many of the bottles there as I could and eventually selected a couple to take back to Miami. (No point buying easily obtainable malts at duty-free shops when the rare malts of G & M were at hand!) Triumphantly, I met Bern and Madeleine and gloated over my purchases. We then went for a pub lunch and, of course, a malt.

That evening, my energy restored by a decent night's sleep and my enthusiasm rekindled by Gordon and MacPhail's huge selection, I tried the Scapa again. Remarkably, in the finish of my first sip I thought I detected—could it be?—bitter chocolate! It was very faint; I could not be sure I wasn't imagining it. But as I savored both that dram and another, I became more and more convinced that the discovery was genuine.

Now I'm not a psychologist; I have only a layman's under- standing of the psychological phenomena of suggestion, wishful thinking, perceptual illusion, and the like. It could easily be said that I talked myself into the taste of chocolate that night. Bern, acute as always, suggested it, and I couldn't deny it with any conviction. Had I imagined it? Perhaps. Does it matter? I'm not sure. Plenty of the tastes and other characteristics we associate with particular malts are as real, and as "objectively" discernible, as can be: the smokiness of Ardbeg, the peat and salt of Lagavulin, the iodine and tar of Laphroaig (pronounced *lah-FROIG*), the rich silky smoothness and balance of Macallan. But the ability to discern taste is highly variable and changeable: not only do the native perceptual abilities of individuals differ, but time of day, mood, and a thousand other variables impinge upon and affect this ability. The more subtle the taste in question, the more difficult it is to detect it. That's one reason why an expert like Michael Jackson is so valuable a guide: his acute powers of flavor detection, combined with his deep knowledge of malt and his remarkable ability to put his taste and smell discoveries into words, serve as a guide for the rest of us (although taking his word for it is not without some risk). So, was there a bitter chocolate taste in the Scapa? Well, I devoted the rest of that week's evenings to the study of that question. During those evenings I discovered many other qualities in the Scapa. By the time that quarter-bottle was gone, I had become a believer, and Scapa remains one of my favorite malts, despite my agreement with the general opinion that it is not one of the greats. Its dry, salty, grassy, cereal flavor—along with that teasing, elusive bitter chocolate in the finish—reminds me always of the pleasures of that week.

To leave our flat we had to drive a few hundred yards down a dirt road to the main thoroughfare running between Elgin and Rothes. Just north of that intersection on the main road was a lovely old hotel. We didn't pay much attention to it at first, but after driving past it several times, we agreed that we ought to take a look around. So one evening, after our day's exploration was done, we walked down to the hotel, hoping to find a bar and a malty aperitif.

We were not disappointed. The hotel was old but elegant, and the bar was full of dark wood, stuffed chairs and settees, and a very respectable selection of single malt. As we were chatting with the bartender, explaining the reason for our presence and discussing the malts he had behind the bar, a man came over, introduced himself to us, and invited us over to the table where he and an older man— his father—were sitting, enjoying a dram. It turned out that they were locals and had been coming to the hotel bar in the evening for years. I admitted my jealousy—by now I had already become completely taken by this magical place—and we had a wonderful conversation about Scotland and the place of single malt in Scottish life. They told us many stories about their malt experiences, the most remarkable of which was their routine practice of buying quarter, half, and even full casks from the various local distilleries. Sometimes they bought with friends, sometimes just for themselves. This was their equivalent of table wine—good, inexpensive malt for daily consumption. For something a bit more polished or unusual, they came to the hotel. Needless to say, they had an intimate knowledge of the malts distilled in the immediate vicinity. One of these was Glen Grant—just a few miles away, and one which, it turned out, we all liked. The younger man—I cannot remember his name—then gave me the best suggestion I have ever received. "Go down to the village of Craigellachie, cross over the bridge ("designed by the great Scottish engineer Thomas Telford," according to the Bible) which crosses the River Spey, go left, go right, go a few hundred yards after you're sure you must have missed it, and you'll find an old pub. They have a beautiful 35 year old Glen Grant behind the bar. The owners, an elderly couple, both have the shakes, and when they pour a dram it's always a large one. You'll not find any tourists there, but you will find some fine whiskies." I thanked him for the tip and directions, and after a while longer we said good-bye and walked home for the evening. (The Scapa was getting better and better!)

Well, how could I not try to find that pub? It was now near the end of my week, but I had to get there if I could. Bern thought that this was probably a bit too much, even for generous and understanding her, so she made an excuse to stay home (something about having to pack for the long journey south the next day), and I went off toward Craigellachie.

It took a while, and I did indeed think I must have missed it, but eventually I found the pub. Inside were a handful of patrons, each sitting alone, nursing their drinks in silence. Their glances as I entered were not welcoming. But having come this far, I wanted at least to taste that Glen Grant before departing. So I made my way to the bar, which was at that moment unattended. Sure enough, the Glen Grant was there on the shelf, along with several other interesting-looking bottles. In due course an older woman emerged from the back. She was short, with pinkish skin, white hair, and a warm smile—this was a woman at peace with her place in the world. Feeling better immediately, I explained how I happened upon her remote establishment, and we spent a few minutes trying to figure out who the man in the hotel bar might have been. She satisfied herself that she knew the man and his father, and in due course poured me a dram of the Glen Grant. As was predicted (but not mentioned), her hand shook when she poured, and I ended up with a generous glass. As I sipped, we chatted about malt, and she had all the conversational skills for which bartenders are famous. She seemed genuinely interested in the conversation, although the pub was too small to keep our conversation private, and the sentiments I felt emanating from my fellow customers as I heard myself talk were all along the lines of "what rubbish—get this Yank out of here so I can enjoy my drink in peace!"

In due course I finished my dram, and, mindful of both the dour mood of the other patrons and the need to get back to help Bern pack, I reached for my wallet to pay. At that moment I was confronted with a surprising question: "Do you know where you are?" Was this a philosophical test, I wondered? "Well, I think so: in Craigellachie, in your pub, just finishing this marvelous Glen Grant." "No, that's not what I mean," she said. "I mean, do you know that the Spey and the Fiddich meet just here?" The Spey, the river from which Speyside gets its name, and the Fiddich, another great whisky river that lends its name to Glenfiddich, the distillery that led the way in the marketing of single malts both within and outside Scotland? I was immediately struck by the significance of the spot. This kind woman explained that the rivers met about a hundred yards behind the pub; that the ground was rough and that I'd have to climb a fence or two, but that no one would mind if I did. Thanking her for this remarkable piece of local knowledge, I made my way back to the parking lot and, after a nanosecond's reflection, into the woods behind the pub, setting off for the spot. I had to get to it if I could.

God in a Dram?

It was a gray day and had begun to rain lightly while I was inside. The ground was wet and slippery as I made my way toward the rivers. I fell more than once, my jeans getting dirtier as I went. After a few minutes I thought I heard moving water, and soon I could see one of the rivers through the trees and brush. As I made my way toward it—as it turned out, the Spey—I thought I could make out the other, off toward the right. I headed for the area at which they meet, and, in due course, with muddy shoes and jeans and considerable anticipation, I reached the spot.

Like most philosophers, I have studied and routinely teach the traditional arguments for and against the existence of God. Indeed, a main impetus on the road to becoming a philosopher was the consideration of the design argument for God's existence, put forward by our rabbi in response to my demand for some reason to believe in God's existence when I was thirteen. My father had died that year, and I went to synagogue twice a day—early in the morning, before school, and again at dusk—for a year. That experience, and of course the death itself, prompted serious doubt; the argument was the rabbi's way of responding to it. (These early morning events did have a silver lining—a shot of shnapps or Canadian Club after the service on Monday and Thursday mornings, the weekdays the Torah is read, got me used to the burning warmth of straight liquor.) The result, in my case, was twofold. First, the argument's weakness was clear—even my thirteen-year-old self was able to recognize its many weaknesses, and I quickly realized that if this was the best that could be offered in its defense, in the face of human death and suffering, God's existence was doubtful in the extreme. Second, I became increasingly impressed with the power of philosophical analysis to address such questions and of philosophical arguments to answer them. In the event, I became both an atheist and an aspiring philosopher. By the time I visited that pub, I had for many years considered myself to be a professional (since I was paid to think, read, write, and teach about the subject) atheist. I did my best to keep my personal views from my students and to find strengths in pro-theistic arguments (and have in fact found many); still, my atheism was firm.

Nevertheless, my experience at the spot where the rivers meet can only be described as "spiritual." To the south, the Spey—the most important and famous whisky river in the world—stretched to the horizon. To the southeast, the Fiddich did the same, while where I stood it fed into the Spey as the latter continued its journey north to the North Sea, not far away. Crouching low, the waters nearly filled my field of vision, with just the gray sky above. I followed the rivers back in my mind's eye, imagining them as they flowed past the many distilleries we had seen that week. In that spot I couldn't help but be aware of the many centuries during which these waters, and the whisky produced from it, had been essential to the lives of the people of this place. Surely, it seemed, this is the way this place, and these lives, were meant to be. I felt a profound peace, and a sense that the universe, here at least, was as it should be. I sat there for a while, gazing at the gently flowing water, as this peacefulness flowed through me.

Eventually, my thoughts turned more prosaic as I contemplated the ways in which these rivers contributed to the making of malt whisky. Before too long I returned to the real world, and thought about driving back to Bern and Madeleine. I looked around one last time, taking in this moving river-scape, and prepared to hike back through the woods to the car. Before I left, I waded toe deep into the water where the rivers joined, and picked up a small smooth stone as a reminder of the spot where the Fiddich meets the Spey. It sits on my desk to this day, and often prompts a welcome reverie.

My experience that day did not turn me into a theist. But it did give me some sympathy for the power of what is often called 'religious experience'. I don't believe such experience has anything to do with a God, at least as traditionally conceived. But as a powerful human phenomenon, no doubt best understood by students of psychology and culture, it is undeniable.

Back to Reality

More than fifteen years have passed since that trip to whisky heaven. My enthusiasm for single malt continues unabated. I still seek out new single malt tastes and experiences, and travel to Edinburgh and Cadenhead (and other great malt shops in the United States and in Europe) as often as I can. I still consult my old tasting notes in the first edition of the Bible, though I'm now on the fifth (and final edition, since Jackson has recently passed away). My collection of single malt has grown to a respectable size, with a fair number of relatively unusual expressions. It usually contains a range of expressions of my favorites—Ardbeg, Caol Ila, Port Ellen, and most of the rest of Islay; Springbank, the legendary Campbeltown distillery; both Scapa and Highland Park from Orkney, and Talisker and several other malts from the other islands; and Glen Garioch, Dallas Dhu, and others from Speyside and the rest of the Highlands. I hasten to point out that this is a drinking collection, not an investment—the bottles are open, not stored away in anticipation of cashing in for future profits.

Not long after returning to Miami from this journey, I discovered that some university colleagues—a chemist, and a sociologist—shared a fondness for (the regularly available 16 year old) Lagavulin. Having acquired not long before a cask strength expression of it, I suggested a comparison tasting of the two bottles. A very enjoyable evening led to an informal search for other colleagues with an interest in single malt, and we gradually found people from all around the university who shared our enthusiasm. We formed the Single Malt

Tasting Group, which meets once or twice each semester (though it is currently "on sabbatical"). The e-mail list contains the addresses of over sixty faculty and friends from all around the university—many from the arts and sciences departments, but also from the schools of medicine, law, business, and communications—and beyond. Like most universities, meeting people from other departments, let alone schools and colleges, is increasingly unusual, so the group serves an enjoyable social function. Inevitably, our conversations include a healthy dose of university gossip, but we do our best to keep at least some of the focus on the malt. We've had distillery tastings (comparing several expressions from the same distillery), regional tastings (Islay, Islands and Speyside being favorites to which we regularly return), and as many theme tastings as we can come up with. The more zealous among us search the duty-free shops and the famous malt shops around the United States and Europe when the opportunity presents itself. Occasionally, the conversation turns to "malt stories." When I told this one, our creative writer from the English department harassed me until I wrote it up. The result is what you have just read.

UNIT III

The Metaphysics and Epistemology of Whiskey

11

As a Good Bartender Might
Whiskey and Natural Kinds

Thomas W. Polger

> The second principle is that of division into species
> according to the natural formation, where the joint is,
> not breaking any part as a bad carver might.
>
> —*Plato,* Phaedrus

The world is replete with things of many kinds. There are mountains and trees, cats and dogs, houses and castles, flowers and weeds. And there are whiskeys.

We human beings are remarkably adept at sorting the things of the world into various categories, types, or kinds. Small children quickly learn to sort objects according to their shape, size, color, number, and more. Before long we sort things in innumerable ways: by ripeness, by sweetness, by cost, by beauty, by weight, by familiarity, by luster, and so forth.

Some of the distinctions that we draw seem to be in the world, or in nature; they "carve nature at its joints" as the expression goes, and as a good butcher does according to Plato. The differences between mushrooms and trees, cats and dogs, or silver and gold seem to be of this sort. Philosophers call these sorts of categories natural kinds. Other categories seem to reflect more about human beings and our peculiar habits than about the world we inhabit: the beautiful things, the shiny things, weeds, things that go bump in the night, things within one kilometer of the Eiffel Tower. These are among the non-natural kinds. To call them 'non-natural' is not to say that they are supernatural, spooky, or mysterious; nor is it to deny that there are things of such kinds. It's just to say that they don't categorize the world "according to the natural formation," as the quotation from *Phaedrus* describes. Given the human aptitude for inventing or discovering new categories, it is perhaps inevitable that some will express our own interests and preferences rather than any facts about the world considered independently of those interests and preferences. It might even be that most of the categories we employ in daily life are "non-natural" in this way, i.e., that they express our own interests and preferences.

The particular kind of thing of interest herein is whiskey. Or, better yet, the kinds of things that are of interest herein are whiskeys—bourbons, Scotches, Irish whiskeys, rye and so on. Is whiskey a natural kind? Does the category *whiskey* carve nature at its joints? What about bourbon and Scotch—are they natural kinds?

We are interested in natural kinds for many reasons. One reason is that we simply want to know about the world we live in. We want to know about its natural features as well as those that are dependent on us. A second reason is that the natural kinds, among the features of the world, seem to be the most basic or fundamental. It is commonly thought that all of the nonbasic kinds of things in the world depend upon the basic natural features of the world. Third, the natural kinds are useful. In particular, they appear to be especially effective for formulating accurate explanations and predictions in science and in everyday life. No doubt there are other reasons to be concerned about the natural kinds.

It seems to me that there are at least two basic ways that one could settle once and for all the question about whether whiskeys are natural kinds. One tactic would be to provide a philosophical account of natural kinds, and then see if whiskeys have the features that natural kinds are supposed to have. Another tactic would be to assume that whiskeys are natural kinds if anything is—what could more obviously "carve nature at its joints" than the distinction between whiskey and vodka, after all—and then formulate an account of natural kinds that vindicates this assumption. These tactics either begin with or end with a fully formed account of natural kinds, and that is a tall order. Any general account of natural kinds will be contentious.[1] And even if we assume that whiskeys are natural kinds, a general account of natural kinds has to be responsive to much more than that one assumption. So let us not attempt to settle once and for all the question of whether whiskeys are natural kinds. Rather, let us consider some of the features that natural kinds are supposed to have, and ask whether whiskeys or varieties of whiskeys have them. We won't settle the question for all time, but perhaps we can get a sense of whether whiskeys are more like natural kinds or non-natural kinds.

Kinds and the Symptoms of Natural Kinds

First, we need to say something about kinds in general. I began by saying that there are many kinds of things in the world. But what are kinds?

Consider the word 'bourbon'. How many letters are in the word 'bourbon'? At least two answers seem acceptable: seven, and five. If we count each token, that is, each particular letter, then there are seven (b, o, u, r, b, o, n). If we count each kind, that is, each type of letter, then there are five (b, o, u, r, n) because 'b' and 'o' are each repeated. So there are seven token letters and five letter types in the word 'bourbon'. The original question (How many letters are in the word 'bourbon'?), it turns out, is ambiguous: it can be interpreted as asking about token letters or about letter types.[2] Most people are already familiar with the distinction between letter tokens and letter types, though perhaps they don't know it by name. If you are playing Scrabble, you must form words containing at least two letters. This rule applies to token letters. Some Scrabble dictionaries will allow the words 'aa' and 'mm' to be played. If you were to deny that 'aa' and 'mm' are legal Scrabble words, it would be because you doubt they are words at all, not because you believe that they are words that contain only one letter.[3] But other games count letter types or kinds rather than letter tokens. If you are a player on the television game show *Wheel of Fortune*, you try to solve a puzzle by guessing letters in a hidden word or phrase. You earn prize money for each letter of the type you name that is in the hidden word or phrase. So if the word is 'bourbon' and you guess the letter 'b', you earn prize money for each token letter of the type 'b' in 'bourbon'. If you guess 'b', you would be cheated if they revealed only one of the tokens, such as '– – – – b – –'. This is because you understand that you are guessing letter types, not just letter tokens. One could easily imagine a game similar to *Wheel of Fortune* but in which contestants had to guess letter tokens. Crossword puzzles are something like this.

Now that we have set out the general idea of tokens and types or kinds, let's focus on those 'b's and 'o's in 'bourbon'. What makes the two 'b's tokens of the same letter type, or kind? This is just a particular example of the question: what makes any thing a member of any kind at all? One can imagine that the world contains no kinds, that everything is entirely distinct from everything else, except perhaps in belonging to the so-called kinds 'things' or 'stuff'. The traditional philosophical doctrine of nominalism holds something like this. In its most simplistic and least plausible version, nominalism is the view that there are only things and words, and we apply some words to more than one thing. Concerning *whiskey*, the crude nominalist would claim that there is no further explanation for why we apply the word 'whiskey' to more than one thing; that's just how it is.

But many of us think that there is an explanation for why words or concepts apply to more than one thing. The answer is that they have something in common. But saying what that "something" is turns out to be devilishly difficult. Take our running example of letter tokens and letter types. Let us suppose that there is, after all, an answer to the question: what makes the two 'b's tokens of the same letter type, or kind? And let us suppose that that answer has to do with the tokens having something in common, or being alike in some way. What way? Maybe they have the same shape? But we quickly notice that can't be quite right because there is also a letter 'b' at the start of this sentence, but it is not the same shape as the other 'b's in this sentence. The capital 'B' is not even similar in shape to the lowercase 'b'. And that letter can be printed in different fonts, or written in cursive handwriting, or scrawled by a small child, or gestured in sign language.

Shape, as it turns out, is not the common factor among members of letter types. Perhaps shape is a common factor for some other kinds of things (such as baseballs or tennis courts), and perhaps not. The important lesson is that being a member of a kind often involves having one or more characteristics that qualify a thing for being a member of that particular kind. These characteristics are what philosophers think of as the essential properties of a kind of thing—the properties that are had by all members of a kind without which a thing would not be (or would cease to be) a member of that kind. The essential properties of mousetraps include, we might think, that they have the function of catching or killing mice. The essential properties of diamonds include being a certain kind of carbon lattice molecule. And if I invent a new kind—for example, by stipulating that a 'qwafp' is anything that is sitting on my desk at a certain time—then it is an essential property of qwafps that they are or were located on my desk at that time. If whiskey is a natural kind, then there must be some common feature that is had by all and only whiskeys.

Many of us suppose that diamond is a natural kind—one of the kinds that categorize things "according to the natural formation" as in the *Phaedrus*—and that made-up kinds like qwafp are not natural kinds. For natural kinds, the idea is that there is some fact about the world or the object itself that makes it a member of the kind. Think about chemical elements like silver and gold or molecular substances like water and diamonds. Atomic kinds are distinguished by their atomic structures: gold has the atomic number 79; silver has the atomic number 47. Molecular kinds are distinguished by their molecular structure: water has the molecular structure H_2O; diamonds are crystals formed of tetrahedrally bonded carbon atoms. If something does not have the atomic number 79, it is not gold; if it does, it is. Atomic number is essential to element kinds; and atomic number, we suppose, picks out a fact about the world that is quite independent of human interest.[4]

Whether whiskeys are more like diamonds or more like qwapfs seems to depend on whether the essential properties of whiskeys depend on human interests or not. But how can we tell which essential properties are in the world in itself (as it were), and which are dependent on human interests? This is the tricky part, the part that calls for the invocation of the sort of general theory of natural kinds that I cannot defend herein. Rather than fret over this lacuna, let us instead take up what we have handy. We can at least note some of the features that various theories of natural kinds value, and treat these features as symptoms of natural kinds by which such kinds can be identified, however imperfectly. What are the symptoms of a natural kind? I will focus on the following four, which I will clarify below: first, natural kinds are explanatorily fertile; second, natural kinds serve as the evidential basis for predictive generalizations; third, natural kinds are governed by laws of nature; and fourth, natural kinds are the objects of "rigid"

general terms. Each of these symptoms requires some brief explanation before we can consider whether they are features exhibited by whiskeys.

The first symptom, that natural kinds are explanatorily fertile, is just a fancy way of saying that they figure in good and useful explanations. Gold is an explanatorily useful kind, whereas qwafp is not. I can explain why some mechanism works as it does in part by citing the fact that it has parts that are made of gold, for example, that's why it conducts electricity as well as it does. In contrast, nothing is explained by citing the fact that something is a qwafp—not even, on pain of circularity, that it is called qwafp. Is whiskey an explanatory kind?

The second symptom is related to the first. Natural kinds figure in explanations and also in predictions. If I know that something is gold, and I know some facts about it (e.g., that it conducts electricity well), then I can make some predictions about other gold things. And I can cite as evidence for those predictions the fact that my original observation was of a sample of the kind gold. In contrast, no matter how much I observe a qwafp, I will not be able to generalize or "project" the evidence from that sample into predictions about other qwafps. So two symptoms that a kind is a natural kind are that it figures in useful explanations and accurate predictions. Is whiskey a predictive kind?

The third symptom might just be a way of summarizing or explaining the first two: it is frequently thought that for a kind to be a natural kind there must be some laws of nature that cover members of the kind. Of course, some law of nature will cover them—gravity covers every material thing, after all. But here we are concerned with laws that cover the members of the kind because they are members of the kind. For example, one might think that it is a law of nature that water boils at 100°C, or that diamonds can cut glass. These kinds of generalizations might be the foundation for the explanations and predictions that I have called the first two symptoms of natural kinds. Are there any natural laws concerning whiskeys?

The last symptom of natural kinds is that they are often named or referred to by what philosophers call "rigid" general terms. The easiest way to understand this idea is to contrast them with terms that are not rigid. Compare the expressions 'the first person to set foot on the moon' and 'Neil Armstrong'. As it happens, both of these expressions pick out the same person. But it did not *have* to be that way—the Soviets might have won the space race or Buzz Aldrin might have stepped out first. That is, it might have been that Neil Armstrong was not the first person to set foot on the moon. Were that the case, 'Neil Armstrong' would still refer to Neil Armstrong; but 'the first person to set foot on the moon' would not refer to the same person, because 'the first person to set foot on the moon' would refer to whoever was the first person to set foot on the moon. Proper names like 'Neil Armstrong' refer to the same things no matter what—they designate particular persons "rigidly." Expressions like 'the first person to set foot on the moon' are not rigid in this sense; they refer to different things in different scenarios. Natural kind terms are thought to be like names, in that they refer to the same kinds of things regardless. So 'gold' would refer to the same kind of stuff (namely, gold) even if the laws of nature were different from what they actually are.[5] Does 'whiskey' refer rigidly?

With these symptoms in mind, we can ask: how many of them does whiskey have? And how many are had by particular varieties of whiskeys? Do the distinctions among whiskeys, and between whiskeys and other things, divide the world as Plato supposes a good butcher—or bartender—should?

First Pass: Liquor, Beer, and Wine

The store where I buy beer, wine, and liquor is organized according to the kinds of things that are stocked in each aisle or area. There are aisles for different wine varietals, for wines from Spain or from Australia, for beer, for soft drinks, and so forth. There is an aisle for Scotch, an area for bourbon, and designated shelves for Irish, Canadian, and rye whiskeys. Some of the areas are larger and some smaller. The store's organization gives the impression that one is walking through a giant periodic table of beverages. It seems that these retail distinctions could not be clearer and that they surely mark natural formations of the world. But how does whiskey fare on the criteria for natural kinds outlined above?

To begin, consider whether the category *whiskey* is explanatorily fertile or evidentially useful in formulating predictive generalizations. Are there truths about whiskey that do not apply to other distilled spirits? It is tempting to appeal directly to the distinctive tastes of the various beverages. But two problems lurk. The first is practical: is it true that whiskeys all have a reliable taste, such that one can formulate explanations and predictions about them? It is hard to think of some claim that I could make about the taste of whiskeys that would apply to all of them and to nothing that is not a whiskey. It's doubtful that all and only whiskeys are smoky, oaky, peaty, or have a toasted grain taste. But suppose there were some such feature that could be explained or predicted by the fact that a beverage is a whiskey. A second problem awaits: how something tastes is, to some degree, dependent upon the taster as well as upon the stuff in the world. How a whiskey, beer, or wine tastes may depend on what kind of critter I am, on my own peculiar genetically and environmentally sculpted taste buds, and on what else I am eating and drinking at the same time or have been eating or drinking lately. Tastes are good candidates for what philosophers call *secondary* or *response-dependent* qualities. These are features of how things affect us; and they seem to be features of us or of our relationships to things, rather than of the things themselves. Although it is less likely, tastes might even be entirely subjective experiences of one individual that just happen to be stimulated by things that contact the olfactory and gustatory sense organs. Could it be that the taste of whiskey to me is the same as the taste of beer to you?

It's also extremely unlikely that there are natural laws that apply only to whiskeys. Perhaps we could think of laws of nature that apply only to distilled spirits, brewed beverages, or wines. But even that is a stretch. The problem for finding the kinds of lawful, explanatory, or predictive generalizations about whiskeys is that the category seems to pick out things according to how they are produced rather than according to the features of the resulting product. This is also a hint as to what sorts of commonalities they might in fact have, and a possible way of saving the idea that whiskey is a natural kind.

First, if facts about how something was produced can count as features of the thing itself, then maybe there is a common feature to all and only whiskeys: whiskeys are distilled liquors—unlike beers and wines—and they are those that are produced from a grain mash—rather than from potato or from fruit. (We might also specify that it is distilled to around 70% alcohol, or that no additional flavorings are added, as in a gin head.) We would no doubt have to adjust our parameters to get this category just right, but it seems promising. It is at least as promising as finding a category for biological kinds like hearts and lungs. Infamously, it's not the case that all hearts have any obvious features in common. They come in many shapes, sizes, and configurations. And it is an unfortunate medical fact that it is not even the case that all hearts pump blood—for some hearts fail to do so, or cease to do so, and do not thereby fail or cease to be hearts. A broken heart is a heart just the same. If hearts have anything in common at all, a good candidate might be that they are produced and maintained by natural selection because their predecessors pumped blood often enough in the evolutionary ancestors who had them. And one can offer some—plainly fallible, but nevertheless useful—explanations and predictions about hearts based on this historical fact. We can say, for example, that many hearts will pump blood, at least in ordinary or ideal circumstances. Or we can explain why creatures like us have hearts rather than not. And so on.

If this kind of historical feature is good enough to make hearts natural kinds, then perhaps our whiskey can qualify as a natural kind on the grounds that it must be produced in a certain way. We can perhaps predict whether a certain apparatus will produce whiskey rather than vodka, gin, or wine. And we can perhaps explain why some substance is a whiskey, or a whiskey with particular qualities, by citing the fact that it was produced in a certain way.

And this brings us to the fourth criteria for natural kinds. For among the kinds of things that are referred to by "rigid" designators are some that have a particular sort of historical essence: namely, their origins are essential to them. Some philosophers believe that particular human beings have their origins essentially—I could not have different parents than I do, for example.[6] 'Thomas Polger' always refers to a person with that history and thus always to me.[7] If my children had different parents, they would be different children. So *these* children, *my* children, must have the parents that they in fact have, the origins that they in fact have, essentially. Proper names, as I said earlier, are rigid designators. And 'heart' might be like this: something a lot like a heart that was not produced and maintained by the historical process would not, strictly speaking, be a heart. And if whiskeys are like hearts, then 'whiskey' might be like 'heart'. If so, then 'whiskey' is a rigid term as well.[8]

If we're in the right ballpark, then whiskey satisfies one or two of the usual criteria for being a natural kind, and maybe even all four if we are willing to allow historical features to figure in our explanatory and predictive generalizations.

Second Pass: Bourbon, Rye, Scotch, and Irish Whiskeys

One problem with treating whiskey as a natural kind is that there are many kinds of whiskeys: bourbons, Scotches, Irish whiskeys, rye whiskeys, Canadian whiskeys, and more. Some of the differences among these things are incidental. But other differences are relevant to the features that make them all whiskeys while also making them different kinds of whiskey. It seems that there is more than one way to be a whiskey. We may wonder whether there is any one feature (or set of features) that all and only whiskeys have in common. Whiskey is a good candidate to be, as philosophers say, multiply realized. This is why we had trouble thinking of explanations, predictions, or natural laws that apply to all and only whiskeys.

Even if whiskey is not a natural kind, perhaps some of the kinds of whiskeys are themselves natural kinds? This may seem paradoxical, but it is quite common. Consider the kind 'rocks'. Probably rocks fail to satisfy any of the four criteria outlined above. There are not explanatory or predictive generalizations that apply to all and only rocks, there are not laws of nature concerning rocks, and the term 'rock' is not rigid. But diamond and jade are both kinds of rocks, and arguably each of them is a natural kind that satisfies most or all of the criteria. So it is possible for a general or superordinate kind that is not natural to include other more specific subordinate kinds that are natural. Perhaps whiskey is like this.

The suggestion is promising, but not without its own problems. Many types of whiskey do not seem to be good candidates for being natural kinds. This is because their "defining" features include more than just how they are made and of what, but also where they are made. Scotch must come from Scotland, Irish whiskey from Ireland, and so forth. But these locations are themselves politically variable. That the political boundaries salient for whiskey-lovers have remained relatively stable is an accident of history. The same was not true through the twentieth century for all of the wine-growing regions of France and Germany. And even today the official extent of even the great French wine-growing regions is up for negotiation.[9] So it's hard to see how, say, Scotch can be a natural kind if it must be produced in Scotland, and *Scotland* is not a natural feature of the world, independent of human interests and peculiarities. And national boundaries are surely dependent on human interests. The trouble is that there are few natural generalizations, predictions, and laws that depend on whether something is located or produced inside or outside of a political boundary, as though gravity were different inside and outside of Scotland. Being from Scotland is much more like being within a kilometer of the Eiffel Tower or being a thing that goes bump in the night than it is like being a substance with the atomic number 79.

Of course, we human beings are interested not only in the natural properties of stuff but also in its non-natural properties: being shiny, being bitter, being from Ireland, and so forth. So it's easy to understand why we distinguish Scotch whisky from Irish whiskey. But that does not assure that the distinction carves nature at its joints.

Bourbon is a somewhat better candidate for a variety of whiskey that is a natural kind. This is because bourbon is characterized by its production process and by the ingredients of the mash that is fermented and distilled—it must be a grain mash containing at least 51% corn. Thus, if grain types are natural kinds, a good case is to be made that bourbon is a natural kind. But contrary to common belief, bourbon does not have to be made in Bourbon County or even in Kentucky. Now it's true that for something to be labeled as bourbon in the United States, it must be produced in the United States. But this is like passing a law that says stuff called gin has to be made in England. Such a stricture on bourbon seems to have more to do with trade policy than with the identity of the stuff.[10]

One way of salvaging the geographically specialized whiskeys as natural kinds would be to argue that those geographic boundaries are good indicators of some other feature of the product that is not so humanly dependent as national boundaries. The idea would be that the human laws are crude approximations of the deeper truth. For example, with wine one might suppose that the authorities that fix the geographic range of vinicultural appellations are not creating those regions but are merely trying to correctly record a real distinction already present in the world. This would require taking seriously the idea that *terroir* contributes some distinct (but perhaps indescribable) quality to the product. A similar claim could be made for whiskey production, I suppose. I'm not sure how plausible this would be, particularly in light of the way that distillation erases many of the traces of *terroir* that are supposed to be preserved in fermentation. But it is a possibility worth considering.

Conclusions, Such as They Are

We have not settled the question of whether whiskey—or bourbon, or Scotch, or Irish whiskey—is a natural kind. But we have garnered a better understanding of what the answer hinges on. At least two key questions require answers: can natural kinds have their origins or methods of production as essential features? Do geographic locations of origin contribute essential features to whiskeys, or can natural kinds have their relations to particular geographic locations as essential features? I don't know the answers to these questions. I'm sure that not every distinction drawn among beverages qualifies them as natural kinds, but I would like to think that whiskey—bourbon in particular—is one of them. Surely Plato's good butcher would enjoy a good whiskey.[11]

NOTES

The chapter epigraph is taken from Plato, *Phaedrus*, Benjamin Jowett (trans.), http://classics.mit.edu/Plato/phaedrus.html (accessed July 24, 2008), 265d.

1. See, for example, W.V.O. Quine, "Natural Kinds," in *Ontological Relativity and Other Essays* (New York: Columbia University Press, 1969); Ian Hacking, "A Tradition of Natural Kinds," *Philosophical Studies* 61 (1991): pp. 109–126; or Richard Boyd, "Kinds as the 'Workmanship of Men': Realism, Constructivism, and Natural Kinds," *Rationalität, Realismus, Revision: Proceedings of the Third International Congress, Gesellschaft für Analytische Philosophie*, ed. Julian Nida-Rümelin (Berlin: de Gruyter, 1999).

2. One could also say that there are two kinds of letters in 'bourbon', consonants and vowels. The example of token letters is adapted from David Armstrong's example of token words in *Universals: An Opinionated Introduction* (Boulder, CO: Westview, 1989).

3. The term 'aa' designates a kind of lava; 'mm' is a word used to express pleasure or satisfaction, especially concerning a food.

4. Of course we have many such interests, but those interests do not make the facts about atomic number what they are, as my interests make the facts about qwafps what they are.

5. See especially Saul Kripke, *Naming and Necessity* (Cambridge, MA: Harvard University Press, 1980); Hilary Putnam, "The Meaning of 'Meaning'," in *Language, Mind and Knowledge, Minnesota Studies in the Philosophy of Science*, Vol. 7, ed. Keith Gunderson (Minneapolis: University of Minnesota Press, 1975), and reprinted in *Hilary Putnam, Mind, Language and Reality: Philosophical Papers*, vol. 2 (Cambridge: Cambridge University Press, 1975); and Scott Soames, *Beyond Rigidity: The Unfinished Semantic Agenda of Naming and Necessity* (New York: Oxford University Press, 2002). But for doubts about this theory of reference, see David Lewis, *On the Plurality of Worlds* (New York: Basil Blackwell, 1986).

6. This controversial view is often associated with the work of Saul Kripke (cf. *Naming and Necessity*) and subsequently Nathan Salmon, *Reference and Essence* (Princeton, NJ: Princeton University Press, 1981). For doubts, see the concerns surveyed in Salmon, as well as in John Hawthorne and Tamar Szabó Gendler, "Origin Essentialism: The Arguments Reconsidered," *Mind* 109 (2000): pp. 285–298.

7. Suppose for the sake of the example that I am the only person who in fact has this name—which is true as far as I know.

8. This introduces the possibility of what some philosophers would call "swamp whiskey"—something just like whiskey but which is not genuine whiskey. It would be a kind of whiskey forgery. The truth is that philosophers worry too much about such doppelgänger substances. Donald Davidson introduced the idea of "Swampman," a duplicate of himself that was not born and had no developmental or evolutionary history, but simply popped into existence out of swamp gasses, in "Knowing One's Own Mind," *Proceedings and Addresses of the American Philosophical Association* 60 (1987): pp. 441–458.

9. Jacob Gaffney, "Champagne Region Set to Expand," *Wine Spectator*, March 14, 2008, www.winespectator.com/Wine/Features/0,1197,4296,00.html (accessed July 24, 2008).

10. If it does not, then perhaps rye whiskey is an even better candidate for being a natural kind. There seems to be no geographic requirement on rye whiskey.

11. I would like to thank Steve Geisz for introducing me to bourbon and for many philosophical conversations involving whiskey. I'd also like to thank my in-laws for their support and for their family tradition of always giving whiskey and socks for Christmas. Finally, I must thank my wife (who managed not to give birth until I was done working on this essay) and children (who managed to sleep while I revised it).

12

Heisenberg's Spirits
Tasting Is More Uncertain
Than It Seems

Jerry O. Dalton

I've talked to a great many whiskey enthusiasts over the twenty years that I've been a distiller at Jim Beam and Barton Brands. Some of them were writers and critics, real aficionados. Some of them were whiskey icons like Booker Noe, Jim Beam's grandson; Jimmy Russell of Wild Turkey fame; and Elmer T. Lee of Buffalo Trace—all of them acknowledged masters with bourbons named after them. But the majority of the folks that I did tastings with and talked to were just plain people who enjoyed their bourbon to the point of wanting to know more about it. Because of my tenure as master distiller at two different distilleries, I was considered to be an expert in all aspects of bourbon, including tasting and evaluation. I was often asked questions about whiskey in general and bourbon in particular: how to drink it, what properties to look for, and, most difficult of all, which of the whiskeys that I produced as well as those of my competitors did I prefer. I was always hesitant to answer such questions, especially the ones about which bourbons are better. For my own bourbons it was like asking a father which of his children he liked best. For other whiskeys, if I stated a specific preference, I ran the risk of being pilloried by Marketing for admitting that we had competitors, let alone that they made good bourbon.

I finally realized that my problem with questions of preference ran deeper than I thought. I suspect that the people who asked me about bourbon were not asking for my opinion because they wanted to know more about me. Instead, their queries could be distilled down to a fundamental question. Are some whiskeys better than others? The answer is more complicated than it seems.

I will show in the following sections that the question encompasses not just the whiskey but also the person tasting it. The Heisenberg Uncertainty Principle and how it relates to the taster/tasted system will be discussed. A few near-absolutes that affect whiskey quality perceptions will be mentioned and how even these bad actors produce uncertain results. I will cover some objective measurements that distillers use to produce a consistent product. The difficulties of tasting and evaluation will be explored, especially those related to objectivity. I will discuss critics' evaluations and how they affect the consumer and the whiskey. The final section will show that the answer to the question of which whiskey is better is as close as the nearest liquor store.

Are Some Whiskeys Better Than Others?

I often frequent the bourbon shelves in liquor outlets as a matter of professional interest. I enjoy surveying the many brands available and watching especially for new offerings with which I am not familiar. I have also noticed that there seem to be two types of shoppers. One is the person who comes down the aisle, makes a beeline to the whiskey of his or her choice, picks it up and is gone. The other type is the person who drifts down the aisle, staring at the array of whiskeys and occasionally pulling down a bottle to read the label.

It was probably while watching one of these small dramas in a liquor store with an uncertain consumer holding an unopened bottle that I thought of a lesson from quantum theory and how it applied to the situation at hand. We will discuss this lesson on uncertainty in the next section.

The Certainty of Uncertainty

There is a lot of uncertainty afoot in the world these days, what with wars, terrorist attacks, and shock and awe at the tab after filling up at the gas station. But I'd bet that there are not many people who know just how blurry things are when examined closely. It was events on a subatomic scale that gave blurriness its due, the Heisenberg Uncertainty Principle. Heisenberg shook the foundations of physics and chemistry when he showed that the exact position and momentum—that's velocity with some mass thrown in—of a particle cannot be measured simultaneously. It turns out that the particle, an electron, for example, must be hit with a beam of energy, light or otherwise, in order to measure anything about it. When it is hit with energy, the particle takes off for parts unknown or at least uncertain, thus changing its velocity and position. It can never quite be pinned down.

You might argue that the principle is irrelevant because subatomic particles have little or nothing to do with quaffing a wee dram or knocking back a shot, depending on which side of the Atlantic you are enjoying your whiskey. To get to the heart of it, we have to leave the spooky world of quantum mechanics and move back into more familiar realms. The Uncertainty Principle in its broadest, most philosophical form says that the observer and the observed can't be separated. A thing has to be disturbed in order to measure it or even look at it, which is taking its measure, in a way. So that means that we are never truly separate from anything of which we are aware. No matter how objectively we try to see something, its edges blur, as do our own, and we become part of what Heisenberg would have called a system. We interact with the other parts of the system and likewise they interact with us. So it is with the taster and the tasted. Like beauty and the beholder, whether a given whiskey is better than others depends on the taster. To a person accustomed to Scotch, bourbon might seem too sweet or grainy. To an avowed bourbon drinker, Scotch and even Tennessee whiskey might be too smoky. A vodka aficionado might think that tequila tastes like weeds and a tequila fan might think vodka tastes like nothing but alcohol (as technically speaking, it should). The first law of absolutes is that there are none (that are absolute), which will be discussed in the next section.

There Are No Absolutes

All of these considerations force us to recognize that we're not considering just the whiskey in answering the question; we are considering a system consisting of a consumer interacting with a libation. This brings in the concept of quality. When we talk about "better" bourbon, we're really dealing with quality, which has two components: manufacturing quality—absolute conformance to product specifications; and quality of design—which means that the product, be it bourbon or a BMW, must meet customer requirements (Heisenberg just showed up). Customer satisfaction, which is a major part of modern quality management system standards such as ISO-9001, hinges on giving the consumer the whiskey that she wants, when she wants it, and at a price that she's willing to pay. If the consumer wants moderately priced, 4-year-old bourbon that he will use to mix with cola or to make Whiskey Sours, then that's what the distiller should offer. At four years of aging, the bourbon will be lighter in character and will be less complex and nuanced than the same bourbon will be at eight years. In a mixed drink, especially one with citrus or sugar, the sharp-edged "bite" of younger whiskey may, in fact, be necessary for the spirit not to be lost among other tastes and aromas. At the same time, the complex subtleties of older whiskey may disappear into a forest of flavors. Offering a "better" 8-year-old bourbon with a higher price to this consumer would produce no enhanced satisfaction and more likely would have the opposite effect.

My point is illustrated by an impromptu tasting in which I was involved about twenty years ago. The technical director of a large (now defunct) spirits conglomerate had brought an important Japanese purchasing executive to Kentucky to visit some of the distilleries that were producing bourbon for his company. We were having drinks at a historic old Bardstown tavern when the technical director decided to have the executive taste two whiskeys, one of which was classical sour mash bourbon with rye as the small grain. The other was a popular wheated bourbon, so-called because it used wheat as the small grain instead of rye. We tasted the regular bourbon first, and when asked his opinion the Japanese gentleman made a few polite comments about its taste and aroma. We then tasted the wheated whiskey. The technical director, whose conglomerate owned the distillery producing the wheated bourbon, pressed the executive for a response, which was at first not forthcoming. Finally, with remarkable candor, the Japanese gentleman said that he didn't think that the Japanese people would recognize the wheated whiskey as bourbon. He speculated that perhaps it would be more like sherry to them.

In this account, both of the bourbons were sound, high-quality whiskeys with no big flaws in aroma or taste profile. Bourbon drinkers might prefer one or the other, depending on their individual tastes, and would rate their preference as "better" in a head-to-head comparison. But to the Japanese executive, one was not even recognizable as bourbon.

So what constitutes a good whiskey, that is, one that is better than others? At this point we are forced for the most part to abandon absolutes with only a few possible exceptions. I mention these because, in my experience, there are some things that seem to be almost universally unacceptable to whiskey drinkers.

The first thing is must. Must is that character in aroma that we associate with wet basements, rotten logs, damp wallpaper in old closed-up houses, and, closer to the whiskey business, musty or moldy grain. It is a character that will come through fermentation, distillation, and aging and generally is the kiss of death for whiskey. If a batch is bad enough and if one tastes the whiskey in spite of the odor, it lingers on the tongue and even seems to concentrate in the finish or aftertaste of the whiskey. Distillers go to great lengths to screen grain for must, and it is very seldom that musty whiskey makes it to market. If it does somehow, it always produces customer complaints.

There are two compounds that do occasionally find their way into the finished product, and like must they always cause consumer dissatisfaction. One is trichloroanisole, TCA for short, which vintners and wine drinkers identify as cork taint. My perception of cork taint is that it is similar to must with a sharp, pungent medicinal note thrown in to add insult to injury. Oddly enough, cork taint was not a factor in bourbon in recent years until "better" upscale bourbons were presented in bottles with cork closures.

Finally in this whiskey rogue's gallery, there is geosmin. Geosmin is found in stagnant water and is often associated with decaying vegetation. It produces an earthy sort of wet-dog odor and taste when it is present even at very low levels in whiskey. Like must and cork taint it lingers on the palate and concentrates in the aftertaste. Most people don't like it when they find it in their drink.

At high enough levels all three of these compounds seem to turn people off. But even these bad actors can't be presented as absolutes because some people are much less sensitive to them than others. As a result, whiskey that one person might reject outright might be classified as better by another person who detects good qualities and misses the bad. I will return to sensitivity later.

One last thing about quality—manufacturing quality, specifically—approaches the absolute. It is consistency.

Manufacturing specifications include a product organoleptic (taste and aroma) standard. Each lot bottled should be indistinguishable from the standard. There is still some uncertainty there because of the vagaries of mixing, processing, and bottling in large volumes. Furthermore, even highly trained taste panels can have a collective off day. That notwithstanding, I would tell my audiences at tastings that if they liked my bourbons, they would still like them years from now unless *their* tastes changed.

Are there no objective properties of "better" bourbon in particular? We'll cover that next.

On Objective Measurements

How do we distillers measure and specify our products beyond alcohol strength, color, and clarity? In some regards we are wildly sophisticated in our measurements compared to the early distillers. Congeners, often called fusel oils, are higher molecular weight alcohols produced in fermentation. At moderate levels they enhance flavor and at higher levels they enhance hangovers. At least one old whiskey song pays tribute to congeners (with more rhyme than reason, since they are colorless) by saying, "if the whiskey's too red, it'll swell up your head." We measure congener levels using gas chromatography to separate the various compounds of interest and can do so easily down to parts per million concentrations. Different distillers measure other components based on their experience of what is important to their particular product. There may be as many as ten or fifteen compounds specified and routinely measured for a given bourbon. But when we make an exacting and exhaustive analysis of whiskey, we can find literally hundreds of components, all of which may have some impact on flavor and aroma. To say that a particular compound, benzaldehyde, for example, introduces a cherry note to the bourbon is true to a degree but simplistic when one considers the hundreds of potentially synergistic interactions in which it participates in the barrel and later, the bottle. In my experience, it is a short step from a clean, sweet "honey barrel" perception in bourbon to a sweet but rancid-butter perception of a fermentation gone bad or to the sweet, turpentine characteristic often found in whiskeys that were too long in the barrel. So an objective measure of a compound known to smell or taste like a particular thing in no way guarantees that an identifiable note of that thing will be detectable in the organoleptic profile of the whiskey.

We can and do specify maximum and minimum levels of various compounds in bourbon for the sake of product consistency. The distiller works constantly to remove uncertainties produced as a result of bourbon being a product of a natural process. No two fermentations are exactly the same. There are variations in distillation that happen in spite of the best efforts and controls of the distiller. Barrels are all different because they are made from wood that grew in different places and under different conditions. At the end of the aging process, every barrel of whiskey is as unique as a fingerprint. All of this is taken into account and averaged out as much as possible by the quality control in processing and bottling. But in the final analysis we make our batches based on taste panel evaluations in blind tastings against product standards. Furthermore, we hope that our taste panel members are diversified enough to be a fair representation of the consumers of our products, thus acknowledging again the importance of the taster-tasted system.

We've discussed some of the vagaries of a natural process and how they affect whiskey, but what about the other half of the system? In the next section we will discuss some of the factors and uncertainties that affect tasters.

Taster Uncertainties

The topic of tasters and tasting is worthy of an essay in itself. Even that is an understatement considering that there are entire books written on sensory evaluation and statistical analysis of the results. My discussion here is intended to cover the middle ground between the Saturday night drinker intent on getting "about half smoked," as Booker Noe termed it, and the sensory evaluation taste panel member who is highly trained to identify notes in organoleptic profiles.

A person who is interested in tasting for the purpose of discovering a better whiskey has a certain sensitivity to various flavor and aroma components and a certain amount of experience in recognizing them. Almost everyone would recognize the aroma and flavor of vanilla outright and most would recognize coconut or orange, for example. But put those notes singly or collectively in with dozens of other competing notes of various intensities, and it becomes more difficult to single out one from the other. That being said, I have to wonder how many people other than experts and critics deconstruct their perceptions of whiskey, searching for a hint of hazelnut or a touch of damson plum. For my part, I taste bourbons and other whiskeys looking for balance with no overbearing notes. My view of a better whiskey is one that, regarding specific notes in the profile, is comparable to a really good choir in which no single voice sticks out and each section is appropriately strong but does not dominate any other. But this just reinforces the argument that the taster is part of the Heisenbergian system, since my preferences are valid only for me and are based in my own set of sensory evaluation tools. It is true that there are whiskey flavor and aroma components present at levels that can be measured by objective means. But I have seen the *same product's aroma* described by renowned experts with comments ranging from fiery and assertive, through sweetish and light, and ending with smooth and refined. Given that experts apply their own standards (and biases!) to evaluation, it makes it all the more important that we taste for ourselves, thus applying our own standards (and biases!).

Further uncertainties are introduced to the system because of variations in the taster. Certain things are obvious. One doesn't try to evaluate whiskeys just after eating a spicy dish or having a mint. Smoking, colds, and allergies interfere as well. I quit wearing aftershave lotion almost as soon as I got into the business, which is to no avail if the person who precedes you in the tasting booth is heavily scented with perfume or cologne.

There are some amazing misconceptions held by people who are earnestly trying to find better whiskey. I was told at one presentation that I was giving that you should cup your hand over the tasting glass when nosing the whiskey to gather the aroma. Hopefully, I minimized that particular uncertainty by suggesting that the scent of the dog, or the cat, or whatever else one might have most recently touched could easily prevail over the profile of the spirits. I have also been told that you should not let the whiskey touch the tip of your tongue when tasting to avoid being overpowered by the spirits. Since the tip of the tongue is where one perceives sweet notes, I never understood that direction and never tried to follow it.

But after years of tasting groups of samples at a fixed proof in identical glasses and in a controlled environment, I became aware of what I call the second sample syndrome. I found that I tend to rate the second sample that I taste in a flight of whiskeys lower than the first. It doesn't happen every time, but in a large number of tastings it becomes significant. I found that I could offset this tendency by swishing a composite of the whiskeys in the flight in my mouth just before the actual tasting. I have no idea if this is a general phenomenon or a personal idiosyncrasy, but it is an indication of one more factor influencing nominally objective evaluations.

There are many factors that make subtle, small-scale perturbations in the taster-tasted system. Color clues, proof at which the whiskey is tasted, temperature of the sample, even the shape of the tasting glass have some influence on the evaluation. To compound these uncertainties, the system is not closed. That is to say that there are external influences that affect the search for better whiskey. My final word on variations in the taster is a customer complaint that I once received. The customer said that he had gone to dinner and had a few drinks before eating. He also explained that he had a couple of drinks with his meal, which consisted of a large steak and all the trimmings. He had a drink or two with his dessert (rich, no doubt). His complaint was that the last drink that he had of several after-dinner cocktails made him sick. I should add that the complaint was written with a shaky hand in pencil on a grocery bag. We will discuss the somewhat more reliable evaluations of experts and critics in the next section.

The Critic's Choice

It might be argued that judgments by experts and critics don't change the product, but they do. Returning to Heisenberg's Principle, in the subatomic world the particle gets hit with energy and takes off for Kansas to be with Dorothy and Toto. In the macro world, the effect of experts and critics is not as fast but just as real. The direct effect is that a particular brand of whiskey will be changed over time by the distiller if enough real experts and critics judge the whiskey to be inferior or low quality.

I have no doubt that some experts and critics are really expert. Those who are have superior palates and broad experience in tasting. But sometimes the critics have carefully enhanced reputations that far outstrip their abilities. I had a visit one time from a world-renowned critic who was known for almost miraculous ability to objectively analyze and even recognize various whiskeys in blind tastings. He visited with me for the greater part of a day, tasting my wares and asking questions about my distilling methods. As he left he asked me to give him one bottle of each of the bourbon brands that I was making at the time so that he could carefully evaluate them and report his findings in the book that he was writing. I complied and he reported quite favorably on one product, saying that it was a great 4-year-old and well worth the price. Another 4-year-old bourbon didn't fare nearly as well, however. As I recall, he judged it to be harsh to the point of being more qualified as furniture stripper than as sipping whiskey. The thing that stuck in my mind was that all of the differently labeled, 4-year brands that I had given him were carefully mixed to be statistically indistinguishable from a single product standard. It left me with an undying skepticism about critics' evaluations and especially those with scores attached. It also made me wonder about the value and validity of the deconstruction of whiskey profiles into notes such as white pepper, black courant, Golden Delicious apples, and cured tobacco.

Critical opinion, whether or not it is based in objective and expert evaluation, has an indirect effect as well. These forces and others, such as marketing campaigns, change some con-sumers' perceptions of the whiskey. Ultimately, the cumula-tive effect of these changes in perception will translate to a change in the whiskey as the distiller tries to adjust to con-sumer preferences. Whether the changes are direct or indirect, the critic and the marketing department become part of the taster-tasted system and alter it thereby.

Given Heisenberg's Uncertainty Principle, one might argue that all whiskey preferences are subjective since the taster and the tasted are inseparable. We can't really talk about taste except in our own terms. In doing so we must acknowledge that my perception of orange peel will almost certainly be dif-ferent from yours. An aroma that reminds you of buttered popcorn may remind me of rancid butter. I may prefer Scotch because of its rich peat character while you avoid it because it smells like iodine. In the face of real differences in vari-ous whiskeys and the taster's perception of them, debate on preferences seems fruitless and counterproductive. It might enhance understanding and camaraderie among spirits enthu-siasts (and hold down on fights in bars) if we took a phenom-enological approach. In my capacity as a distiller I found that by setting aside my own biases regarding bourbon and listen-ing to ordinary folks talk about their perceptions of my offer-ings gave me valuable direction in developing new bourbon products. It was far more important for me to temporarily suspend my personal frame of reference and preferences in order to hear what the consumer really wanted than to hold myself up as the know-it-all expert. Nothing instilled the required openness and humility in me like hearing one of my better-selling upscale bourbons described as rotgut or watching a person make a face and roll her eyes upon tasting whiskey that was too strong for her. Striving to understand the taste and aroma experience of a person is more informative, especially for the distiller, and more likely to have a positive outcome, than a debate on the proposition that I have better taste than you do.

Heisenberg's Spirits

So, which whiskeys are better than others? The answer can be found at any reputable spirits outlet. If you look at the offerings there, you will see an incredible array of choices even in a moderately sized store. There are broad whisk(e)y categories: Scotch, bourbon, rye, Canadian, Irish, American blends, to name a few. Within the bigger categories there are dozens of labels representing various distilleries, strengths, ages and mash bills. All of the different whiskeys that you see are "better" to some particular group of consumers who cast their votes with money by buying their preference. The ones that are not better will soon disappear from the marketplace. The ones that remain might be thought of as Heisenberg's spirits.

13

One Bourbon,
One Scotch, and One
Buddhist Theory of No-Self

Steven F. Geisz

There's a bottle of Scotch whisky on the table. It's single malt, aged 15 years. Good stuff. I want to indulge, but it's late and I'll feel pretty rough in the morning if I do. The whisky is here and now. The hangover is there and then. What should I do?

Common sense says be careful. Hangovers are bad, and I'm not as young as I used to be. If I drink my fill now, I'll regret it tomorrow. Thus, I should take it easy on the bottle. I can drink and enjoy, but only in moderation.

But I'm struck by a different line of thought. Why worry about my future self? Why not think of him as someone other than the me of here and now—someone connected to me, of course, but separate enough to make a meaningful difference in my current decision making? I'm living in this very moment. My self of tomorrow morning will be living then. Even if I drink more than is prudent, it won't be me who deals with the aftermath. It'll be my self of tomorrow morning, and the consequences of my actions will be his problem.

Perhaps it's not nice to bequeath a hangover to my future self. Perhaps it's mean or even wrong. But what has he done for me? Not much. So, why worry about his troubles—especially when doing so will prevent me from enjoying the single malt that's the most salient feature of my present moment? Why isn't it just his dumb luck for being in the wrong place at the wrong time? Those are the breaks, future self of mine. I'm sure you'd do the same to me, if given half a chance.

This way of thinking is appealing, to be sure, but it seems too good to be true. Yes, I can label the me of tomorrow a "future self" and think of him as someone other than the me of right now, but that's a mere linguistic trick, and a danger- ous one at that. Isn't it? Self-serving wordplay notwithstand- ing, my future self will be me in all relevant ways—right? Won't his troubles be mine, at least when I get to that place in time? If I drink too much, surely I will be the one to suffer the consequences.

I hesitate. I ponder the bottle. What to do? It's not that I'm overwhelmed with a compulsion to drink. I'm well practiced in temperance these days. Rather, I'm struck by the worry that temperance itself might be irrational, that the common- sense advice might rest on a problematic view of the self through time. Why shouldn't the me of this present moment be treated as importantly different from the me of some future moment—even if the future moment is mere hours away?

Bourbon, Karma, and the Cats

I think back to a trip I took a few years ago. My partner and I spent our spring break on a pilgrimage to the bourbon distilleries of northern Kentucky. At the Buffalo Trace distillery in Franklin County, we learned about the rick house cats. In the rick houses—the warehouses where barrels of aging bourbon are stored—live a handful of lucky cats. They sit around, watching the barrels, breathing oak- and whiskey-infused air, and (at least as I imagine it) plucking woozy, bourbon-soaked mice from the floor and popping them into their mouths while contemplating life and their good fortunes. I recall thinking to myself that if some straightforward, nonmetaphorical account of karma and reincarnation turns out to be true, then coming back as one of the Kentucky rick house cats would be pretty sweet. Not a bad gig, all things considered.

Now, I should confess: I don't remember whether I actually saw those rick house cats with my own eyes. Perhaps I just saw a mouse, and then deduced (or simply made up) the rest. Or maybe I saw neither the cats nor a mouse, but instead just heard about that little whiskey-soaked ecosystem from the man working as the distillery's tour guide (which, by the way, is another gig that wouldn't be bad to have). Indeed, my uncertainty runs deeper. Though I think that I was the one who made the connection between the cats and the metaphysics of karma, I'm not even sure about that: my partner thinks she had the idea first, and she's often right about these things. All I know for sure is that at some point about six years ago, she and I (or perhaps I should say, one of her past selves and one of my past selves) were at the Buffalo Trace distillery (should I say, at a past "self" of the distillery?), and somehow there arose the thought that cats, bourbon, and the karma-driven cycle of reincarnation hang together.

Now I sit here staring at a bottle of whisky, feeling a sort of vertigo. Those karma-privileged rick house cats show at least one way in which a metaphysical theory of Buddhism might be connected to whisk(e)y: bourbon goes with rick houses, rick houses go with cats, and those cats go with the metaphysics of reincarnation, at least in my mind and in the mind of one of my previous selves. That particular chain of connections is whimsical at best, but the troubling indefiniteness of my memory connections to my self of six years ago and the current uncertainty of my connections to my self of tomorrow morning both point the way to another, perhaps more serious, connection between Buddhism and whisk(e)y drinking, stemming from the Buddhist commitment to *anatman*, or "no-self." Buddhism famously claims there is no self, or at least no self of the sort that is supposed to hang around and last as an unchanging, abiding entity in which personal identity is located.[1] If Buddhism is right and there really is no continuously existing self, then it seems that my somewhat facetious, (current) self-serving rationalizations about drinking my fill and leaving the consequences to my self of tomorrow morning might have a serious grounding in one of the central commitments of Buddhism.

From No-Self to Whisky Indulgence?

Now, Buddhism doesn't promote overindulgence in drink.[2] Nevertheless, the idea that there is no real individual self that exists through time lends at least surface-level credibility to my speculations about current, future, and past selves. Perhaps this one piece of the Buddhist puzzle can be used, on its own and torn away from other Buddhist practices and ethical commitments, to justify some imprudent consumption of fine Scotch whisky in the present moment.[3] Here, then, is what I propose: I will sketch out a rough-and-ready account of the Buddhist conception of no-self, and then I'll consider whether this account of no-self might give me a reason (or at least an excuse) to tell my future self that he's on his own.

Buddhism says all phenomena are marked by the Three Characteristics ('*trilakshana*' in Sanskrit).[4] The first characteristic is transience, or impermanence ('*anitya*' in Sanskrit, or '*annica*' in Pali): Everything will change and ultimately disappear. The second characteristic is suffering, or "unsatisfactoriness" ('*duhkha*' in Sanskrit, or '*dukkha*' in Pali): Everything is or gives rise to suffering in one form or another (i.e., it all pretty much sucks). The third characteristic is *anatman*, or no-self ('*anatman*' is the Sanskrit word; in Pali it's '*annata*'): Nothing has a continuing sort of self-existence (whatever exactly that is); everything is empty of self.

These Three Characteristics are presented as a package, but I will focus on the no-self characteristic, since that's most relevant to my current dilemma. To say that all phenomena are marked by no-self is to say that everything lacks a certain kind of self-standing essence. Things are interconnected with and dependent upon each other in ways that undermine the ordinary sense many of us have that the objects around us exist as individual, more or less independent things. Though this third characteristic is introduced as being true of *all* phenomena, the most startling implication is what it says about each of us. According to the Buddhist view behind the Three Characteristics, each of us lacks any permanent, individual self that persists through time. There is no eternal soul, no Cartesian mental substance, no deep psychological ego in need of protection or analysis,[5] no anything that might seem to be a real me that continues on through time.

How can that be? One way the no-self idea is defended is by asking us to look for the self and report on what we find. According to Buddhist texts, the process goes something like this: We look around, trying to find something that is the self. It might seem as if it has got to be somewhere, after all. However, as we look, we only find changeable stuff. Our bodies change, and change in ways that make it unlikely that anything about our bodies—even that special part of our body that is our brain—can serve as a self, as a *me* that exists as a thing and continues through time. If there is nothing about our bodies that can do the work, then perhaps there is something distinctively mental about us that might serve as the self. However, even assuming for the sake of argument that our minds are different from our brains, the contents of our minds change even more noticeably than our bodies. According to Buddhist texts, no matter where we look, we won't find anything stable enough to do the work that the self is typically thought to do. If that's so, the Buddhists say, then we should just jettison the idea of a self: there's no self there, and letting go of the idea that there is will make everything easier in the long run.[6]

There's more to say about the no-self view, but much of that is best left to another time—and, perhaps, to another self (or even to another "no-self") existing at that other time. Whatever exactly it means to say that you and I and everyone else are without permanently existing selves, the standard Buddhist view insists that there is something lacking that I might mistakenly be thinking is there when I make plans or strategize or worry about the future. Planning, strategizing, and worrying seem to require that I think there is some real entity—the self—that is capable of serving as the locus of my self concerns, both at this moment and in the future. Acceptance of the Buddhist no-self claim seems to require that I give up being concerned with my future self in the way I typically am.[7]

So, suppose the Buddhist account of no-self is true. What then? What, if anything, follows with regard to whisky drinking and temperance?

If there is no continuously existing self extending through time, then it seems that I'm correct in thinking of my self of tomorrow morning as a different person than the me of right now. Any concern I have for my self of tomorrow morning is not *self* concern. I may have *other* kinds of concern for that future person (i.e., the kinds of concern I have for other people) but not concerns for the future self as concerns for *me*. Thus, I shouldn't worry that drinking my fill of whisky now will cause *me* any trouble in the morning; there simply won't *be* a me in the morning. Consequently, I might conclude that I should eat, drink, and be merry, for tomorrow—and even a minute from now—I will be no more.

Momentary Selves

So, if the Buddhist view is correct, there is no continuously existing self but only, at best, a series of momentary selves that do not extend through time in the way that we ordinarily think we do. The full story is more complicated. After all, if the Buddhist account of no-self is true, then there is arguably a difficulty in postulating *any* selves, even momentary ones. The self that continuously exists through time is ruled out by the no-self doctrine, but it might seem that the self of right now and the self of tomorrow morning are both banned, as well, since the no-self view seems to challenge the notion of self entirely.

I want to set this worry aside. Perhaps Buddhist skepticism about the existence of the self through time also requires skepticism about any self at any time, even a momentary self—but if that's true, it only complicates things for me as I search for an excuse to indulge in the whisky on the table. Importantly, my philosophical speculations here are driven by a *practical* concern, that of deciding whether to drink with abandon the whisky that sits before me, and it at least seems that this practical concern is had by a self of some sort that exists at least right now, if not for extended periods of time into the past and future. Therefore, with an acknowledgment that I'm taking only one page from the massive Buddhist playbook, I will assume in what follows that there is something that I can think of as a momentary current self and that there is another something that will exist tomorrow morning that I can think of as a momentary future self, but that never the 'twain shall meet—that is, that these selves are different entities (or maybe even different "entities," with big neon scare quotes to acknowledge their problematic statuses as things), connected to each other only by complex causal chains of various sorts, but not by anything that can meaningfully be called identity through time.

Even so, there are two different ways we might think of such momentary selves. First, we can think of them as truly instantaneous and completely unextended in time, existing for mere temporal points. Second, we can think of them as momentary in that they exist only for a minute or so but are nonetheless extended in time for very brief durations.

If selves are truly instantaneous, then they might be more compatible with the full theory of no-self than selves that are extended for short periods of time. However, truly instantaneous selves bring with them their own problems. How can we make sense of any such self *deliberating* about whether to drink the whiskey, or *deciding* to drink the whiskey and then *following through* with the decision by grabbing the bottle and swigging something down?[8] Such cognitive-plus-mechanical processes take time to play out, even if it's only a few seconds or less. Thus, it seems that thinking in terms of truly instantaneous selves would make it impossible to understand how I—my self of this very instant—could engage in *any* kind of decision-making process. And remember, I'm being driven by a very practical problem of deciding whether or not to indulge. Consequently, I will adopt the second way of thinking about momentary selves, and I'll treat my self of this moment and my self of tomorrow morning as existing for very brief but nevertheless temporally extended periods of time, and I will assume that such brief selves are compatible with the overall spirit of the Buddhist conception of no-self.[9]

A Middle Path of Whisky Indulgence

I now return to pondering the bottle in front of me. I reason as follows: I am here and now, existing for just a short moment in time. I can either drink the whisky or not. If I drink, I can consume in moderation or with abandon. In the short period of time in which I'll continue to exist, there is only so much I can consume, even if I drink heavily. Leaving all other considerations aside, I want to drink with abandon, since such wanton consumption will maximize my short-term pleasure, and short-term pleasure is the only sort of pleasure available to me as a momentary self.

So, why not drink with abandon? According to my current thinking, my future self won't be me—but perhaps I should take his welfare into account in the same way I take the welfare of other people into account. I do not want to force a high-grade, über-intense hangover on him, in the same way I wouldn't want to cause another person living right now to become ill. Would that provide a reason to refrain from drinking too much?[10]

I consider, and I'm not sure what to say. If I don't drink with abandon, I sacrifice my only shot at the full enjoyment I could have by drinking as much as possible in the next few seconds. Once those seconds are gone, I will be no more. That's a big sacrifice, considering the fact that there will be no way for my future self to return the favor. On the other hand, it seems downright wrong to do whatever I want with no regard whatsoever for the consequences of my actions for others, be they momentary selves existing now or momentary selves existing in the future.

I decide on a middle path: I will not do my future self *too* much harm. I will not, that is, purposely act in such a way that he will experience *excruciating* pain. A mild hangover, however, doesn't seem too bad of a thing to foist onto another person, especially since the cost of not sticking him with any hangover is that I'd forgo my only shot at the enjoyment that would come from heavy drinking of fine whisky in the next minute or so. Moreover, in this rough-and-tumble world of momentary selves that cannot strike reciprocal deals with momentary selves of the future, it seems that getting stuck with a mild hangover as a result of a past self's drinking behavior is just part of the cost of doing business. Nothing too unfair about that.

But what about the momentary self that comes immediately after me? If he continues to drink with abandon, won't that cause our self of tomorrow morning to have a really awful hangover? Perhaps, but I can only be responsible for what I do. I've come into existence completely sober, presumably because my past selves didn't take full advantage of their opportunities. If I drink my fill in the remaining time I have, my actions will create a bit of a hangover for my self of tomorrow morning, but not more than that. What the self that immediately follows me does is another matter. If he adds to my whisky consumption in such a way that our self of tomorrow morning gets blasted by a mega-hangover, that's on his conscience, not mine.

This reasoning is perhaps shaky, but time is short, and there are obvious opportunity costs to not seizing the moment. I'll soon cease to exist. If I delay even a few more seconds, I'll lose my chance. Thus, I reach for the whisky. Forget about pouring it into a glass; there's no time for such niceties. I pull out the cork, put the bottle to my lips, and tilt it back. Oh, the sweet joys of living in the moment!

Fleeting Moments, Aging Whisky, and Everlasting Reward

But wait. To my current self's chagrin, I stop to think. There seems to be a very whisky-specific challenge to my plan for self-indulgence that I've not yet taken into account. I think back to instances of whisky drinking by my past selves. As I recall (whatever 'recall' means here), much of "my" previous enjoyment of fine whisky stemmed from an understanding that what I was drinking was something with a long history. Part of what made the whisky taste so good was that I (i.e., my previous selves) knew that what I was consuming was a particular quantity of fluid that—unlike samples of that wan concoction vodka—acquired its taste and color only as a result of aging for many years in a barrel in the Scottish Highlands. In the same way, my full enjoyment of the whisky *right now* seems to require that I think of this particular fifth of whisky as having existed through a considerable period of time. But I also recall that the Buddhist no-self theory says that *everything* lacks the sort of self-existence through time that we often attribute to people. If I accept the full no-self theory, it seems I'll have to reject the idea that the whisky before me has existed for fifteen years or more. It, too, exists only here and now. Perhaps there was a series of previous whisky "selves" that preceded it, but it, like me, has really only existed for a moment or so.

Thus, if I truly accept the no-self theory, it seems that I cannot get enjoyment from the whisky of the here and now by thinking of it as something with a long history stretching back in time. Therefore, I've got a problem: either I accept the Buddhist no-self theory and lose at least some of my motivation to indulge in the whisky in the here and now, or else I keep my full motivation for drinking here and now but lose my Buddhist-derived excuse for intemperance and self-indulgence.

Perhaps I could avoid this problem by limiting my application of the no-self theory only to people, not to all things. Such a move would be inconsistent with the full Buddhist theory, but at least it would allow me to think of the whisky as something that exists through long periods of time, even if I myself do not. However, I'd *still* have a problem: isn't there some sort of practical inconsistency with me living in the moment, treating my history and my future as something lived by other selves, all the while taking pleasure in a momentary experience, the enjoyment of which depends upon temporally extended facts about the history of the fluid I am drinking?

I'm not sure what to say. Perhaps I can make sense of a momentarily existing self having an experience that in some deep way depends upon the experience being of something with a long history. But it seems odd. Alternatively, I can try to reconstruct my thoughts about the history of the whisky in terms of a series of momentary whisky selves giving rise to further whisky selves, and do so in such a way that I can think of my self of this moment encountering a concurrent whisky self and gaining enjoyment, without thereby violating the fundamental spirit of the no-self theory that has got me to this point in my thinking. But that, too, seems strange, and when coupled with the commonsense claim that one should be moderate in one's drinking if one does not want to experience a hangover in the morning, I'm less sure about my recent decision to drink to my heart's content.

But perhaps that doesn't matter, since in the time I've been thinking about the complexities of whisky history and their relationship to the experience of drinking, my previous momentary self has passed out of existence. Another current self is here now, and he can start anew, trying to figure out what to do with the bottle of single malt whisky in front of him that has some sort of difficult to comprehend, apparent fifteen-year history.

At this point, my thoughts turn to a line that one of my previous selves once read. It's a quote from a fictionalized version of country music legend Hank Williams, who reflects as follows: "I stood there, in my dark den, smelling the leather and sipping my Coke, looking at that bright-green yard, and I thought to myself, 'Hank, just this one morning, just this single sunrise, is your everlasting reward.' And, for once, I was right."[11]

Now, I don't know if that really gets it right, or whether it even get things anywhere in the neighborhood of plausibility, but it seems to do a nice job of at least expressing the possibility of a single fleeting moment somehow transcending itself, in terms of significance if not in terms of existence. I can't figure out whether my self of tomorrow morning will be me in any way that should make me concerned about his hangover as if it were mine, and I can't figure out whether I can consistently indulge in the whisky and not worry about my self facing the consequences in the future without at the same time radically altering my enjoyment of this fine 15-year-old single malt. At the very least, I can't figure this out in any timely way that will help the me of the here and now.[12] But I can enjoy this whisky, in moderation, and then sit back and hope that, somehow, someone down the road can make sense of it all.

I admit that this might very well be a cheap way of shirking my responsibility to make some rigorous sense out of the philosophical mess I've made. If so, I'll leave it to a future self to clean things up.[13]

NOTES

The chapter title is an allusion to "One Bourbon, One Scotch, One Beer," a John Lee Hooker song made famous by George Thorogood and the Destroyers. No beer necessary for this essay.

1. No-self is one of the Three Characteristics, discussed below. The Three Characteristics are presented in the *Anguttara Nikaya* (III. 134). See Nyanaponika Thera and Bhikkhu Bodhi, trans., eds., *Numerical Discourses of the Buddha: An Anthology of Suttas from the Anguttara Nikaya* (New York: Altamira, 1999), p. 77. See

also Thanissaro Bhikkhu, trans., "Dhamma-niyama Sutta: The Discourse on the Orderliness of the Dhamma," Access to Insight, www.accesstoinsight.org/tipitaka/an/an03/an03.134.than.html (accessed June 30, 2008). Other translations of relevant passages are available in Sarvepalli Radhakrishnan and Charles A. Moore, eds., *A Sourcebook in Indian Philosophy* (Princeton, NJ: Princeton University Press, 1957), pp. 273–274; and Donald W. Mitchell, *Buddhism: Introducing the Buddhist Experience*, 2nd ed. (New York: Oxford, 2008), p. 34.

2. Indeed, various Buddhist monastic vows involve abstinence from alcohol, and the very notion of Buddhism as a middle path between sensual indulgence on the one hand and spiritually driven self-denial on the other seems to rule out such wanton over-consumption of an intoxicant, even without delving into more nuanced details of Buddhist doctrine. For a quick introductory gloss on how drinking connects to the "Right Action" aspect of the Noble Eightfold Path, see Mitchell, *Buddhism*, p. 56.

3. For a discussion of relations between the Buddhist conception of no-self and Buddhist ethics, see Mark Siderits, *Buddhism as Philosophy: An Introduction* (Indianapolis, IN: Hackett Publishing, 2007), chapter 4.

4. For an overview of the Three Characteristics, see Mitchell, *Buddhism*, pp. 34–38. See also "*trilakshana*" and related entries in Damien Keown, *Oxford Dictionary of Buddhism* (New York: Oxford, 2003); and Ingrid Fischer-Schreiber, Franz-Karl Ehrhard, and Michael S. Diener, *The Shambhala Dictionary of Buddhism and Zen*, trans. Michael H. Kohn (Boston: Shambhala, 1991).

5. See Mark Epstein, *Psychotherapy without the Self: A Buddhist Perspective* (New Haven, CT: Yale University Press, 2007), chapter 2, for a more sophisticated view of the relationship between the ego of Western psychoanalysis and Theravada Buddhism.

6. A main way that Buddhist texts make this argument is by asking us to look at ourselves and surroundings and analyze them in terms of what the Buddhists call the five *skandhas* ('*khandas*' in Pali), or "aggregates." We start looking for plausible candidates for the self. First, we find all sorts of material forms (*rupa*), the stuff of our bodies and all their component parts, including the brain. The material forms are the first of the five *skandhas*. However, according to the Buddhists, if we observe carefully we will find that the material forms of our bodies are always changing, such that none of them—not even our brain—can really count as a self of ours, if 'self' is supposed to refer to some stable, independent thing that exists through time. Thus, following this Buddhist approach, we

set aside material forms, and look to see what else there is that might count as a self. The second *skandha* is sensation. Perhaps, we might think, our selves are located there. But, the Buddhists say, our sensations are constantly changing, and nothing in sensation is stable enough to serve as a continually existing self. The third *skandha* is perception, which we can here think of as differing from mere sensation in that it involves conceptualization of the raw material of sensation. But perception, too, is constantly changing, and changing in such a way that it cannot serve as a self, either. The name of the fourth *skandha* is variously translated as "volitions" or "mental formulations." Whatever volitions or mental formulations are (and the details are not crucial here), they are changing, too, and, thus, cannot serve as a continually existing self. The fifth and final *skandha* is consciousness, something that is supposed to be different from sensations, perceptions, or mental formulations. But consciousness, whatever it is, is always changing, and it, too, fails to provide anything that might count as a self, according to the Buddhists. See the passage from the *Samyutta Nikaya* (III. 66–68), Radhakrishnan and Moore, eds., *A Sourcebook in Indian Philosophy*, pp. 280–281; in Siderits, *Buddhism as Philosophy*, pp. 38–39; and in John J. Holder, trans., *Early Buddhist Discourses* (Indianapolis, IN: Hackett Publishing, 2006), pp. 83–86. For further discussion, see Mitchell, *Buddhism*, chapter 2; and Siderits, *Buddhism as Philosophy*, chapter 3 (especially sections 3.2 and 3.3). For discussions of self and no-self in Buddhism from a variety of perspectives, see the relevant essays in Gay Watson, Stephen Batchelor, and Guy Claxton, eds., *The Psychology of Awakening: Buddhism, Science, and Our Day-to-Day Lives* (Boston: Weiser, 2000); and B. Alan Wallace, ed., *Buddhism & Science: Breaking New Ground* (New York: Columbia, 2003).

7. Within English-language philosophy, a *locus classicus* for philosophical discussions about personal identity through time and its possible relations to Buddhism is the work of Derek Parfit. See Derek Parfit, *Reasons and Persons* (New York: Oxford, 1984), as well as various other essays Parfit has written or coauthored. Parfit's view as it relates to Buddhism is mentioned at the start of the discussion of Buddhist ethics in Siderits, *Buddhism as Philosophy*, chapter 4. For important contributions to philosophical discussions about personal identity through time in general, see the collections of John Perry, ed., *Personal Identity*, 2nd ed. (Berkeley: University of California, 2008); Daniel Kolak and Raymond Martin, eds., *Self & Identity: Contemporary Philosophical Issues* (New York: Macmillan, 1991); and Raymond Martin and John

Barresi, eds., *Personal Identity* (Malden, MA: Blackwell, 2003). My way of framing these issues in terms of relations between a current and future self is indebted to many of the philosophers (or the previous selves of those philosophers) whose work is contained in those three anthologies.

8. For a discussion of how issues of agency play out against a backdrop of a Parfitian account of personal identity (or lack thereof) through time, see Christine M. Korsgaard, "Personal Identity and the Unity of Agency," in *Personal Identity*, eds. Raymond Martin and John Barresi (Malden, MA: Blackwell, 2003), pp. 168–183.

9. For a philosophical account of selves that exist for short periods of time, see Galen Strawson's account of "the Pearl view" in Galen Strawson, "The Self," in *Personal Identity*, eds. Martin and Barresi, pp. 335–377. An earlier version of Strawson's essay appeared in *Journal of Consciousness Studies* 4: 5–6 (1997): pp. 405–428. Strawson briefly discusses Buddhist accounts in his essay. For a more detailed discussion of possible ways of fleshing out the no-self view, see Siderits, *Buddhism as Philosophy*, especially section 4.2.

10. In *Reasons and Persons*, Derek Parfit explores many similar claims about the ethical implications of a metaphysical theory that accepts something like the Buddhist theory of no-self.

11. Dave Hickey, *Air Guitar: Essays on Art & Democracy* (Los Angeles: Art Issues Press, 1997), p. 137.

12. I've been thinking mainly about the implications of the no-self theory, that third of the Buddhist Three Characteristics. Hank Williams's musing about an everlasting reward being present in a fleeting moment points back to the first characteristic, impermanence. Perhaps I need to think more about such impermanence, about whether it undermines the pleasure one might take in whisky or any other food or drink. To take just one example from the texts of Buddhism, consider the following lines from the "Discourse on the Parable of the Water Snake," from *Early Buddhist Discourses*, trans. John J. Holder (Indianapolis, IN: Hackett Publishing, 2006), p. 112: "'And that which is impermanent, is it painful or pleasant?' / 'Painful, Sir.'" Clearly, the Buddhist view is that there is a connection between impermanence and pain, even if there is no permanent self to exist through time and observe things it cares about passing out of existence. And perhaps I should look again at the second characteristic, suffering, and think about ways in which Buddhists say that desire, indulgence, and suffering go together, even in a world without permanently existing selves to stick around and deal with the consequences of indulgent behavior. Here, the Four Noble Truths are crucial. See the text of "Setting in Motion

the Wheel of the Dharma," in *The Connected Discourses of the Buddha: A Translation of the* Samyutta Nikaya, trans. Bhikku Boddhi (Boston: Wisdom Publications, 2000), pp. 1843–1847. Bringing all three of the Three Characteristics into discussion will lead to a fuller consideration of Buddhist ethics, and perhaps that is what is needed to figure out what I should do.

13. Many thanks to Brook Sadler for comments and suggestions (and for letting me have the story about the cats). Thanks to Marcus Adams and Fritz Allhoff for feedback and guidance along the way. In writing this piece, I benefited from a course release made available by a David Delo Research Professor Grant from the University of Tampa.

14

What Do Tasting
Notes Tell Us?

Ian J. Dove

I have a limited budget. To my chagrin this means that I must
mete out my drams in a more or less fiscally responsible way.
I can't afford to own bottles that aren't worth tasting—I can try
them at tastings or at my local whisky[1] club or avoid them altogether. My focus is on what bottles to keep at home to delight
the senses and tickle the palate. Now I face near information
overload with a flood of tasting notes available in compendi-
ums, magazines, and online metasites and blogs. If only these
notes were univocal, I would know what to buy and what
to avoid. Lamenting this surfeit of information to a friend,
she said, "Ian, you're a logician, why don't you turn your
logical powers on the tasting notes?" I'm sure I sensed sar-
casm and derision in the question. I am like a math professor
at the hardware store trying to determine how much fencing
material will enclose the perimeter of his or her yard—I could
use my academic expertise to solve a practical problem. And
so I gathered *Jim Murray's Whiskey Bible, Michael Jackson's
Guide to Single Malt Scotch*, issues of *Whisky* magazine, and
my computer with bookmarks to Malt Maniacs[2] and the like
and settled in to make logical sense of whisky tasting notes.

My goal in this missive is twofold. First, I want to understand what to make of the combination of descriptions and numerical scores typical in whisky tasting notes. Second, because these tasting notes are being used in point-of-purchase marketing, I want to determine how best to use these notes and the associated scores in choosing a dram. Are the marketers tricking me into a bad decision with a brief description and a 90-plus score on the placard hanging over some as yet untasted bottle? To this end, I will appeal to the methods of informal logic. Informal logic, as opposed to formal logic, does not translate an argument into a formal language in order to assess the quality or strength of the inferences. Rather, the techniques of informal logic concern the assessment of reasoning in the vernacular. I will use what are known as argument schemes to assess the use of tasting notes in point-of-purchase marketing. Argument schemes help both to analyze and to evaluate the reasoning. For the informal logician, argument analysis concerns determining whether a given claim contains reasoning, identifying the explicit components of the reasoning, and deciding whether the given reasoning depends upon unstated assumptions, tacit premises, or other nonexplicit elements. Evaluation, on the other hand, concerns the determination of overall quality of the reasoning. Here I wish to discover whether my whisky shop, my bartender, or both, give me good reason to spend on this or that malt.

A Few Words about Words

Have you ever tasted durian fruit? Anthony Bourdain said of durian, "Someone, some New York chef, some day will harness durian's strange and terrible powers."[3] Consider that a hint for the uninitiated. Brett Godfrey, the cofounder of Australia's Virgin Blue airline, complained after a Virgin Blue flight was delayed because someone had put a crate of durian on the flight that it smelled like "something you'd find in your outdoor dunny."[4] What is lacking from Bourdain's hint is the attempt to place the unique taste and odor of durian in a public context—to replace the obscure and unfamiliar with the commonplace and recognizable. This is the position of tasting note writers. They are our tasting surrogates. Their eyes, noses, and mouths taste for us what we haven't or can't. It is, therefore, their duty to trade the unknown for the known. Otherwise, their notes are of little value to us. We require a lexicon of whisky tastes and smells—descriptions that key to familiar tastes and smells. Bananas, strawberries, and pineapples are more familiar, for example, than cherimoya—a fruit from South America that tastes of bananas, strawberries, and pineapples. Hence, describing a flavor as cherimoya rather than as hints of strawberries, bananas, and pineapple shirks one's duty as a surrogate taster. Bourdain, aware of the difficulty in situating a unique smell or taste, first solves, then backs away from his attempt.

> It [durian] smelled like you'd buried someone holding a big wheel of Stilton in his arms, then dug him up a few weeks later.[5]

Then, regarding durian's taste, he writes:

> Imagine a mix of Camembert cheese, avocado, and smoked Gouda. OK, don't. That's not a very good description. But [in] tasting the stuff, one struggles for words.[6]

Notice that Bourdain has attempted to describe the smell and taste of durian in terms of (perhaps) more recognizable aromas and flavors. Whereas Brett Godfrey gave a nonspecific but nonetheless evocative description, Bourdain's description is concrete and specific. Both work inasmuch as they replace the unknown with the known. I leave it to you to decide whether you now want to taste (or smell) durian based on these descriptions.

Still, with whisky tasting notes, the positive ones invite and the negative ones dissuade. That's what marketers count on. Keep this in mind as you read the following two notes from Michael Jackson.

	Whisky #1	Whisky #2
Color:	Full, greeny gold.	Bright greeny gold.
Nose:	Powerfully earthy-fruity aroma. Fruit skins. Fruit in boxes at the market.	Fresh, clean. Very soft "sea air." Wild flowers among the dunes. A picnic at the beach.
Body:	Smooth and syrupy.	Satin.
Palate:	Sweet. Peach, orangey.	Summer fruits. Passion fruit. Zesty, almost effervescent. [name withheld] at its fruitiest.
Finish:	Assertive. Dry. Peach stones. Rind-like. Woody.	The flavors meld, with a late frisson of sharpness.
Score:	[withheld]	[withheld]

As an exercise, compare and contrast each category within the notes to determine an ordinal ranking of these two whiskies solely in terms of the descriptions.[7] I've withheld Jackson's numerical scores to show how difficult it can be to compare quality without them. Nothing about writing tasting notes precludes using verbal quality descriptors such as "excellent" or "swill." Yet, it seems that some whisky writers prefer to let numerical descriptors, such as numbers or stars, do that work for them.

Regarding the color of these two whiskies, I can discern no quality difference. I have no reason to believe that a full greeny gold whisky is more or less desirable than a bright greeny gold whisky.

Regarding the aromas, one may get further. On the one hand, Jackson clearly attempts to situate the aromas within commonplace experience. With #1 we get a concrete description, "powerfully earthy-fruity" and "fruit in boxes." On the other hand, Jackson takes poetic license. Consider #2's "wild flowers among the dunes" and "a picnic at the beach." These phrases evoke an aroma without describing a particular smell; there are, after all, numerous aromas consistent with these phrases. The portrayal is positive and inviting, even without the numerical score.

Jackson distinguishes three elements of taste: body, palate, and finish. Where #1 is "smooth and syrupy," #2 is "satin." I've never put satin on my tongue, but I imagine it is smooth. Hence, there is no way to distinguish these in terms of smoothness. I can assume that if #2 were syrupy, Jackson would have mentioned it. Whether a syrupy whisky is a good whisky I'll leave to you.

Regarding the palate, Jackson is specific and concrete with #1: "sweet, peach, orangey." He is less concrete and more evocative regarding #2: "summer fruits, passion fruit, zesty, almost effervescent." Why is he more evocative with #2? Is it better? Does it have a higher score? Should I purchase it?

There is a giveaway in notes regarding the finish. "Woody" suggests that a single malt has been too long in the barrel. #1 is deficient, but how much? The other elements of the finish neither suggest nor imply a poor whisky. Jackson gave #1 his lowest score: 60.[8] He noted that it, a recent bottling of Ladyburn, is much sought after by collectors, perhaps because of its rarity, though certainly not for its taste. If one is interested in what to buy from a collector's standpoint, it is unlikely that tasting notes will be of much use. Jackson gave #2, Bruichladdich 10 year old, a score of 82.[9]

A whisky tasting note is a promissory note regarding what to expect in the bottle. If the descriptions are too abstract, too unfamiliar, or too generic, they are unhelpful. Yet, descriptions that are specific or concrete or evocative are helpful, even when provided as part of a marketing campaign.

Of Numbers, Numb Skulls, and Numbskulls

I love whisky scores. Every year that Jim Murray updates his annual *Whiskey Bible*, I look forward to reading that some malt has improved or declined. Numeric scores are a simple way to signal perceived quality but not the only way. Jim Murray says of one, "If the nose doesn't get you, what follows probably will. . . . Grim doesn't quite cover it."[10] That one scored 66. Or, on the other side of the spectrum: "Befitting the great distillery this unquestionably is. Forget some recent disappointing bottlings: this is the real thing!"[11] Surely, this would count as an endorsement. One needn't see the score (it was 95). However, in terms of reasons to buy, scores sell. Take a trip to your local purveyor of fine malts and you will see that the sale of whiskies can be a downright Parker-esque[12] experience. Point-of-sale placards descry this or that rating. On a recent visit to my favorite shop, every single malt had a placard with a score above 90. Seeing this many high scores is mind-numbing. Ask your bartender to recommend a single malt, and he or she is likely to tout some score as indicative of what to try. In Michael Jackson's *Guide* and Jim Murray's *Bible* alone, we are treated to more than three thousand scores. So, what do the scores mean?

Michael Jackson is careful with his range of numbers. Indeed, one can hardly find a malt worth avoiding in his explanation.

The pleasures described above cannot be measured with precision, if at all. The scoring system is intended merely as a guide to the status of the malts. Each tasting note is given a score out of 100. . . . In this book, a rating in the 50s indicates a malt that in my view lacks balance or character, and which—in fairness—was probably never meant to be bottled as a single. The 60s suggest an enjoyable but unexceptional malt. Anything in the 70s is worth tasting, especially above 75. The 80s are, in my view, distinctive and exceptional. The 90s are the greats.[13]

Jim Murray is less guarded with his scores, as shown below.

Score	Description
0–50	Nothing short of absolutely diabolical.
51–64	Nasty and well worth avoiding.
65–69	Very unimpressive indeed.
70–74	Usually drinkable but don't expect the earth to move.
75–79	Average and usually pleasant though sometimes flawed.
80–84	Good whisky worth trying.
85–89	Very good to excellent whiskies definitely worth buying.
90–93	Brilliant.
94–97	Superstar whiskies that give us all a reason to live.
98–100	Better than anything I've ever tasted![14]

Of course, marketers aren't (usually) fools. You won't see a point-of-sale placard touting a score of 60 with a quote from Michael Jackson "Woody," or Jim Murray's "Grim doesn't begin to cover it." The lowest score in Michael Jackson's complete guide is 60 for the now defunct Ladyburn. Jim Murray also gave it a 60. Since 60 for Jackson means that the malt is enjoyable and for Murray this means that it is nasty, the score needs a key. Murray and Jackson do their readers a great service by clearly stating the meaning of their scores.

Still, knowing the key wouldn't count as definitive evidence for purchase. Here is a different set of two single malts, each as scored by Jackson and Murray

	Whiskey #3	Whiskey #4
Jackson's score	95	95
Murray's score	95	92

Which one to buy? Knowing only that these two whiskies are highly regarded by two well-seasoned malt writers isn't enough to decide. Most of us have other constraints on our buying habits. At my local shop, #3 sells for about $70, while #4 is over $300. If money were no object, which would you buy? What if one is a peat monster from Islay and the other warm Highland? The numbers can't stand on their own.

Moreover, what's the difference between a 92 and a 95? The answer, "three points," is meaningless when I'm standing in the aisle or at the bar trying to decide how to spend my wife's hard-earned money. Can my palate distinguish those three points? I think not. Are the malt writers lying with such fine-grained distinctions? I don't know. There is a worry that a 100-point scale begs for *false precision*. False precision is the fallacy that occurs when one states a numerical figure at a level of precision beyond its meaningful application. If you asked me how much my car cost, it is false precision to give you a number to ten decimal places. False precision is a rhetorical maneuver meant to lend artificial strength to a claim.

If there is no key to what the numbers (or stars) mean, then the score is meaningless. Jackson and Murray tell us what they mean. But other writers aren't as kind. Yet even with the explicit key, numbers aren't as objective as numerical data is in other realms. Jackson's scores seem more like subjective impressions—like a summary—of the overall tasting experience. His scores would be no less useful had he used a ten-point scale without decimals. Murray's scores are the sum of four separate scores. Still, one should be wary of making overly fine-grained distinctions on the basis of close scores.

On Experts, Authority, and Firsthand Experience

Even if numerical scores weren't ubiquitous, the would-be enthusiast faces another difficulty; whose tasting notes to consult?

There are two widely accepted experts: Jim Murray and the late Michael Jackson. There are other possible experts as well.

Jim Murray notes the nose, taste, finish, and balance of a whisky while Michael Jackson notes the color, nose, body, palate, and finish. The combination of body and palate for Jackson should be roughly comparable to Murray's taste and balance. Both score the whiskies on a 100-point scale. Murray's scores are the sum of the scores for his four categories, each worth up to 25 points. Jackson's scores, on the other hand, aren't necessarily the composite of scores for the individual categories. For example, Jackson doesn't consider the color any indication of quality, though he doesn't discount the way a whisky looks.

> I do not suggest that one color is in itself better than another, a particular subtle hue can heighten the pleasure of a fine malt. We enjoy food and drink with our eyes as well as our nose and palate.[15]

Jackson may sometimes weigh one category more heavily. For example, he gives Cragganmore's 12 year old a score of 90.[16] Recall that a score in the 90s indicates one of the *greats*. Regarding the nose of this version, he writes, "the most complex aroma of any malt."[17]

I don't believe that either Murray or Jackson has special powers of discernment regarding whisky. Rather, they both have (nearly) unrivaled experience in tasting a variety of single malts. They are as close as we can get to *authority*. With that in mind, compare Jackson's and Murray's tasting notes for Aberlour a'bunadh (59.6%)—a single malt from the Aberlour Distillery that aged between ten and fifteen years in sherry casks.

In this case, we have both writers' notes for the same whisky. There are similarities. For example, they both note sherry in the nose. But there are differences as well. Where Murray smells overripe mangoes, Jackson smells mint and pralines. Mangoes, especially when overripe, do not smell of mint. What do you do if you hate mangoes but love mint?

Aberlour A'bunadh (59.6%)	Michael Jackson	Jim Murray
Color	Dark orange	NA
Nose	Sherry, mint, pralines. Luxurious, powerful.	Firm malt and sherry but punctuated by overripe mango and rich honey tones. (23/25)
Body	Full, creamy, textured, layered.	NA
Taste	NA	Immediate spice and then an eruption of honey and barley with some liquorice diving in. A soft dispersal of peat around the palate adds an extra surprise. (23/25)
Palate	Rich, luxurious, and creamy, with a hint of mint and cherries behind.	NA
Finish	Nougat, cherry brandy, ginger, faint smoke.	The intensity remains at first but quietens as vanilla makes its mark and some cocoa trickles in. (22/25)
Balance	NA	Brilliantly balanced and displaying a fruity-malty and mildly peaty complexity which is jaw-dropping. (23/25)
Score	86	91

Besides their experience with a variety of whiskies—Murray's latest book claims to have notes for over twenty-seven hundred whiskies—is there anything else that makes someone an expert? Probably not. But Murray and Jackson don't agree across the board. For example, Jackson consistently rates whiskies in the Macallan line higher than Murray does. This suggests a method for using tasting notes from these two experts. First, find whiskies on which they disagree. Taste them yourself. Determine whether you agree more with Murray or with Jackson. After a few such tests, you may find more commonality in taste with one over the other.

Perhaps the notion of expertise or authority is the wrong evaluative concept. Instead of expertise or authority, tasting notes supply descriptions of the experience. To push a legal analogy, we might want to think of the authors of tasting notes as eyewitnesses rather than expert witnesses. For an eyewitness, the law requires merely honest reporting. Expert witnesses must be certified before a court will allow their testimony. Eyewitnesses needn't have any expertise at all. Instead, they have firsthand experience. In the case of tasting and smelling whisky, a tasting note author need only taste and smell the malt, then report his or her impressions. In terms of argumentative force, an eyewitness is, perhaps, less convincing than an expert.

Informal Logic and Whisky

Informal logic[18] concerns the goodness or badness of reasoning. A marketer, by providing scores or descriptions, wants you to draw a conclusion: buy this. The form of such arguments is simple. The premises (or evidence) include the explicit score or a brief descriptive note. Our job, as both consumers and philosophers, is to determine the strength of this appeal.

For arguments that appeal to authority or expert testimony, one should wonder whether the source is an expert on the subject. This can be incredibly difficult to determine. Just because Michael Jackson and Jim Murray are commonly reputed to be experts doesn't guarantee that they are. To gauge whisky expertise and the strength of appeals to such expertise, consider the following critical questions:

1. Does the person have special training or knowledge that qualifies him or her as an expert on the topic of whisky?
2. Is the expert consistent?
3. Is the claim recent?
4. Is the expert objective? (Is there any reason to think that the person making the claims has a personal interest in your purchasing this or that whisky?)
5. Do other experts agree with the claim of this expert? (Does Murray agree? What about Jackson? Or the Malt Maniacs? Or . . . ?)

Answer the first question in terms of experience. Although it is possible for a neophyte to predict quality, it isn't likely. The second question concerns whether the producer of a score uses the same criteria in the same way to produce all tasting notes.

The third question concerns the timeliness of the claim. Although whiskies don't mature in the bottle, there are differences, though perhaps minute, from year to year. So, for example, the heather honey taste of a 12 year old Macallan from five years ago may be masked by heavier sherry notes in the future. Proximity in time matters.

We find questions like the fourth one in trials. Are you less swayed by an expert when you find out he or she was paid for that testimony? The same is true with marketing testimonials. If an expert was paid to endorse a product, one should wonder about the objectivity of the resulting review.

The last question is, perhaps, the most interesting. As was noted above, Murray and Jackson don't always agree in their assessments of whiskies. But, even when they do, that isn't a guarantee of quality. Instead, it is evidence. Here is where the combination of score and descriptive note becomes important.

We cannot expect the experts to agree perfectly across all dimensions of analysis. If Murray scores some whisky 88, while Jackson scores it 85, one would be hard-pressed to say that they disagreed about the quality. Since we have their explicit keys, we can tell when they agree or disagree.

An affirmative or positive answer to the five questions suggests, though it doesn't guarantee, quality reasoning. A negative answer to any one question undermines the strength of the argument. The more negative answers, the less strong the argument.

If tasting notes are like eyewitness testimony, different critical questions apply.[19] This form is known as a *position to know*. In a position to know argument, a person in a position to know, see, hear, taste, smell, and reports her firsthand experience. Because the person explicitly reports what she experienced, one can take that as evidence. For such reasoning we want to know first whether the taster really did taste the whisky. Second, we want to know if the person has competing interests that might undermine her reliability. Third, we want to know if anyone else similarly experienced the whisky. Here is an argument of this form.

> Jim Murray claims that Lagavulin (16 year old) is worth buying—he scored it 95. He tasted it in the course of writing his latest version of *Jim Murray's Whiskey Bible*. Therefore, Lagavulin is worth buying.

Jim Murray did taste Lagavulin (16 year old)—surely he isn't lying. Jim Murray is reliable—there is no reason to discredit him. And Michael Jackson agrees with Murray's assessment—he scored it 95 (his highest rating). Therefore, I should accept, maybe with some reservation, that Lagavulin (16 year old) is worth buying.

Critical Questions at the Point of Purchase

Marketers want you to buy their products. They probably don't care about the reason you buy their products except insofar as knowing that will help them to sell you more of their products. This is not so different from other of our interactions with the world. In general, we are inundated with attempts at persuasion. Moreover, most people want to make informed decisions. One of the tools in an informal logician's toolbox is what are called argument schemes.[20] Roughly, an argument scheme is an aid for identifying reasons, discerning patterns in reasoning, finding hidden assumptions, and assessing the quality of reasons. The scheme itself is a template. A scheme contains a list of critical questions to aid the process of analyzing and evaluating reasoning. I like to think of argument schemes as guides that keep you from being taken advantage of. Argument schemes help detect bad reasons. So, we should develop argument schemes for use with tasting notes.

For the present purposes, let's focus on point-of-purchase marketing and tasting notes, though we could examine any marketing effort that appeals to tasting notes and scores. We need a list of critical questions, the answers to which will lead to a decision as to whether to buy a product on the basis of tasting notes and scores. This assumes that we are dealing with an explicit marketing tool, like a placard or stand-alone visual. Here are the questions:

1. What is the product? (If you can't tell, reject the ad.)
2. Is a score provided and sufficiently high? (If not, reject the ad.)
3. Is the source of the score provided? (If not, reject the ad.)
4. Is a descriptive note included? (If not, reject the ad.)

The first question concerns a curious use of tasting notes. Imagine a placard that simply says that Michael Jackson scores the Macallan 90 plus. This is true for a wide swath of the Macallan line. However, it isn't true of all expressions of the Macallan. Since I cannot determine the specific product in the ad, I reject it.

The second question probably never receives a negative answer in practice. As noted above, marketers aren't stupid. It would be crazy for a shop to use Jackson's score for Tobermore to market that whisky, though the note without the score is sufficiently lacking in evaluative measures as not to be a hindrance. Still, to see, "Jackson claims 68 out of 100," isn't a ringing endorsement—it's like bragging about receiving a D.

The third question brings us back to the idea of experts and authority. If we can't identify a claim's maker, we can't use the previous questions to determine whether the claim's maker is an expert.

Lastly, the descriptive note enhances the raw score by allowing us to judge whether a high score warrants further investigation. Many of Jackson's 90-plus malts are from Islay. This usually means peat. A description can cancel that expectation, which could open new and previously unthought-of possibilities.

Concluding Remarks

If you find yourself in the aisle of your local shop with no idea of what to buy, the marketers have already won. You are in danger of becoming Buridan's ass—a mythical beast that died from dehydration because it couldn't decide which of two equal but mutually exclusive water sources to choose. Or worse, you will make a decision solely on the basis of the information available at the shop.

Instead, consider the following:

1. Taste what you can: you'll know what you like and more importantly, what you don't.

2. Read what you can; more tasting notes are available today than ever before.

3. Remember, marketers are neither your friends nor your enemies.

4. Trust your taste.

Enjoy!

NOTES

1. I'll use 'whisky' rather than 'whiskey' throughout as I focus on Scotch whisky notes. Nothing should hinge upon this choice.
2. The Malt Maniacs Web site, www.maltmaniacs.org (accessed June 17, 2008).
3. Anthony Bourdain, *A Cook's Tour* (New York: Ecco Books, 2002), p. 171.
4. "Smelly fruit sparks airline alert, CNN.com," www.durianpalace .com/newsmedia/DTA/durian_terror_alarm.htm (accessed June 30, 2008). An outdoor dunny is an outhouse.
5. Bourdain, *A Cook's Tour*, p. 169.
6. Ibid.
7. One problem with this exercise is that we may be trying to derive an *ought* from an *is*—a fallacious maneuver known as Hume's Is/Ought Problem or the Naturalistic Fallacy, from work of the philosopher David Hume. The notes are descriptive, but, it seems, we want normative, i.e., evaluative, information. We are trying to cross the fact/value divide. However, insofar as nearly every tasting note is scored, there is a sense in which the notes are evaluative. It is the combination of descriptions and scores that makes an overall evaluation. If this is correct, then one needs to try to make evaluative sense of the descriptive information—Hume be damned.
8. Michael Jackson, *Michael Jackson's Complete Guide to Single Malt Scotch: A Connoisseur's Guide to the Single Malt Whiskies of Scotland*, 5th ed. (New York: Running Press Book, 2004), p. 323.
9. Ibid., p. 151
10. Jim Murray, *Jim Murray's Whiskey Bible* (London: Dram Good Books, 2008), p. 91.
11. Ibid., p. 149.
12. The wine writer Robert Parker is credited with popularizing numerical scores for wines. I can't remember a time when shopping for wine wasn't a maze of placards containing scores.
13. Jackson, *Michael Jackson's Complete Guide to Single Malt Scotch*, p. 84.
14. Murray, *Jim Murray's Whiskey Bible*, p. 8.
15. Jackson, *Michael Jackson's Complete Guide to Single Malt Scotch*, p. 84.
16. Ibid., p. 194.
17. Ibid.
18. One way to distinguish informal from formal logic concerns the distinction between natural language and formal language. The former category contains languages like English and French whereas

the latter are languages constructed for the purposes of investigating this or that formal property. These languages might be thought to model some natural languages, but that is unnecessary. Some informal logicians see informal logic in competition with formal logic as a theory of argument assessment, see for example Stephen E. Toulmin, *The Uses of Argument* (Cambridge: Cambridge University Press, 2003), p. 6ff or Ralph Johnson, *Manifest Rationality: A Pragmatic Theory of Argument* (Philadelphia: Lawrence Erlbaum Associates, 2000), p. 59ff and especially p. 78ff. I do not. Rather, I take formal logic to be part of the informal logician's tool kit. The informal logician is concerned with assessing reasoning as it occurs. When a formal logician uses formal logic for this purpose, he or she is also an informal logician in my sense.

19. Since a neophyte's notes are probably of limited value, one might be tempted to fuse the questions regarding experts with these questions.

20. For a systematic account of argument schemes, see Douglas Walton, *Fundamentals of Critical Argumentation* (Cambridge: Cambridge University Press, 2006).

UNIT IV

Ethics and Whiskey

15

The Virtuous Whisky
Drinker and Living Well

Richard Menary

You hold in your hand a glass of Caol Ila (12 year old). You twist the glass up to the light and admire the pale straw-colored liquid refracted through the deep cut grooves of the crystal. The glass is brought toward the nose and you take in the pungent phenolic aroma: smoky, peaty, a classic Islay malt. A drop of spring water is added to free up the esters, the aromas change subtly, and now it is time to take that first sip.

You are a virtuous whisky drinker. You have learned to discriminate a variety of tastes and smells and know the difference between an Islay and a Speyside. You have developed your sensory virtues—being able to apply your senses in the right way to the sensory qualities of the whisky. The virtues, what the Greeks called *arete*, are simply useful abilities that can be exercised well or badly. There are moral virtues such as courage, intellectual virtues like open-mindedness, and sensory virtues for discriminating tastes and smells—what I shall call the aesthetic virtues. The virtuous whisky drinker exemplifies all three.

Realizing our virtues is not the same as whisky snobbery; in developing, cultivating, and exercising our virtues we make for ourselves a good and happy life. Not only is it a pleasure to appreciate whisky in a virtuous way, it is also a wonderful thing to share in the appreciation of whisky while in the company of other virtuous whisky drinkers. A dram is best taken in friendship, and friends complete the good life. If Aristotle[1] were alive today, he would surely see the truth in this, because Aristotle knew that virtue and friendship play important roles in a well-lived life.

Happiness: What Makes for a Happy Life?

I once made the acquaintance of someone at a party in London who had developed a particular way of drinking whisky. The party was winding down and the topic of conversation had moved on to favorite whiskies. He related that he was sometimes given bottles of single malt Scotch as presents; in fact, he was the recent recipient of a lovely old bottle of Glenlivet—a fine expression of the classic Speyside malt. Not being the type to return an unwanted gift, he attempted to drink the liquor and enjoy it, and he claimed that he had found a way of doing so that made the whisky quite potable. He described his habitual taking of whisky as follows: first, he would add a liberal amount of whisky to a glass, and then add a generous portion of ice; and second, he would top up the glass to the brim with Coke!

I found that hard to take. Polluting a particularly fine old Glenlivet with sugary carbonated water until all that was left of its complex aromas and tastes was a dull alcoholic note somewhere below the overwhelming taste of sweet confection—it's equivalent to pouring icing all over a fillet steak because you have a sweet tooth. Fortunately, there was no whisky on hand for him to demonstrate his habit or else I may not have been able to control the desire to rescue the imperiled bottle from his rubbery grip.

Why should I care about this individual's habit? He clearly enjoyed the concoction; the sweetness of it was a taste that he liked, so what caused me to care? Isn't he just doing what he likes, what he finds enjoyable? Life is just about doing things that give us pleasurable sensations, right?

There is a particular conception of happiness at work here; that happiness is equivalent to pleasurable sensations and that any such sensations will do. Consequently, we do things that give us pleasure in order to be happy. As the British utilitarian Jeremy Bentham put it: "Prejudice apart, the game of push-pin is of equal value with the arts and sciences of music and poetry. If the game of push-pin furnish more pleasure, it is more valuable than either."[2] If drinking Glenlivet with Coke furnishes my acquaintance with more pleasure than Glenlivet without Coke, then it is better for his happiness that he does so. This is the hedonistic conception of human happiness.

However, there is another conception of happiness, one that is far older, and in my view far wiser, and comes down to us directly from Aristotle. Aristotle's conception involves the notion of living well over an entire life, rather than the notion of a fleeting psychological state as defined by the hedonistic conception.

According to Aristotle, living well involves developing our moral, emotional, and rational characteristics. For to live well, we must make choices as to how to act in various circumstances. In his *Nicomachean Ethics*, doing good and living well are intertwined. Happiness is the sum total of a life; it is the measure over a human life of how far we have achieved our goal of living well. Therefore, we would be wrong to think that happiness is merely a fleeting psychological state. Aristotle's concept of happiness cannot be confused with a purely mental state of euphoria, nor should it be confused with the fleeting sensation of pleasure. Rather we should think of happiness in terms of flourishing, or "fulfillment."

The happy life is one in which the person is fulfilled or flourishes over the whole of his or her life. Aristotle thought that we would live well when we were able to engage in activities that required us to exercise our virtues. That in doing so over a lifetime we would develop a character that is easily recognizable because our actions would proceed from strong character dispositions, or virtues, such as calmness, critical acumen, and taste. Acquiring these virtues of character and acting from them might require patience and hard work, but the sense of fulfillment we get from them makes the virtuous life a pleasurable one.

Now Aristotle was a serious soul, so he didn't write much about the aesthetic virtues; the moral and intellectual virtues were his playground. The word 'virtue' is apt to conjure up images of abstemious types admonishing others for enjoying the occasional dram. Taken together we might wonder how a well-lived life in Aristotle's sense could ever have room for the aesthetic virtues, which push in the direction of hedonistic delights. But Aristotle was well aware of the importance of pleasure to a well-lived life, and while pleasure is not the sole, or even primary, aim of living well, it is a welcome result of our virtuous activities. As he puts it: "like the bloom that graces the flower of youth."[3]

I agree with Aristotle that there is more to life than doing what feels good; we often pursue goals that are not simply pleasurable sensations. I want to suggest that becoming a virtuous whisky drinker is not simply seeking after pleasurable sensations. Being a virtuous whisky drinker is taking pleasure in directing our senses at the complex array of tastes and smells that the beautiful dram affords us. My acquaintance enjoyed his sweet alcoholic mix, but almost any alcohol would have been as good. He wasn't interested in distinguishing the oak, peat, and candied fruit flavors in the whisky itself. This was because he wasn't yet a virtuous whisky drinker, he hadn't taken time to develop his aesthetic virtues where whisky was concerned. If he had, and for all I know he has now, he would have discovered a new range of pleasurable experiences and a new set of virtues for discriminating tastes and smells. He would have added a new dimension to his life that would have made him happier. Who would have thought that all that was possible through taking a little time over a dram?

246

Wherefore Virtues?

I bet you have skills, and I bet that you enjoy putting those skills to work. Furthermore, I bet that you are particularly pleased when you exercise your skills particularly well. It is just the same for virtues, for virtues are like skills in that they are capacities that we exercise well or badly. But more than this, virtues are dispositions of our character; they make us who we are. Let me put it like this: everyone has the capacity to feel anger, that's not to say a great deal, but we get more interested when we meet people who are very calm in difficult circumstances and, by contrast, when we meet irascible characters who fly off the handle at the merest inconvenience. The virtue in this case is to have a settled state of character where we feel anger, and act according to that anger, to an appropriate degree given the circumstances. The virtue is not the capacity itself, that is, the capacity to feel anger, but rather it is how we exercise it in the given circumstances.

Now imagine a friend who is tolerant and open-minded; someone who is not only open to new ideas and experiences but also approaches them carefully and with critical acumen. They may be open-minded, but they are not gullible. This friend has intellectual capacities that you and I might share, the ability to understand new ideas and the ability to think critically about them, but our friend exercises them particularly well, which is why we commend him for his open-mindedness, his tolerance and critical acumen; he is intellectually virtuous.

Like skills, these virtuous states of character need to be developed through a fair amount of training and refinement. They require some knowledge of what the virtues are, and we are motivated to acquire them because they are worthwhile characteristics to have. But how does whisky fit into this picture, you might ask? Well, just as we have virtues aimed at moral excellence and virtues aimed at intellectual excellence, we also have virtues aimed at sensory or experiential excellence: the aesthetic virtues. The virtuous whisky drinker has acquired the necessary aesthetic virtues to appreciate the full range of sensory experiences that a beautiful dram has to offer. This is not a matter of simply seeking a pleasure hit; the simple immediate gratification of my sugar-obsessed acquaintance is not at all the same thing.

For example, when you are developing a skill, you train and practice until you get it right. This is frustrating, sometimes dull, and often painful, but you persevere. Why? Because youknow that when you have successfully acquired the skill, you will have a new range of experiences open to you, you will be able to do something new and you will be able to do it well. This is pleasurable, yes, but it is not a simple matter of immediate gratification. Virtues are like skills; they take time to acquire, but once we have acquired them we gain new and interesting abilities.

Let me illustrate this idea with an anecdote about whisky. When I first started drinking single malts, I began with some of the gentler, fruitier Speysides such as Glenmorangie. A friend told me that I should try a whisky from Islay, so I did, and it was a shock. This was something entirely different; the intensity of the dry, smoky medicinal flavors was both new and overwhelming. I had first tried Lagavullan but was then introduced to Laphroaig, which is, perhaps, the most unforgiving of the Islay malts to someone with an untested palate. I could not understand Laphroaig; it seemed altogether too medicinal, unctuous, and overwhelmingly peaty, but I persevered. I had always drunk my drams from a classic whisky tumbler, and still do on an evening in an easy chair with a good book, but once I started to use a proper whisky tasting glass, more like a sherry glass with a rounded bottom and long tapering sides,[4] things began to change. The combination of aroma followed by taste broke the conundrum for me; with some water added, the estery sweetness and hint of the sea became much more apparent—this wasn't just some medicinal peat monster, this whisky had soul!

Laphroaig and I are now the closest of friends, and for years I have returned to her generous and rich flavors, so much so that I very nearly refused to get on the second leg of a flight from Heathrow to Sydney. After disembarking at Bangkok airport, for refueling of the plane, I was not allowed to take my bottle of quarter-cask Laphroaig back on board! I was told that it would be held in perpetuity for me if I were ever to return to reclaim it. So if you ever happen to be in Bangkok airport and are in need of a dram, you might make an inquiry into its availability.

The parallel between virtues and skills is that they take time to develop and the training and habituation can be daunting, even unpleasant—when I first tasted Laphroaig it was not a pleasant experience. However, we persevere because we want to develop a new ability and to enjoy a new range of experiences. The aesthetic virtues require us to apply our senses actively to the flavors that whiskies so abundantly afford. So let's look at the aesthetic virtues in more detail and how they function well for the virtuous whisky drinker.

Aesthetic Virtues

For nosing and tasting whisky, something like the Glencairn glass[5] or a copita nosing glass is best. They allow for the best combination of the senses, sight, touch, smell, and taste, for appreciating the particular qualities of the whisky. Although sight and touch have a role to play in appreciating whisky, by far the most important senses are smell and taste. This is interesting, because taste and smell are the neglected senses of philosophy. Philosophers and psychologists have written far more about the sense of sight than they have about all of the other senses put together. For our purposes, the neglected senses take center stage.

Taste and smell are responsive to chemical structure. We can taste and smell because of chemoreceptors in the mouth and nose, which are sensitive to the chemical properties of different molecules. Tastes are detected by taste receptors, which are located in the taste buds, and these taste buds are found most particularly on the tongue. The taste buds contain cells that are receptive to different kinds of taste, such as sweet, sour, and bitter tastes—these are the crudest and most general notions of tastes, and we shall look at less crude tastes in a moment. While the tongue has around nine thousand taste buds, the olfactory epithelium in the nose has millions of olfactory receptor neurons.[6]

It should come as no surprise that our sense of smell is very important for our sense of taste, and the senses of taste and smell work in harmony. A familiar, if unpleasant, demonstration of this interdependence of taste and smell is apparent when you have a bad head cold, which affects your sense of taste because it directly affects your sense of smell. This is because the more complex tastes, other than bitter, sweet, sour, are a function of food vapors traveling from the mouth to the chemoreceptors in the nose. Where whisky's concerned, the nose knows.

As an avid whisky drinker you will be aware of the variety of flavors that one can detect in a dram. Pip Hills (the founder of the Scotch Malt Whisky Society) gives a nice table of the kinds of flavors we can find in whisky by using our senses of taste and smell.[7]

Easy

Smoky: peaty, phenolic, medicinal
Fruity: apples, pears, bananas
Floral: heather, rose, geraniums
Vanilla: toffee, vanilla pods
Pungent: hot, peppery
Cereal: hay, grass, porridge
Musty: cellars, cork, mothballs
Harsh: bitter, astringent

Not So Easy

Soapy: candles, wax
Sulphury: rubber, drains
Caramel: toffee, burnt sugar, treacle
Nutty: coconut, almond
Woody: newly sawn timber, resin, pine
Sour: vinegar, cheese
Sweet: cloying, sickly

These flavors are the effect of chemicals such as esters (usually associated with fruit and sweet flavors) and phenols (usually associated with smoky flavors) upon the chemoreceptors in our mouth and nose.

In acquiring aesthetic virtues, we are developing the sensory abilities to recognize these flavors in our favorite drams. The best way of habituating our senses to detect these flavors is by tasting whiskies of different character side by side.[8] This is something you probably already enjoy doing, and here is a quick look at two fine, but very different whiskies I happen to have available for tasting.

The first is the 12 year old Caol Ila, from Islay, which demonstrates sweetness and peaty smokiness on first nosing and tasting. It's also spicy and peppery in the mouth, but nowhere near as pungent as Laphroaig. There are some delightful grassy notes in the aftertaste. By contrast the 15 year old Glen Garioch, from the Highlands, is all heathery, honeyed sweetness on the nose, with none of the smokiness of the Caol Ila. There's quite a bit of maltiness on the palate along with that honey and heather, and a hint of peat. There's a bit of spiciness, but nothing to compare with the Caol Ila. They are very different whiskies: the Glen Garioch is a sweet, almost demure, whisky, while the Caol Isla is bolder and spicier, definitive of the islands.

The contrasting flavors of these whiskies allow our senses to become attuned and habituated, because the flavors stand out against one another. We shall now be in a better position to detect and appreciate them when we meet them again in the future.

Skeptics might deny that we really taste or smell anything quite so precisely; they might wonder how we can develop the precision and sensitivity that the aesthetic virtues demand. In answering such a question I am reminded of Sancho Panza, Don Quixote's squire, who relates a story about two master wine tasters in his family.[9] Upon being asked to judge the quality of a reputedly fine barrel of wine, the first master declared that it was a good wine but suffered from having a leathery flavor. The second declared that it suffered from a hint of iron. This caused some consternation, and the masters were assured that the barrel was clean and nothing had been added to the wine that could give it these flavors. Upon emptying the barrel, a small metal key with a leather thong was found in the bottom.

The Scottish philosopher David Hume took this story to show that there are qualities of objects that are fitted to produce certain sensations in us—and he was right, for the chemoreceptors in our mouth and nose are activated by the different chemical structures of molecules that pass through them. When we develop the aesthetic virtues, we are attuning the senses to discern the different sensations that those qualities (differences in chemical structure) produce in us. This is why acquiring and exercising the aesthetic virtues is so satisfying, and it's something that anyone with a mouth and a nose can learn to do reasonably well.

However, acquiring the aesthetic virtues is a process that takes time and requires practice and constant attention. Hume believed that we can develop an aesthetic taste in the sense that we would say that "she has great taste in art" or "he has great taste in whisky." This is a good description of the aesthetic virtues as states of character; the virtuous whisky drinker has taste because he or she can taste well.

Just as we admire people for their characteristic calmness under duress, or their open-mindedness and acumen in argumentation, we admire people for their taste in art or their appreciation of whisky. Not only do they possess a character with a certain style, but they are also able to do things that we admire particularly well. That is why we praise their characters with virtues such as calmness, acumen, and taste.

It's about time that I give some examples of aesthetic virtues that a virtuous whisky drinker ought to have. We have already looked at what I shall now call analytic virtues, where we employ an active sense of taste and an active sense of smell to our whiskies.[10] Actively smelling and tasting allows us to analyze the various flavors of a whisky. Alongside this we should expect an ability to concentrate on those flavors as we experience them. Furthermore, we should expect a little wit and linguistic flair in describing these experiences.[11] I think there's also room for a little imagination here because we will want to recombine the flavors that we have analytically reduced to components to form an impression of the whisky as a whole. Finally, we will hope to be guided by an aesthetic wisdom that we have developed over the years. Unlike practical wisdom, aesthetic wisdom's function is not to deliberate about how we can best achieve our goals; rather, it is the ability to consider and evaluate our sensory experiences on the basis of our past experiences and upon our knowledge of what makes these experiences good or bad ones. For example, we'll begin to notice off flavors in our whisky when something has gone wrong in the making of the whisky or its storage.

One can imagine a virtuous whisky drinker who can analyze the flavors of the whisky, describe them in a witty and stylish way, compare this whisky with others she knows in her imagination, and apply this knowledge to her evaluation of the quality of the whisky. This is someone you would want to spend time with, to taste whisky in the company of, and to compare experiences of different whiskies with. This is someone you'd like to have as a friend, someone you admire, and most of all someone who is fun to have a few drams with.

Whisky and Living Well

I hope you will agree that it is worthwhile making room for the aesthetic virtues in the happy life. Normally, the focus of discussion of the good life is on moral and intellectual virtues, and they are very important to a philosophical account of living well. But doing good deeds and reasoning well will not by themselves make us happy. Actively experiencing the world, taking enjoyment in the active use of our senses, is also a very important part of a life well lived. Whisky is such a beautiful drink because it affords such a wondrous array of tastes and smells that nothing else can match for variety. Consequently, nothing can match it for the active use of our senses; fine-tuning our senses to all of these wonderful flavors takes time and is its own reward.

Aristotle's most important idea was that living well and flourishing are achieved by virtuous activity. Acquiring and exercising the virtues makes for a flourishing person. If

Aristotle is right, and I certainly believe that he is on to a good thing, then it seems to me that the aesthetic virtues are as important a set of virtues as moral and intellectual virtues. Hence, being a virtuous whisky drinker is a contribution to our happiness, to living well. It is delightful to engage actively the world with our senses. The excellent deployment of our senses to discriminate and enjoy the different flavors of whiskies *is* living well. However, one cannot live well on one's own, even if you have a bottle of Bowmore to keep you company.

A Dram and a Friend Are Never Very Far Apart

Aristotle tells us that friendship is a kind of virtue, or implies virtue, and is also necessary for living well. For friends extend our current range of experiences; we can recognize in them virtues in which we wish to share. However, we also care for our friends for their own sake and not because they are useful to us; we will put their interests before our own. A virtue, friendship allows for a deep expression of altruistic emotions, of concern and care for our friends. It also allows for a deep sense of identification between friends, which comes about through shared experiences and interests.

A great joy in life is to share and explore interests with our friends, and what better way to do that than by sharing and enjoying a dram together. While we may take great satisfaction in developing our aesthetic virtues, what use are they if they are never shared, never put to use in company? To be able to share experiences and discuss them with our friends is an important part of what makes a life well lived. The virtuous whisky drinker prefers to take a dram in the company of his or her virtuous friends. Thus, whisky plays a dual role in a life well lived. It helps us actively use our senses, to attune virtuously them to all the various tastes and aromas of all the different varieties of whiskies. It also allows us to share these experiences with our friends, and that makes for shared happiness.

I have the great fortune of having many virtuous friends, and some of them love whisky, too. One of my closest friends—and the best man at my wedding—does not particularly enjoy whisky, but I remember many very pleasant evenings with him sampling the various whiskies I was enthusing about at the time. I can also think of some special whisky friends and many occasions on which we shared the fruits of our aesthetic virtues together. Whether it be blind tastings in Sydney at the home of our friends John and Doris; or a late night tumbler of Lagavulin with Dan in his study when we lived in Hertfordshire; or a dram of *whiskey* with my father (who grew up not far from the Bushmills distillery) when I lived in Northern Ireland, with Hayley who worked for various whisky companies when we lived in Maida Vale in London and always had a special bottle put aside for visitors, but especially at home with my wife, Sarah, enjoying whisky in each other's company. Her wit, intelligence, and good taste have taught me so much about the value of being a virtuous whisky drinker.

NOTES

1. All references to Aristotle are from Aristotle, *Nicomachean Ethics*, trans. J. A. K. Thomson (London: Penguin, 2004).
2. Jeremy Bentham, *The Rationale of Reward* (London: J. & H. L. Hunt, 1825), p. 206.
3. Aristotle, *Nicomachean Ethics*, p. 263.
4. See, for example, the Glancairn glass, discussed below, specially developed for nosing and tasting whisky.
5. The Glencairn glass can be viewed at the Glencairn crystal Web site, www.glencairn.co.uk/portal/ (accessed July 5, 2008).
6. See, for example, Richard Axel, "The Molecular Logic of Smell," *Scientific American* 273.4 (1995): pp. 154–159.
7. Phillip Hills, *Appreciating Whisky: The Connoisseur's Guide to Nosing, Tasting and Enjoying Scotch* (Glasgow: HarperCollins, 2002), p. 41.
8. I won't be able to go into any great detail about the best techniques for doing this and recommend books such as Pip Hill's that do have a great more detail on the subject.
9. Miguel De Cervantes, *Don Quixote* (New York: Penguin Classics, 2003).
10. Pip Hills spends a lot of his book describing how to do this.
11. It is of course possible to go to descriptive excesses, hence a little wit helps!

16

Nasty Tempers
Does Whiskey Make People Immoral?

Dave Monroe

The theme that whiskey produces mean, violent drunks pervades and shapes the classic Clint Eastwood Western *Unforgiven*. Eastwood's character, William Munny, a reformed villain turned pig farmer turned bounty hunter, remarks at several points that part of his reformation involved giving up whiskey—which we are lead to believe played a causal role in his wickedness. Whiskey, it seems, is at least partially to blame for William Munny's evil past, and it triggers a mean-spirited, truculent, and lethal side of his personality. This is especially evident near the end of the film, when Eastwood's character discovers that his closest friend has been killed by Little Bill, the tyrannical sheriff portrayed by Gene Hackman. Munny immediately starts drinking whiskey, triggering a startling reversion to the despicable killer who kills women, children, and "everything that walks or crawls." After downing a copious amount of firewater, Munny exacts his revenge, casually and remorselessly gunning down several men.[1]

I believe that this theme from *Unforgiven* represents a prevalent, deeply ingrained American attitude about whiskey, namely, that it produces mean drunks.[2] Whiskey has a reputation for being a tough guy's drink, made for the strong, salty, and sadistic. Whiskey is frequently associated with immoral behavior of sundry sorts, including (but not limited to) barroom brawls and domestic violence. Granted, alcohol in general is also associated with these things, but whiskey seems to be singled out among other libations in that many believe that whiskey more readily causes such base behavior. Thus, the belief that whiskey produces mean drunks seems to suggest that whiskey has a special property, which we shall call mean making, that other alcoholic beverages, like wine coolers, lack. We will call this the mean property thesis (MPT).

On the grounds of this supposed special capacity to create mean, potentially immoral, drunks, one might conclude that whiskey itself is immoral and should be avoided, perhaps even legislated against. In this essay, I will argue against this conclusion, noting that there is no evidence of any such "property" in whiskey. I will further suggest that alternative explanations of the correlation between whiskey and immoral behavior, if it exists, are more plausible. I will argue that the cultural attitude itself is partially to blame, though ultimately the blame for bad behavior rests with the drinker, not the drink. It is the occurrent or dispositional mental attitudes of the imbiber that cause him or her to get nasty—that is, they get mean because they *think* they will, either consciously or unconsciously. As a coup de grâce, I will argue that even if whiskey does have mean-making properties, that fails to establish the immorality of consuming it.

First Round: Barkeep, Will This Whiskey Make Me Mean?

The first question we must address is whether whiskey causes people to become ill-tempered in a special way. By 'special way' I simply mean in a way over and above the normal ways in which any alcoholic beverage can activate our more primitive urges and lower our inhibitions. Is there some characteristic or property in whiskey that affects us over and above alcohol? Was William Munny a despicable son of a bitch because whiskey made him so, and can it do the same to us? In short, it is unlikely.

Contrary to the hopes of evangelical teetotalers and conservative prohibitionists, there is a lack of scientific evidence to suggest that there is a "mean-maker" in whiskey not present in other drinks. While researching this essay, I could not find any scientific results that would support the Mean Property Thesis, which leads me to suspect that the prevalent thinking about whiskey is mistaken. If there is a Mean Property, it ought to be the sort of thing we could scientifically discover and explain, and the lack of evidence should serve as a red flag to us.

Note, however, that mere lack of evidence *for* the Mean Property Thesis does not make the claim false, and a lack of scientific evidence is insufficient to rule out the existence of such properties. Perhaps the lack of evidence is due to a lack of research; if experiments to test the thesis have not been conducted, it is obvious that there could not be any real "evidence" about mean-makers. Thus, it could be that the lack of evidence just shows a lack of effort on the part of scientists and is thus no indictment of the MPT. Moreover, a defender of the MPT is within rights to point out that it is impossible to *prove* that mean-makers in whiskey do not exist, and further, point to the scientific practice of positing unobservable entities as explanatory machinery in theories. An ardent defender of the MPT might argue that sociological data relating whiskey and domestic violence, assuming that the rate is higher when the assailant consumes whiskey than other intoxicating *boissons*, is best explained by positing a mean-making property.

By way of response, we should note that the rational choice when lacking evidence for some claim, one way or the other, is suspended judgment or agnosticism. To draw a positive conclusion from a lack of evidence is to argue from ignorance, which is fallacious reasoning we should work to avoid. From my position, we should say that we do not know for certain whether whiskey has mean-makers. The hypothetical MPT supporter, though, has appealed to outside evidence to support the positive claim that mean-makers exist; it is consistent with and helps support other data concerning whiskey and domestic violence, say, and thus is not strictly arguing from ignorance. The real issue is whether a relationship between whiskey drunkenness, meanness, and other immoral behavior really is best explained by reference to some special property of whiskey. If this were the only way of explaining such phenomena, then the MPT supporter is within rights to believe that mean-makers exist. If, however, there are alternative explanations that do not involve positing additional properties, then the principle of parsimony suggests we should prefer the latter.[3] I think that alternative explanations are at hand and will discuss them in the next section.

Second Round: Send a Shot to the Mean Property Thesis at the End of the Bar

Suppose you are William Munny at the end of a long day of bounty hunting filled with revenge killings in outhouses, dodging bullets, defending the honor of prostitutes, worrying about your kids and diseased livestock, pining for your dead wife, and listening to a whimpering young braggadocio lamenting his first kill. As a chaser, when finally compensated for enduring all this, you learn that your best friend has been murdered. Add a little firewater to the recipe, and you will get an explosion.

As is by now familiar, the MPT explains this, at least in part, by a special objective fact about the whiskey Munny consume: it makes him mean. The alternative explanations I favor, which are consistent with one another and thus could both be true, hold that something inside Munny explains his reaction. There is an essentially subjective component,

I claim, to whether or not whiskey tends to make one meaner, nastier, or more violent than other drinks.

The first alternative is a "mixed drink" consisting of two "mixers." I put them together on the basis of one similarity: they are occurrent mental states of the imbiber. On one hand, Munny could go off when he consumes whiskey because he specifically believes that whiskey will make him mean at the time he drinks it. That is, he has an occurrent belief about the effects whiskey will have on him. One can imagine Munny, or anyone for that matter, thinking, "Wild Turkey makes me ill-tempered, so I shall drink it so I can get mean— Bartles & Jaymes wine coolers and Mike's Hard Lemonade just won't cut it for what I aim to do." In this case, the imbiber is a bit like Jekyll drinking the potion that transforms him into Hyde, or like Popeye eating his spinach. A tough person wants to get tougher and believes that the whiskey is the trick. This occurrent belief creates an expectation that then shapes and creates the experiences Munny, or anyone else of like mind, will have. What we expect to experience or perceive often powerfully influences what and how we see and feel the world around us; this phenomenon has long been observed and documented in both the history and psychology of perception.[4] So, if Munny really believes that drinking whiskey will make him nasty, it will. Note, though, that one could believe this of nearly anything, and to the extent that one is affected, it is largely a matter of the inner workings of one's own mind. Thus, if one believed that wine coolers make him or her more confident, or that Triscuits make one randy, chances are those expectations would be subjectively confirmed. That is to say, what one believes an object will do is to some extent arbitrary—so it is no fault of that thing that one misuses it.[5]

On the other hand, it could be that the drinker is already in a foul mood, as suggested by Munny's situation above. If one is already in a rotten state of mind, testy and ready to fight, adding any alcoholic beverage to the mix is likely to exacerbate, rather than mollify, one's affective state. As we all know, alcohol is like a megaphone for our feelings: they are amplified to the point of being obnoxious when we are drunk. Sometimes it is a love fest, during which we proclaim our undying friendship for mere acquaintances or partner up with people we otherwise would not. More notoriously, the darker side can amplify: frustration, anger, jealousy, and so on reach crescendo. This, too, would explain why one gets mean while drunk on whiskey. However, this is not limited to whiskey since it is true of any alcoholic libation. The moral of this story is not "Don't drink whiskey when you're in a bad mood"; rather, it is "Don't drink alcohol when you're in a bad mood." Thus, this explanation still merits attention, though it is more generally focused since it does not invoke some property over and above those shared by any alcoholic beverage.

Notice that both of the above mixers reference the occurrent mental states of a drinker just before or while drinking. In neither case is it whiskey specifically playing the crucial role in explaining why so-and-so acted thus-and-so. The second alternative explanation for why whiskey produces mean drunks is slightly more complex; while it still involves the beliefs or mental states of those drinking, it refers not to occurrent beliefs but to the power of background, subconscious, dispositional beliefs to produce expectations.

Third Round: It's Not Just the Whiskey Talking

Many of the things we believe are not conscious at any given moment—we do not, for example, consciously believe that we are not William Munny (at least until you just read that proposition). However, when circumstances are such that we must call upon our beliefs in order to think them consciously or to assert them, what we believe comes to the fore and occurs to us. Nevertheless, we do believe these propositions are true and that things are as they are even when we are not actively thinking them. These are dispositional beliefs, and they constitute the vast majority of what we believe.

Among the beliefs lurking in the background of our minds are powerful ones that shape the way we fundamentally interpret and interact with the world around us. Some of these beliefs may never have seen the light of our consciousness yet nevertheless have powerful clout over those facts and beliefs that we subsequently accept, and over our actions. In fact, many of these background dispositional beliefs go a long way toward forming our sense of self-identity, agency, and situation. A further curious fact about most of these background beliefs is that they are not often ones we consider for ourselves and are generally implanted in us from without. We have a tendency to adopt unreflectively "popular beliefs" or "common sense" as fact and to accept them without thought. Most of the time this process is innocuous; sometimes, though, as we all know, things can get ugly when we fail to think about what we believe and why.

Such beliefs also seem to have a built-in confirmation bias, much like Munny's occurrent belief about whiskey making him mean. Given that these beliefs structure our experiences, and the fact that these beliefs are frequently implanted and widely shared, the experiences of individuals, and the group, will be similar and tend to support the already held dispositional beliefs. That is, once one of these beliefs takes hold, there is perpetual feedback from our everyday experience that reinforces the "truth" of the belief in question. So, for example, if one lived centuries ago and learned that the earth is flat, very little short of a conceptual revolution would change one's mind since almost anyone could ask about the matter would confirm what you already accept.[6]

I suspect that the belief that whiskey causes people to be nasty tempered and violent is a dispositional background belief of this sort. It does not approach the lofty heights of framing our view of reality, in the way that religious or irreligious beliefs can, but it certainly seems to be a widely held belief in America, almost to the point of being "common sense."[7] Since our background beliefs can guide our actions, even when they are unconscious, one might explain whiskey's tendency to rile people up by reference to the deeply ingrained belief itself.

In other words, it need not be the case that Munny actively thought that drinking whiskey would make him mean or that he was in a bad mood—it may just be that the beliefs in the background of his mind asserted their influence and shaped his thoughts and behaviors when conditions were right. The belief is thus fortified as confirming experiential evidence piles up, further perpetuating the cycle.

The latter explanation also helps explain the meanness phenomenon without appealing to some unidentified characteristic of whiskey, but it differs from the purely subjective occurrent belief explanation in that what lurks in the background is a shared public belief. Thus, there is an objective component to the dispositional background belief explanation that is missing in the other alternative.[8] This helps make sense of the scope of the MPT, that is, why it seems to be so widespread and not merely a local occurrence. On the downside, this explanation is much more difficult to test; it is a daunting task to judge another's background beliefs from a third-party perspective. Nevertheless, I maintain that this approach has the advantage in metaphysical simplicity over the MPT because it does not turn to additional mind-independent properties of "things" for help.

Another important point is that there's nothing inconsistent in asserting one or both of the psychological explanations for the same individual simultaneously. William Munny could be in a terrible mood, actively believe that whiskey will make him mean, and believe that in the background of his mind all at the same time. So, it may be that one or more of these explanations apply to a single case and may work together to offer us a more robust picture of what's afoot with the mean whiskey drinker.

Who's Paying the Tab?

Given the lack of evidence for mean-makers, and the fact that we can explain the whiskey curmudgeon's behavior in simpler ways, I suggest that we reject the idea that whiskey

has any properties that make it specially morally objectionable. Remember that I mean whiskey has no properties in
addition to those that might make alcohol in general morally
offensive. There is no doubt that heavy drinking factors into
many social evils. My claim is not that whiskey does not play
a role in such things, but merely to point out that whiskey
does not bring any extra potential immorality to the shot
glass with it.

So where should we place moral blame for what someone
besodden with whiskey and foul-tempered does? The obvious answer is not on the drink but on the drinker. There is
nothing inappropriate, odd, unprecedented, or contradictory
about holding a drunk responsible for what he does even
when he is smashed—and citing a lack of full agency has
never worked as an excuse. This is particularly true if our
explanation of one's whiskey meanness is the result of occurrent mental attitudes. If someone believes whiskey will make
him mean and prone to violence and drinks whiskey for that
reason, then that person is worthy of heavy moral censure.
For this person, the whiskey is a means to willful immoral
conduct. By the same token, we should be less outraged at
a guy who is in a bad mood, drinks too much whiskey, and as a
result gets angrier. We still hold him responsible for whatever
he does, maybe admonishing him to eschew alcohol when he
is testy, but we would be incorrect if we classified him as the
black-hearted, immoral jerk the first guy is.

What about the riled up whiskey drinker who does not
have an occurrent mental state influencing his behavior? Can
we hold a person accountable for what he does given unconscious background beliefs? The answer is yes. Simply because
one unreflectively believes something is right does not make it
the case that it actually is. Take racism or sexism, for example. Many people erroneously believe that discrimination on
the basis of race or gender is perfectly good form—though
we know it is wrong, even if on the sparse basis of justice and
treating relevantly similar things alike. In addition, we can
hold responsible the agent who, as a result of background

beliefs, unconsciously gets mean when drinking whiskey for getting drunk enough to let it affect him or her thus.

Let us suppose, though, that a supporter of the MPT objected in the following way. She might point out that it may someday be discovered that there is a property in whiskey that does affect our brain chemistry in such a way that the MPT's version of things pans out. If that day comes, would we then be forced to conclude that whiskey is more morally objectionable than any other spirit? As far as I'm concerned, the answer is no, unless the mean-makers ultimately turn out to be sparks of Satan's unholy essence.

I resist the notion that material objects, once they come into existence and no longer rely on a thinking mind for their per-sistence, have any sort of moral standing separate from how persons interact with them. To brainwash you into seeing things my way, consider the following thought experiment.

Imagine a god named Fred owned our world like a per-son might own a house and that this god wanted to sell our world to his neighbor, Tom. Like anyone wanting to show-case a property, Fred wants to show Tom his world without its inhabitants, who are bound to foul up the sales pitch. To mitigate this problem, Fred constructs a model world just like ours in every respect save for the fact that it is wholly unin-habited. Everything, including man-made artifacts, is present but the people. Tom, liking the model but not liking people, buys the model world from Fred, despite the latter's objec-tions (secretly, Fred doesn't really like his people very much either and is trying to be rid of the immoral little rascals). Now we have two worlds, one inhabited by people and the other not. When we consider the world without people, it seems a stretch to think that anything in that world has moral status or genuinely the subject of moral judgment. Could we even say of nuclear power, bombs, firearms, or whiskey that they are immoral or wrong in such a world?[9]

This thought experiment doesn't completely settle the mat-ter, but it does show us what we believe about what has moral status and what doesn't, that is, that things, regardless of their properties, are not morally charged until they interact with persons. More technically, brute states of affairs consisting in merely material objects do not have intrinsic moral values. Whiskey, all by itself, is no more "immoral" than your couch. The manner of its use may color our judgments; for example, we may say that whiskey is beneficial or good if used for medicinal purposes like disinfecting wounds, or, conversely, that it is destructive or evil when one misuses it as William Munny does. However, our judgments of whiskey here seem to be an extension of our judgments about some agent's actions—the whiskey is an instrument that someone uses for a certain end, and it is the individual or the ends that should be the focus of our moral approbation or scorn. The same is true of your couch, which is capable of being used for weal or woe. The point is that we should hold people morally responsible; that is, restrict our moral judgments to persons, actions, and ends, and avoid pointlessly condemning mere material things.

Furthermore, if we were to discover that whiskey has properties that increase the likelihood of our behaving badly, we would simply have more reason for holding whoever drinks it responsible for what they have done. One is not forced to get drunk on whiskey or consume it in lieu of other alcoholic beverages, and if one overdoes it knowing that it may have an adverse affect on him, moral blame for any immorality still lies with him.

Thus, it seems to me that even if whiskey had mean-makers, it would still be far from clear that this would ground any special moral objections against it. Our moral judgments are better situated against those who abuse whiskey.

Last Call

One may point out that whiskey still has the reputation that it does, and if that reputation is contributing to inappropriate behavior, it may still be worthwhile to condemn drinking whiskey. After all, if the effect is the same—namely, people getting nasty and brutish when drunk on whiskey as opposed to other drinks—who cares whether the underlying explanation is some special property of the thing or an engrained background belief? Are we not better off getting rid of the stuff? Why not cut the head off the snake? If people do not drink whiskey, it will not matter what they think will happen when they do. Problem solved!

That is one way of dealing with the issue, but it seems a little ham-fisted and paternalistic for those of us who like living in a free society. Obviously, another of our deeply ingrained American beliefs is that we have the freedom to pursue any good we wish so long as we do not interfere with the freedom of others to do likewise. This ideal is not perfectly realized in our actual society, and neither is its status supreme among moral standards, yet it is an ideal that we should respect. The aforementioned solution pays this ideal no respect, and for that reason I reject it. Alternatively, we could work to dispel some of the power of the misguided myth that whiskey causes meanness—which is, in fact, the aim of this essay. It is a less drastic way of attempting to solve the problem, one that requires patience, time, and the willingness to help people think about what they are drinking and about some of their unquestioned beliefs. It also has the benefit of respecting the freedom of individuals to pursue their own good.

In the end, I think I have given reason to reject the thesis that whiskey has special properties that make it more morally objectionable than other alcoholic beverages. So, the next time you are at the bar with a friend who claims that whiskey turns him into William Munny, I hope that you will have profited from reading this essay. Bottoms up![10]

NOTES

1. *Unforgiven*, Dir. Clint Eastwood, Malpaso Productions, Los Angeles, 1992.
2. Some interesting remarks about the relationship between violence, whiskey, and popular belief can be found in Gilles Vandal, *Rethinking Southern Violence: Homicides in Post–Civil War*

Louisiana, 1866–1884 (Columbus: Ohio State University Press, 2000), p. 171.

3. The Principle of Parsimony, or Ockham's Razor, is a normative principle in theory construction that tells us that other things being equal, the simplest explanation is best. An interesting defense of this principle as a synthetic a priori truth appears in Richard Swinburne, *Simplicity as Evidence of Truth* (Milwaukee, WI: Marquette University Press, 1997). I leave it to you, the reader, to decide whether you accept this principle on this basis or another, or whether you reject it entirely.

4. An insightful and interesting analysis of the psychology of expectation applied to emotive states and music appears in David Huron, *Sweet Anticipation: Music and the Psychology of Expectation* (Cambridge, MA: MIT Press, 2006). There is, of course, a disanalogy between the expectation's role in musical response and that of alcohol, since biochemistry plays a role in the way alcohol affects human persons. Nevertheless, the account of expectations stands on its own.

5. We should note, too, that this explanation is testable and has precedents for so doing. One could proceed with placebos and measure the manifestation of the behavior "caused" by the actual object—be it whiskey, wine coolers, or Triscuits.

6. Thomas S. Kuhn, *The Structure of Scientific Revolutions*, 3rd ed. (Chicago: University of Chicago Press, 1996). Kuhn's work is a classic discussion of how concepts in science constrain explanations and how these concepts change over time.

7. I attempted to poll people in the most unscientific way to support this point. Most of my students last semester agreed with the MPT, and so did my recently departed father, and so does my brother—a bar manager for fifteen years. Most seemed to think that whiskey caused mean-spiritedness and bad behavior. I obtained my results by asking loaded questions and sampling about fifty people. As I said, very unscientific but funny.

8. For a similar discussion of the way background structures of the mind shape our experiences, see John Searle, *The Construction of Social Reality* (New York: Free Press, 1995).

9. There are those who disagree with the intuition to which I appeal here, especially in the context of environmental ethics.

10. I would like to thank Marcus Adams and Fritz Allhoff for the patience, insights, and suggestions that helped me shape this essay.

17

Whisky and the Wild
On Preserving Methods and Distilleries

Jason Kawall

In 1992 the renowned Rosebank distillery outside of Glasgow was mothballed. Similarly, in 1984 the doors of the Port Ellen distillery on Islay were closed, one of several distillery closings that occurred in the early 1980s. Should we care about losing such distilleries given that so many other distilleries, long since forgotten, have also disappeared? Distilleries, like other businesses, come and go. Kilchoman, a new distillery on Islay, has begun to produce spirit, Angostura Limited is reopening the Charles Medley bourbon distillery in Kentucky, and a Dutch consortium will be reopening the currently mothballed Speyside distillery, Glenglassaugh. So what exactly is lost when a distillery closes?

Related questions arise when we consider the loss of traditional methods and practices in producing whisky. Bowmore and Laphroaig continue to perform some of their own malting using more traditional methods, though they—like the other

Islay distilleries—now use barley malted at the industrial Port Ellen maltings. Is this use of traditional methods best seen as a mere show that might be of interest to the tour groups that pass through? The question is pressing as few people, if any, would be able to taste a significant difference in the final product, regardless of where exactly the malting occurred. What if the malting were no longer done on Islay but instead somewhere cheaper in Eastern Europe? Would anything of value be lost?

Finally, we may wonder about preserving whisky as a spirit, as such. Consider the following words from Vijay Mallya, the head of United Spirits Limited (a major owner of several Scottish distilleries): "I'm not suggesting radical changes, but maybe natural additives could be used to make it [Scotch] more exciting for this young target market."[1] Mallya believes added flavorings could make whisky more appealing to younger people and more competitive with wine, vodka, and other spirits. Are there any good reasons for whisky lovers to reject such proposals?

My goal in this essay is to show how these questions, which might be of interest to whisky drinkers, may be profitably compared to parallel questions that arise for people concerned with certain environmental issues. In particular, I will argue that we should care about preserving traditional distilleries and styles of whisky by drawing upon a set of analogous concerns and arguments from the domains of environmental ethics and aesthetics. We can treat distilleries as akin to species of living things; even if there are plenty of species, and even if most species in the past have gone extinct, there are still good reasons to value individual species now. With respect to maintaining traditional techniques, even if they have no significant effect on the taste of the end product, I will draw on arguments from environmental and other areas of aesthetics to argue that there are still important values at stake. A key point will be that we can appreciate whisky as a drink as such but also the process by which it is made and the history behind it.

The Analogy between Species and Distilleries

We can begin by developing briefly an analogy between distilleries and species. In both cases we are considering entities that many of us see as being of value and worthy of preservation. In treating distilleries as analogues to species, we can treat different lines or expressions of whisky from a given distillery as being akin to subspecies. Thus, Bruichladdich's Infinity line would be one of its subspecies, while its Links expression would be another. In turn, individual bottles of whisky can be seen as akin to individual members of species. The analogy is not perfect, of course, but it is surprisingly rich.[2]

Distilleries, like species, evolve and adapt over time. Distilleries will change owners and modify their whiskies (and equipment) for changing markets and tastes as their circumstances change. For all of this change, there will still be a common lineage and shared features. Bunnahabhain, opened in 1881, began by distilling highly peated whiskies but switched to a very lightly peated whisky in the 1960s to better suit certain blended whiskies, particularly Cutty Sark; more recently, Bunnahabhain (pronounced boon-ah-IIA-ven) has started to distil again a highly peated spirit in addition to its less peaty expression/subspecies.[3] It has evolved in response to competition and changing circumstances, yet it is still identifiable as Bunnahabhain.

The success of a species is largely a matter of how adaptations over time allow its individuals to succeed in the circumstances they face. Similarly, as a distillery changes, its ability to flourish and survive will largely depend on the quality of the individual bottles of whisky produced by the changing methods, managers, mash bills, and so on. Still, there are exceptions. An erupting volcano might kill off the most promising species and individuals in an area—rapid climate change might wipe out an otherwise healthy species. Recessions or changing ownership can lead to the extinction of strong distilleries producing good whisky—as in the cases of Rosebank and Port Ellen.

271

Species in ecosystems, though often in competition with each other, need populations of other species in order to flourish, and distilleries also profit from the existence of rivals. How? First, having a healthy range of competitors provides more general interest in whisky. A rye drinker might be inspired to try a Scotch; a Speyside drinker could develop a taste for peaty Islay whiskies. Second, having rivals can spur distilleries to produce better whisky: if others are producing fine spirits, remaining distilleries will need to produce good products also or risk extinction. If the local rabbits become faster, the local foxes had better adapt in some way or risk dying out. Third, there are cooperative ventures. For example, the shared needs for malted barley from the Islay distilleries keep the Port Ellen maltings running (and provide convenience and economy for the distilleries). Many distilleries are part of "whisky trails" and work together to attract tourists to their region. Having a range of distilleries helps keep bottlings, coopers, and other required supplemental businesses open and profitable. Finally, and perhaps most important for Scottish distilleries, there is the role of their whisky in blended whiskies. Indeed, for most Scottish distilleries, the majority of their whisky will be used for blends and not sold as single malts. The distilleries need blends to survive, and the blends, in turn, require a wide range of whisky from distinct distilleries with a range of expressions in order to achieve their distinctive characters. These latter relationships might be seen as akin to symbiotic relationships in ecosystems, like the relationship between flowering plants and the insects that pollinate them while feeding.

We can now consider how thinking about species and environmental concerns might help us understand why traditional distilleries, methods, and styles of whisky would be worth preserving. How might the analogy help guide our thinking?

Aesthetic Value

Our starting point will be aesthetic value, a form of value often associated with the arts and with nature. The nature of such value is contentious, but for present purposes we can use the following characterization: an object has aesthetic value insofar as the contemplative experience of it, as such, appropriately produces a positive response (such as pleasure) in us. Paradigmatically, when we think of aesthetically valuable objects, we think of those that are, for example, beautiful, fascinating, or graceful; objects that produce pleasure or similar positive responses when we experience them.

The most obvious loss when a distillery closes is the production of that whisky, that is, individuals of that species. There is intrinsic aesthetic value to the whisky in individual bottles of whisky (this is why we drink it), and when a distillery closes, we will have no more individuals of that kind. Of course there might be similar whiskies with similar tastes, but we would still lose the unique value of the whisky of the closed distillery. Similarly, if the polar bear species (*Ursus maritimus*) were to go extinct, the obvious loss would be the loss of individual polar bears. Even if there were other bears, there would no longer be polar bears with their striking, beautiful white coats and their unique adaptations to harsh arctic conditions.

Beyond the aesthetic value of the whiskies they produce, there is aesthetic value to distilleries as physical entities—in the architecture of their buildings, in the beauty of their copper stills, and so on. Hence, in part, the popularity of distillery tours even among nonwhisky drinkers. When a distillery is mothballed or fully closed, its buildings and equipment fall into disrepair and decay, and the aesthetic value of the physical structures will gradually be lost. There is not a parallel on the side of species here.

Next, there is aesthetic interest to the processes involved in producing whisky—the work of the maltsers, the stillmen, and so on. We can admire the skilled work involved, the current instantiations of demanding crafts with long histories. In the case of species, we can look at the often-fascinating behaviors in which members of a species engage in order to flourish: their techniques and methods of survival.

There is aesthetic interest in the histories and lores of distilleries. We learn about their origins and locations, their struggles and successes, past expressions, and so on. There is generally a wealth of interesting stories related to how a given distillery has evolved into its current status over time. Again, this parallels the intriguing stories of evolution and adaptation in the natural world—consider Darwin's famous work on the unique species of the Galapagos.

We thus find at least four sources of aesthetic value in considering whiskies: first, the whiskies themselves, as drinks; second, the distilleries as physical entities; third, the crafts involved in producing whisky; and fourth, the stories and lore of distilleries. In a later section we will consider how knowledge of these latter three can enhance our appreciation of the whisky we drink. But first we will turn to another basis for valuing distilleries, drawing more directly on work in environmental ethics.

Goodness in Variety

The contemporary philosopher Ben Bradley has investigated the question of why we should care about preserving endangered species. In particular, he considers the case of the snail darter, a small fish found only in Tennessee, once threatened with extinction. Bradley makes the following proposal:

> The snail darter in [a world with a variety of species] contributes to the diversity of that world. The world is intrinsically better with the snail darter than without, and by more than the intrinsic value of the snail darter. The snail darter has contributory value, in virtue of its contribution to the variety of organisms in that world.[4]

On Bradley's proposal we should preserve individual species because they add to the overall valuable diversity of species on our planet. How would this apply to distilleries? Beyond whatever intrinsic aesthetic value there is to a distillery and its whiskies, the distillery and its whiskies also contribute to a valuable variety of distilleries and whiskies in the world. As such, they have contributory value. Irish whiskies, Japanese distilleries, mellowed Tennessee whiskies, and so forth contribute to a valuable variety. The current proposal is that such variety is valuable in itself, intrinsically. And, of course, the more distilleries and whisky expressions that exist, the more variety that exists.

Why think that variety in itself is a good thing? A number of philosophers, going back at least to Gottfried Leibniz in the early 1700s, have embraced a principle of *bonum variationis*, that is, "goodness in variety."[5] The idea is that other things being equal it is better to have a range of different goods, rather than simply an equivalent number of the same good. Suppose you could choose to have your favorite whisky be the only whisky in the world and have it available everywhere. Initially, it may seem that you should welcome this—after all, it is your favorite. But it should quickly become clear that this would be extremely boring. Compare: imagine the only music available in the world was your favorite song. It would be the only song played on the radio, and by angry teenage bands, and the only song available on karaoke machines. Would you still listen? You might now and again, but surely you'd listen to music more, and enjoy it more—including your favorite song—to the extent that there were other songs available. Similarly, even if we prefer peaty Islays, we should welcome the existence of rye whiskies, and partake of them on occasion. We should welcome having a range of different kinds of whisky from a range of different distilleries from around the world. Other things being equal, variety is valuable.

But a worry comes to mind. If we value variety as such, would this mean that we should try to preserve every distillery no matter how incompetent, and every variety of whisky simply for the sake of having variety? And would we need to embrace Mallya's proposal of flavored whiskies designed for younger drinkers? After all, such products would add to the variety of whiskies (or near whiskies) in the world. We might imagine a young person, Claire, who cannot stand

Glenfarclas, but who would enjoy it if it were premixed with a sweet strawberry syrup and had a neon pink color that looked fabulous in dance clubs.

In response, note that while variety is valuable, it is not the only value with which we should concern ourselves, and it can be outweighed. If a given whisky is terrible, there are better uses of time, money, and other resources. Similarly with old or rare whiskies, distilleries, or methods: adding to variety in the world is just one concern among many. To have a wide range of horrible disease-causing bacteria adds to the variety of species in the world, but presumably this value can be outweighed by their negative impacts—we need not try to create and embrace as many diseases as possible. Thus, even while we value variety, this does not yet force us to welcome every awful whisky, whisky-based trendy drink, or distillery that comes along. Some can happily be put to rest.

Still, we can consider Mallya's proposal in more depth. Flavored whisky variants might well appeal to many younger people, so why think the value of such variety would be outweighed? There are a few reasons. Even if those producing whisky were interested only in making money, there are different ways of doing so. For example, one could try to sell large quantities of cheap goods at a small profit, or one could instead focus on selling smaller quantities of higher quality goods at a higher price. Mallya's vision seems to reflect the first approach—trying to appeal to as wide a market as possible, but whisky (particularly Scotch) seems most naturally suited to the second approach. Given the years of aging involved in producing whisky, the comparatively high costs of production, and so on, whisky is, by its very nature, going to be an expensive product compared to many other alcoholic beverages. It is also one with a complex, rich character that often appeals only to those with more mature tastes; but Mallya needs to remember that younger people eventually grow up. One can have a flourishing business with excellent high-quality products—there is no need to water things down simply to sell mass quantities.

We can approach the current point from a different angle by comparing reproductive strategies across species. Some species, including many plants and fish, tend to produce very high numbers of low-quality offspring, in the sense that the majority of the offspring will fail to survive to adulthood; the strategy is simply to produce sheer quantities of young. On the other hand, some species, including humans and most mammals, instead focus on producing a few offspring into which the parents invest a great deal of energy. Rather than producing tens of thousands of offspring every year, humans invest in a few offspring much more heavily. Whisky is a species best suited to following this latter strategy—producing fewer specimens but with a greater investment of resources. And it is not as if whisky is struggling—several mothballed distilleries are being reopened, new distilleries are cropping up, and global sales of whisky are increasing significantly.

Finally, if we reject the kind of variety proposed by Mallya, are we instead left with a conservative approach that allows nothing to change? Rather, there are simply better ways of seeking variety. For example, Bruichladdich is well known for being quite open to experimentation. Many are eagerly anticipating Bruichladdich's Octomore line—intended to be the peatiest whisky from Islay (with a peating level of 129 phenol ppm in the malt in 2003).[6] Of course some of these experiments will work, and others will not. But they remain true to the nature of whisky as a complex spirit, requiring time and effort to produce properly. Similarly, Glenmorangie has been leading investigations into different finishes to whiskies—first aging them for ten years in bourbon casks, then finishing them for a short period (perhaps a couple of years) in port, sherry, or other casks. There is thus room for innovation and further valuable variety in whiskies.

Relevant Histories and Knowledge

Why else might we care about traditional distilleries and techniques? As noted above, there is aesthetic interest to distilleries and whisky making beyond the basic value in the whisky that is produced. The distillery buildings and equipment can be beautiful, often in the midst of striking terrain. We can admire (aesthetically) the careful work of the managers, still-men, and other craftspeople involved. And distilleries often have rich, compelling histories.

Knowing about these histories and techniques will shape our appreciation of whiskies themselves. Compare Robert Elliot's remarks concerning the appreciation of wilderness:

> People who value wilderness do not do so merely because they like to soak up pretty scenery. They see much more and value much more than this. What they do see, and what they value, is very much a function of the degree to which they understand the ecological mechanisms which maintain the landscape and which determine that it appears the way it does. . . . Knowledge of this kind is capable of transforming a hitherto uninteresting landscape into one that is compelling.[7]

Similarly, the current proposal is that knowledge of how a whisky is produced and of the particular history and techniques of a given distillery can change and improve our appreciation when we sit with the whisky in hand.

How would such knowledge improve appreciation? To begin, if we know about the production of a particular whisky, we can attempt to pick out particular elements when we try it, giving a focus to our appreciation. In some cases, such knowledge will lead us to search for aspects of our whisky that we might not otherwise have noticed. For example, if we know that a distiller's edition of Lagavulin is double matured—first in American oak, then finished for its final months in casks that held sherry produced from Pedro

Ximinez grapes (an especially sweet, sticky variety)—we can search for distinctive sherry tones as we drink.

Second, such background knowledge can improve our appreciation of a whisky by allowing us to better understand it and to place it in a broader context. Compare: knowing that a given play is intended as a satire can help us interpret it properly. Knowing the way of life and adaptations of an animal can help us understand and appreciate its actions. Knowing that Tennessee whiskies are intended to be smooth (given the sugar maple charcoal mellowing of the spirit that occurs before it is placed in barrels) helps us to understand and appreciate what a distillery is attempting to achieve in its whisky.

Third, coming to know about a whisky's origins and history can make us more interested in the whisky itself; in turn, this may lead us to pay more careful attention to it. To illustrate, consider the following facts about moose:

- Only male (bull) moose grow antlers; these have an average span of four to five feet and weigh around fifty pounds. More remarkably, moose lose their antlers every fall after rutting season, so the antlers grow to this size in the course of approximately six months every year.

- Moose have long dewlaps (or bells), which are folds of hair-covered skin up to twenty inches long that hang from their necks. It is widely believed that males use their dewlaps to spread their scent to attract females during mating seasons—males wallow in urine-soaked mud, and the dewlap becomes covered in it.

Notice a few things. First, this background knowledge may lead us to pay more attention to the moose's antlers and dewlaps. People tend to notice the antlers in any case, but the dewlap is often overlooked; thus we now may pay attention to a feature of the moose that we would not otherwise have noticed. Second, if we notice mud on the dewlap of a male moose, we can better understand why this would be so— we can place aspects of the moose's appearance and behavior in a broader context. Finally, we might be more curious when we see a moose. We'll pay more attention—we'll remember the dewlap, how quickly the antlers grow, and so on. There is an interesting biological story here that will lead us to be more thoughtful and appreciative should we encounter a moose.

Consider now a few facts about Highland Park, a renowned distillery located on the windswept island of Orkney:

- "The most northerly malt distillery in Scotland, Highland Park was founded in 1798 by Magnus Eunson, a man who managed to reconcile being a preacher by day and a smuggling moonshiner by night."[8]

- "Made up almost entirely of decomposed heather, [Orkney's peat] may just be the key to the whisky's extremely evocative aroma."[9]

- "Samples of Orkney peat have relatively more carbohydrate derivatives whereas those from Islay have lignin derivatives more prevalent. Overall, the conclusion is that there is a different chemical fingerprint in the peat which will probably make a difference to the overall flavour of the whisky."[10]

Here again background knowledge can shape our appreciation. We may now pay more attention to the particular peatiness of Highland Park and attempt to see if we can pick out heather tones. We might find a Bowmore or other Islay whisky in order to compare them. Second, we can place the whisky as an island whisky—we can expect a different character than we would if we were drinking a Lowland malt or a Canadian rye. There is a wider context that helps guide our appreciation. Finally, we may be more interested in trying Highland Park now, given its shady origins, unique location, and so on; and this interest on our part may well lead to a more focused, careful appreciation of the whisky.

We thus find another reason why we should care about losing traditional methods and distilleries. They shape the whisky we drink and our appreciation of it. The whisky in our glass comes to us with stories attached. When a distillery is closed, many of these stories are put to an end. When a distillery stops malting its own barley, a particular line of a long-standing craft is lost, and the craft itself, as a valuable tradition, becomes still rarer and risks being lost. The resulting whisky loses some of its interest as its method of production shifts to the ordinary and industrial, and the whisky becomes detached from its traditions. Similar concerns would apply to those whiskies produced on Islay but that are now frequently aged entirely on the Scottish mainland (for example, Caol Ila and Lagavulin); such whiskies seem less interesting and genuine as Islay whiskies because they stray from the tradition of being aged by the sea on the island itself.

Still, there is a worry lurking here. Doesn't the closing of a distillery in fact often create a certain mystique and increase interest in its whisky? For example, remaining bottles of Rosebank are rapidly increasing in price, and people are intrigued by the potential that was lost with the closing of Port Ellen. Perhaps it is better that distilleries close—they and their whisky may then come to take on something of a legendary status.

Considering a parallel case applied to species can illuminate where the objection goes wrong. To welcome the closing of a distillery is akin to welcoming a species going extinct. True, the remaining individuals of the species would thus become more rare and interesting. We could imagine remaining members of the species scattered in zoos, unable to breed due to living in captivity. People may well pay more attention to these creatures and pay quite a bit in order to see them. But surely we would not be wise to allow most members of a species to die off in order to make the few remaining creatures more rare and valuable; instead, by securing the population, we will provide for the continued existence (and aesthetic appreciation) of the species for years to come. Similarly, an open distillery is better: it can continue producing bottles of whisky that will continue to provide a great deal of enjoyment to whisky drinkers for years to come; there are other ways for a distillery to build up a reputation and mystique than by being shut down. Any increase in interest due to a tragic early death would typically be outweighed by the loss of longer-term goods.

Another issue to consider is the following: why should we prefer some stories and histories to others? That is, why should we prefer that some malt used in making a whisky has been malted at the distillery, itself, using traditional methods? The key point here is that we can aesthetically appreciate the methods and techniques of whisky making themselves. To hand-turn malt is a long, labor-intensive practice that goes back centuries, requiring a careful eye on the part of malters. A whisky produced with such malt embodies traditions and histories of craftsmanship in a manner unlike other whiskies, adding to the character and context of our appreciation.

We can turn to a final objection. By emphasizing how knowledge of distilleries and their stories can shape our appreciation of a whisky, it seems we might sell short the appreciation of those who lack such knowledge. Couldn't some people who lack all of this background information still better appreciate the taste and character of a given whisky than others with less developed tastes who merely know a lot about whisky? There's a worry of a misguided elitism, where only the views of those with vast stores of knowledge are respected and the appreciation of whisky by the rest of us is dismissed as shallow and uninformed.

Two main points can be made in response to this objection of elitism. First, we are not holding that a person who lacks knowledge of distilleries and methods cannot make any justified assessments of the whiskies she drinks. A person with refined taste can clearly make sensitive assessments, regardless of whether he or she knows much about the stories behind the whiskies. Our claim is only that having such knowledge can enhance and add to our appreciation of whisky. A person can do well enough without this knowledge, but she would be better off having both sensitive tastes *and* a wide range of relevant background knowledge.

Second, the proposal that we seek out information about distilleries does not amount to a demand for us to become annoying whisky snobs. Rather, it is an invitation to discover more and to enhance our appreciation. When we care about something, we naturally try to learn more about it. Environmentalists and others will tend to enjoy learning about regions that interest them—their geology, their flora and fauna. If we are fans of a particular sports team, we typically enjoy learning about the history of the team (past championships, past players, and various myths and lore associated with the team), as well as its current players, coaches, and so on. Of course we can watch a game and appreciate it without such knowledge, but if we know about these things, we can situate a game in a broader context, shaping and enhancing our appreciation of it.

Conclusion

So why should we care about preserving traditional distilleries and methods in whisky making? First, there are the values associated with having a wide range of distilleries. This contributes to an intrinsically valuable variety in the world, and it also contributes to the health of each of the distilleries, much as species need other species in functioning ecosystems in order to flourish. Second is aesthetic value. There is aesthetic value to whisky itself, to the physical structures of distilleries, to the traditional crafts involved, and in the stories of these distilleries. We find parallels in the natural world, with aesthetically interesting creatures engaging in fascinating behaviors, and with species having intriguing evolutionary histories of adaptation and survival. Finally, for both whisky and living things, knowing how a given individual came to be can enhance our appreciation of the individual. By preserving distilleries and whisky-making crafts we preserve these rich histories—and the world and our whiskies are all the more interesting for it.[11]

NOTES

1. Quoted in Brian Ferguson, "Whisky Trade Chokes as Tycoon Targets Youth with 'Alco-pops'," *Scotsman* (April 24, 2008).

2. A couple of disanalogies: individual bottles of whisky do not typically graze upon or hunt other bottles of whisky; also, while a good case can be made that species are constituted entirely by their individual members, distilleries are not constituted by bottles of whisky (there are buildings, workers, owners, and so on).

3. This, and most information about Islay distilleries in this essay, is drawn from Andrew Jefford, *Peat Smoke and Spirit: A Portrait of Islay and Its Whiskies* (London: Headline Books, 2004).

4. Ben Bradley, "The Value of Endangered Species," *Journal of Value Inquiry* 35 (2001): pp. 43–58, p. 51.

5. Gottfried Leibniz, "The Monadology" (1714), in *G. W. Leibniz: Philosophical Texts*, eds. R. S. Woolhouse and Richard Francks, (New York: Oxford University Press, 1998), pp. 267–283, paragraph 58, for example.

6. Jefford, *Peat Smoke and Spirit*, pp. 179–180.

7. Robert Elliot, "Faking Nature," in *Environmental Ethics: Readings in Theory and Application*, 5th ed., ed. Louis Pojman and Paul Pojman (Belmont, CA: Thomson, 2008), pp. 290–297, here pp. 296–297.

8. Michael Jackson, *Whisky: The Definitive World Guide* (London: Dorling Kindersley, 2005), p. 128.

9. Ibid., p. 130.

10. "The 5 Keystones: The Making of the Best Spirit in the World," Highland Park, May, 2008, www.highlandpark.co.uk/distillery/keystones/key2Peat.asp (accessed June 30, 2008).

11. I would like to thank Spencer Kelly and Gretchen von Schwinn for helpful discussion. I especially thank Claire Sigsworth for very helpful comments and for participating in so much painstaking, hands-on research.

UNIT V

Whisky: A Sense of Place

18

Peat and Seaweed
The Expressive Character of Islay Whiskies

Kevin W. Sweeney

I am immensely fond of single malt Scotch whiskies from Islay, one of the islands of the Inner Hebrides; but my wife detests them. She likes other single malt Scotches from other regions of Scotland, made in a different style. For example, she is fond of the subtle yet spicy flavors of a triple-distilled Lowland malt such as Auchentoshan, and she purrs over Highland or Speyside malts that accentuate qualities of honey and heather such as Glenfarclas or the more complex and aromatic Cragganmore. Yet there is something about the nose and the palate of Islay malts that she considers distasteful. What I find so appealing, but she finds so unpleasant, are what have often been referred to as the signature flavors of the Islay single malts. These whiskies are usually identified as having two characteristic flavors: a smoky "peaty" quality and a briny "sea-air" quality—a smell and taste of the ocean.[1]

As a philosopher interested in gustatory experience, I am curious about why I should enjoy the tastes of Islay malts but

my wife finds them repugnant. This might not seem like a
problem if one follows the commonplace view that there is no
disputing about taste. One hears so frequently that taste is a
personal idiosyncratic preference: there is no right or wrong
taste; just my subjective likes and dislikes and your subjective likes and dislikes. Now, I am prepared to accept that
we all have our quirky preferences. I am sure that our tastes
have been shaped to some extent by past experiences. We have
family and cultural traditions that steer our preferences, and
we approach what we ingest from the vantage of our age.
Coffee and some vegetables with a slightly astringent quality,
such as spinach, might seem horrible to a five-year-old but be
quite delicious to an adult.

What interests me in the case of Islay malts is whether one can
decide voluntarily to change one's dislike of them and learn to
enjoy them. We talk about some foods and drinks being acquired
tastes, but can we decide to acquire them? Or is taste completely
noncognitive? That is, are our tastes determined by causes outside of our voluntary control? Or, can we, on some evidentiary
basis, decide that what we had earlier found repugnant, we are
now going to try to like and, what's more, that we have some
hope of being successful in this enterprise.

So, I proposed to my wife that we visit Islay and see whether
her taste in Islay single malt whisky would change.[2] I was curious about whether visiting Islay might give her some grounds
for changing her distaste for these whiskies and encourage her to
enjoy them. I had spent almost a week on Islay the year before,
touring the distilleries, marveling at the island's varied coastline
and landscape, and developing an appreciation for its history.
In proposing to my wife that we go to Islay, I thought that if
she came to appreciate the beauty of the island, its rural life,
and traditional way of making whisky, she might come to like
these malts. My reason for thinking so is that I believe that the
Islay malt signature flavors of peat smoke and briny sea-air—
the qualities that my wife disliked—are expressive qualities evocative of Islay's distinctive ways of distilling whisky and reflective
of rural life on the island. If she visited Islay and warmed to its

beauty and rural traditions, she might come to like the traditionally distilled whiskies with their expressive qualities of peat smoke and sea air.

Of course, I realized that I needed to be careful not to try to impose my tastes on her. I also realized that to some extent she might see this expedition in the form of a vacation as already trying to influence her taste. However, my wife is a strong-willed woman, particularly with regard to her tastes in food and drink. She is not going to be talked or cajoled into liking something that she detests. She trusts her own judgment, and with good reason, since she has a discerning palate and a true appreciation for fine food and drink. Although we have our different gustatory preferences, we share many of the same views about what we ingest. So, we decided to go to Islay. Even if she continued to dislike Islay malts, the island is so beautiful and just the place for a relaxing vacation. She would enjoy going there for a holiday even if she found nothing new or interesting to like in its whiskies.

For a small island (roughly twenty-five miles north to south by twenty miles east to west), Islay produces a lot of whisky. There are seven major distilleries all making single malt whisky for a world market—quite a large concentration for such a small island. There used to be an eighth, Port Ellen, but it has gone out of business.[3] Bunnahabhain and Caol Ila are on the northeastern coast of the island. Laphroaig, Lagavulin, and Ardbeg are on the southern coast close to the town of Port Ellen. Northwest of Port Ellen on the shores of Loch Indaal inlet is Bowmore, in the town of the same name. Directly across Loch Indaal to the west is the revitalized distillery, Bruichladdich.

The Traditional Peat-Smoke Character of Islay Malts

The first distinctive quality associated with Islay malts is their smoky "peaty" nose and taste that lingers on the palate. What gives Islay whiskies this particular character is that they have been distilled from malted or germinated barley that has been dried with smoke from a peat-stoked fire. The peat smoke infuses the malted barley and lingers in the distilled spirit, producing an unforgettable smoky aroma and flavor. The "peaty" quality does not come from using water with a high peat content to make the mash that is then distilled. That is a myth that commentators on Scotch whisky are fond of exploding. One can use water that has run through a peat bog and has high peat content and still make a whisky without a "peaty" quality.[4] Thus, the "peaty" and smoky qualities that one senses in the whisky are intrinsically bound together or combined. One cannot sense a whisky as having a "peaty" quality without also sensing that it has a smoky quality, at least one cannot if one is able to sense both qualities.

Peat is the traditional fuel that Scottish peasants and crofters have used for centuries in their fireplaces to warm their cottages. When it is burned, the peat, or sphagnum moss, which is found in bogs all over Islay and elsewhere in Scotland, produces a smoke with a pronounced acrid smell. When I smell and taste the "peaty" and smoky qualities of Islay malts, I am reminded of the cottages of rural Islay and the smell of peat smoke wafting from them. I am not alone in making this association. In his remarkable book on Islay and its whiskies—a book that all lovers of Islay whiskies will enjoy and learn much from—Andrew Jefford recalls driving around in the hinterlands of Islay, passing a farm-house and smelling peat smoke. He instantly thought of a young Laphroaig with its assertive peaty aroma and taste.[5] The smoky and "peaty" flavors of Islay malts are sensed as bracing and lingering qualities of these whiskies. They make for an assertive character that one associates with traditional rural life in the Hebrides, that is, if one has at least some idea of such a way of life.

A single malt's phenol content, an index of peat in a whisky that gives rise to our sensing a "peaty" quality, can be measured, although phenol levels drop as the whisky ages. The standard way of indicating the phenol content of a newly distilled whisky is in a parts per million (ppm) scale. So, Bruichladdich and Bunnahabhain make whiskies in a "non-peaty" style that has either no phenol or less than 2 ppm. The 12 year old Bowmore has some "peaty" character but a more restrained content at around 10 ppm. Caol Isla produces a single malt in a slightly "peatier" style than Bowmore. However, whiskies start to exhibit a strong "peaty" flavor with phenol levels above 20 ppm. Laphroaig and Ardbeg both have phenol levels in the mid-20s. Recently, Bruichladdich has produced whiskies with phenol levels above 30 ppm. Other distilleries are also experimenting with making assertively or even aggressively "peaty" malts.

The Traditional Briny Sea-Air Character of Islay Malts

The second flavor said to be characteristic of Islay whiskies is often described as having the briny tang of the ocean, a bracing sea-air quality that conjures up the spray of the Atlantic. Sometimes the nose and palate are described as exhibiting a pungent salty seaweed quality by those, like me, who are fond of it, however, that same quality can also be disparaged as having a "medicinal" or "iodine" taste by those less enchanted or even disgusted with it. Again, like the "peaty" quality, this "sea-air" quality is sensed in the whisky as vivid and assertive, and it prompts me to associate it with the spray and surf of the Atlantic, which one is never far from on Islay.

Other critical tasters have noted this same quality and associated it with the ocean. In his recent guide to Scotch whisky, the knowledgeable and judicious critic Michael Jackson discerns a "fresh, sweet, sea-air aroma" in the 12 year old Bunnahabhain.[6] Other Islay malts (for example, some younger Bowmore malts) are also described as having this "sea-air" quality. This tang of the ocean is most pronounced—aggressively so, some would claim—in the young malts of Ardbeg and Laphroaig. Just as the "peaty" quality of these whiskies conjures up rural Scottish life with peat smoke curling up from cottage chimneys, so does the "sea-air" quality associate those whiskies with a place dominated by an ocean climate, such as the islands of the Hebrides. All seven of Islay's major distilleries are on the shoreline, a requirement dictated by nineteenth-century transportation needs. At that time, all supplies had to be delivered by sea to each distillery's own dock, and barrels of whisky were taken from those docks to the mainland by fishing-trawler-size ships called puffers. However, the day of the puffer is no more. Trucks now carry supplies to the distilleries and haul whisky barrels to the mainland by means of ferries that can accommodate them. Yet most of the distilleries continue to maintain warehouses right on the water; barrels of whisky are separated only by yards from the ocean.

When one visits these coastal Islay distilleries, one cannot help but notice the pungent "salty" aromas prevalent there. They fuse together with the "malty" aromas of the fermenting mash and the "spirity" aromas of the barreled whisky. They often blend with the smoky "peaty" aroma of the malted barley, and together they compose the character and style of a particular distillery's single malt whisky. This "salty," "sea-air," or "seaweed" quality is a rather complex combination of sensed elements. Strictly speaking, one does not smell salt; it is only tasted rather than encountered as an aroma or flavor. Of course, that observation will seem surprising, if not flat-out wrong, to many of us who have fond memories of smelling the ocean and believing that we are sensing a "salty" aroma. The "sea-air" quality is most likely a combination of many olfactorily sensed elements (e.g., seaweed and other tidal scents) that one smells on the shoreline.

Is There an Islay Style of Malt Whisky?

These two qualities (peat smoke and a taste of the sea) are frequently identified in Islay malts, and I have referred to them as their aesthetic signature. Nevertheless, not all Islay malts now have both qualities as assertive components. As noted above by Michael Jackson, the 12 year old Bunnahabhain has the "sea-air" quality, yet there is no assertive peaty component that one tastes in the whisky. One of my favorite Islay whiskies, one of the Bruichladdichies, has a very assertive peaty component but little in the way of that "sea-air" quality. It is also true that the peat-smoke and sea-air qualities are not exclusively found in Islay malts. Peat-smoke and sea-air qualities are neither, as philosophers say, necessary nor sufficient conditions for a whisky to be an Islay malt. Other single malts, not distilled on Islay, can have a "peaty" quality. As several commentators have pointed out, Highland Park, a single malt distilled in the Orkney Islands north of the Scottish mainland, has an assertive smoky character.[7] So does Talisker, a single malt distilled on Skye, one of the Inner Hebrides islands to the north of Islay. Distilled not on an island but on the western coast of the Highlands, the single malt, Oban, has both a "peaty" character and a touch of the "seaweed."

I suppose that one might counter this criticism of the claim for there being an exclusive Islay style of malt by proposing that the "peaty" qualities of Highland Park, Talisker, and an Islay malt such as Laphroaig all show an "island" character, distinct from the Lowland and Speyside styles. And, despite its mainland location, Oban is right on the ocean close to the Hebrides. According to this counter proposal, one might say that since there are seven Islay distilleries and only a few other island distilleries, that Islay malts are the most prominent examples of the "island style." Yet, trying to find a distinctive essence of Islay malts exemplified only by whiskies made by the seven distilleries seems a daunting if not futile task.

Other counterexamples to the exclusive Islay style proposal can be found. Both Michael Jackson and Phillip Hills point out that the Speyside single malt Glen Garioch has a "peaty" quality. They also claim that the distillery has a tradition of making whisky with a "peaty" character.[8] So, it is not unheard-of for a Speyside single malt to have a "peaty" character; however, "peatiness" is not a usual quality in Speyside malts.

Another reason for being suspicious of the generalization that all Islay malts have a "peaty" and "sea-air" quality is that within the last twenty years Scottish distilleries, including ones on Islay, have taken to producing whisky in many different styles. For example, Bruichladdich produces a 10-year-old whisky without a "peaty" character. Yet, it also is interested in making several other very heavily peated whiskies, such as the planned Port Charlotte and Octomore. One of my favorite heavily peated malts from Bruichladdich is a limited bottling called the Norrie Campbell Tribute Bottling, which celebrates a well-known Islay peat cutter. Other Islay distilleries have also experimented with a variety of new styles of whisky. In addition, there is now considerable interest in using different kinds of barrels to age single malts. The traditional barrels used for aging had been either American charred oak barrels used for bourbon whiskey or Spanish sherry. Recently, distilleries have started using Madeira, port, rum, and red and white wine—both sweet and dry—barrels from many different regions to age their whiskies. This has led to producing stylistically innovative whiskies with a new range of qualities and finishes.

This new Scottish experimental interest in making single malt is comparable to New World winemakers experimenting in producing wines from several different grape varietals in a wide variety of different styles ranging from dry to sweet. Such experimentation marks a difference from Old World traditions, where in a particular region such as the Côte d'Or in Burgundy, winemakers have made red wine for centuries from a single varietal, pinot noir. The New World interest in experimentation reflects an independence and willingness to take a fresh look at what kinds of wines to produce. Like these New World winemakers, some Scottish distilleries are also taking a new look at the kinds of whiskies they might produce, although some might object that this innovative interest reflects a corporate concern to promote a broader market share at the expense of established tradition.

Despite the innovative interests of Islay distilleries, single malt distilling is an established artisanal craft as much as it is a scientific or technological effort. Single malts are distilled—usually double distilled—in large copper pot stills. No single malt comes from a contemporary column still such as are now used to make grain alcohol in a continuous and efficient manner. Each distillery uses a slightly different shape and configuration of still, has slightly different accessory equipment, and distills its whisky in slightly different ways. Periodically the stills and condensers need repair or replacement. Great care is taken by the distilleries to duplicate, in as exact a way as possible, the particular shape and configuration of the old still or condenser. So, despite the various innovations, such as in the barrels used to age the spirit, there is some effort expended to maintain the distinctive character of that distillery's whisky.[9]

Even with the wide variety of single malts produced in different styles then, there is some reason to believe, despite the many exceptions, that there is an Islay style of single malt with an aesthetic signature of peat-smoke and sea-air flavors. One reason I cling to holding that there is an Islay character of single malt concerns the particular kind of peat found in Islay bogs. Andrew Jefford maintains that Islay peat is particularly phenolic and has a briny and seaweed quality "which you don't find in other sources."[10] Islay malts, which use this peat to malt their barley and try to accentuate "peaty" and "seaweed" qualities, seem distinctive. So, perhaps there is something to the view that Islay malts, at least traditionally, have a "peaty" and seaweed character. Nevertheless, only two distilleries, Bowmore and Laphroaig, malt and peat smoke the barley they use, and even they peat smoke only a portion of their barley in this traditional way. Most of the other distilleries buy their malted and peat-smoked barley from the big malting factory in Port Ellen, which is at least an Islay source. Bruichladdich, in contrast, gets its malted barley from the mainland.

Peat Smoke and Sea Air Are Expressive Qualities of Islay Malts

As I mentioned earlier, I maintain that the peat-smoke and sea-air qualities of Islay single malts are expressive qualities. That is, expressive qualities have a reference to and association with a broader thematic or psychological context. *Peat smoke* and *sea air* expressively refer to or are associated with the island character and traditional way of life on Islay. Granted, there are new and innovative styles of whiskies, but these qualities are indicative of an older distilling tradition on the island. As expressive qualities, peat smoke and sea air are experienced differently than a quality such as having a "citrusy" or "lemony" flavor. A "lemon" quality in a Scotch whisky has no broader reference to the place of the whisky's origin; the quality is just experienced as an interesting and usually pleasurable quality in its own right. The whisky was not produced in a citrus-producing region, and the flavor does not evoke associations with such a location. It is merely experienced as an identifiable flavor, one similar in some respects to what we experience when we smell or taste a lemon. However, peat smoke and sea air are not simply pleasurable in their own right, at least to some consumers. They evoke the originating location of the whisky. They are *expressive qualities* because they express in a gustatory mode something traditionally distinctive about Islay.

Recently, there has been a comparable interest in the expressive qualities of wines. There has been an interest in qualities indicative of a wine's *terroir*, its vineyard location, the total nurturing environment for the grapes in the wine. For some, the notion of *terroir* is a problematic notion: can one taste location in a wine? A skeptic might say that one can taste fruit, tannin, and crisp acidity, but can one taste a wine's location? To the skeptic one should reply that qualities indicative of *terroir* are expressive qualities. Discovering qualities of a wine's *terroir* allows one to connect the wine to a particular location—a particular region or even vineyard. Thus, sensing the "grassy" and "stony" middle range of a white Sancerre connects the wine to the hills of the eastern Loire, where the wine was made. The acidic tang of a Beaujolais is indicative of the granite hills north of Lyon, where the wine's gamay grapes were grown.[11]

One might say, and some commentators of Scotch single malts do, that the peat-smoke and sea-air qualities are indicative of a *terroir*. In visiting Islay with my wife, I was curious if experiencing the rural beauties of this island with its dramatic vistas of sea and sky, becoming familiar with some of the traditional ways of life on Islay, and tasting the whiskies at the distilleries and local pubs, she would come to appreciate the island and enjoy the qualities of the whisky indicative of that *terroir*. Would visiting Islay allow her to make the connection between the peat-smoke and ocean qualities and the location and traditions that gave rise to those qualities? Can tasting the *terroir* in an Islay malt allow one to develop an appreciation and enjoyment of the whisky? Or, is one naïve to think that if an individual finds a food or drink disgusting or repugnant, identifying the unpleasant taste with a place would make any difference at all in changing one's taste? Does finding out where an unpleasant smell comes from, or finding out about a culture whose food one finds nasty, make one inclined to feel any differently about it, or even encourage one to like it?

Carolyn Korsmeyer has investigated occasions in which people who had previously found a food to be disgusting changed their taste and learned to enjoy it.[12] She notices that a taste for or enjoyment of "high" (haut goût) meats can be developed. The smell of almost rotting meat to many is quite unpleasant, even disgusting. Nevertheless, people do learn to cultivate a taste for "high" meats. Yet how does one go about trying to change one's taste for what one had earlier held to be repugnant? Are the grounds for developing such a taste socially induced or emotionally instigated by cultural values? To what extent can one voluntarily decide to develop a liking for what one had earlier found to be unpleasant or disgusting? Twenty years ago I would have thought it doubtful that popular American taste would find sushi, and especially raw-fish sashimi, to be delicious or even appetizing. However, in the United States, sushi is now very popular. Of course, advertisers have long realized that tastes in food can be created or swayed in new directions.

Like everyone else with whom I am acquainted, I grew up disliking certain foods. Like most people, my tastes in food changed as I grew older; however, one dislike of a food lasted into adulthood. I disliked the taste of eggplant, although I thought the fresh vegetable, with its dark lustrous purple color and sensuous shape, looked beautiful. My dislike of eggplant, I realized, was probably a holdover from some disagreeable childhood experience with it, which I had now forgotten about. It disturbed me that I was not in control of my tastes, but that some experience in childhood controlled and determined my distaste for the vegetable. Other people whose palate I respected liked eggplant; why shouldn't I like it? So, I resolved to learn to like eggplant. It took me a summer to do so, but at the end of the summer I had learned to like eggplant, and like it just as much as other vegetables that were favorites of mine.

Consequently, I believe that taste can be based on a cognitive attitude. Within certain biologically determined limits, we can choose to explore and enjoy what we ingest. Just as we can attempt to form beliefs by critically examining and trying to separate the good from the dubious basis for belief, so can we try to set aside our past alimentary biases and uncritically formed gustatory preferences, and taste with a fresh and open mind, giving what we taste a "fair hearing." There is great pleasure to be had in freshly encountering and objectively approaching all sorts of foods and drinks. Nevertheless, I do realize that often one struggles to achieve this clarity and objectivity of taste.[13]

Was There a Change of Taste Because of the Visit to Islay?

My wife and I visited Islay, and it was as beautiful as I remembered. We drove the back roads of the island, visited the hamlets, hiked in the hinterlands, and walked by the seashore. Along with the smells encountered visiting the distilleries, we became well acquainted with the pungent aromas of peat smoke and filled our lungs with the ocean air. What happened? Was my wife's taste for Islay single malts transformed? Did she exclaim, "The 'scales' have fallen from my tongue. I now realize that I have been completely mistaken about the taste of these whiskies." Hardly!

Her taste in whisky has changed, but only modestly. The principal change has resulted from her separating the peat-smoke quality in a whisky from the taste of "iodine," as she calls it. In her earlier experiences with Islay malts, she reacted to both qualities as a single complex flavor. Encountering the peat smoke in the villages, but especially visiting the Bowmore distillery and seeing and smelling their peat-stoked fire and smoke-dried malted barley, made a positive impression on her. Now the peat smoke seems an emblem of the resourceful, independent Islay people. She has started to enjoy some single malts with a moderate amount of "peaty" quality like Talisker and the less "peaty" malts from Bruichladdich.

Changes in taste often evolve in small increments. Perhaps in the future she will come to like malts such as Bowmore and Caol Isla, which have a slightly higher phenol content. She still objects to strong "peaty" flavors, though, and she continues to find repugnant the assertive ('assaulting' is her term) "sea-air" (iodine) qualities in malts like Ardbeg and Laphroaig. I suspect that she associates that quality with some early disagreeable childhood memory. Instead of identifying the quality with "seaweed" or "sea-spray" as encountered on Islay, she continues to describe it as "medicinal," and—when the quality is especially assertive—she says it smells like old bandages. Yet when asked to sum up her vacation experience, she smiles and says: "Surprised by peat—and other pleasures of the Islay spirit."

NOTES

1. I will use the term 'flavor' in the way that it has come to be used in studies of gustatory experience and alimentation. Qualities that emerge by being sensed by both smell and taste are referred to as "flavors." Very little of what we orally ingest is only tasted; we both smell and taste most of what we ingest. Of course, taste and smell are not the only modalities we employ in experiencing what we ingest.
2. My wife, Elizabeth Winston, who also teaches at the University of Tampa, good-naturedly participated in the project and advised me on writing this essay.
3. There is now a new cottage industry distillery, Kilchoman, which plans to release a single malt in a limited production in 2009. The island of Jura, separated from Islay only by a strait, also has a distillery, the Isle of Jura. While resembling Islay malts, Isle of Jura malts have none of the assertive or pronounced character of some Islay whiskies.
4. See the discussion in Phillip Hills, *Appreciating Whisky: The Connoisseur's Guide to Nosing, Tasting, and Enjoying Scotch* (Glasgow: HarperCollins, 2000), p. 42.
5. Andrew Jefford, *Peat Smoke and Spirit: A Portrait of Islay and Its Whiskies* (London: Headline Books, 2004), p. 337.
6. Michael Jackson, *Michael Jackson's Complete Guide to Single Malt Scotch: A Connoisseur's Guide to the Single Malt Whiskies of Scotland*, 5th ed. (Philadelphia: Running Press, 2004), p. 159.
7. Ibid., pp. 309–310.
8. Hills, *Appreciating Whisky*, p. 42; Jackson, *Michael Jackson's Complete Guide to Single Malt Scotch*, p. 225.
9. For a full account of Islay distilling practices, see Jefford, *Peat Smoke and Spirit*, pp. 5–25.
10. Ibid., p. 197.
11. For further discussion of the notion of *terroir*, see Jamie Goode, *The Science of Wine: From Vine to Glass* (Berkeley: University of California Press, 2005), pp. 25–34.
12. Carolyn Korsmeyer, "Delightful, Delicious, Disgusting," *Journal of Aesthetics and Art Criticism* 60.3 (2002): pp. 217–225; reprinted in Fritz Allhoff and Dave Monroe, eds., *Food and Philosophy*

(Malden: Blackwell, 2007), pp. 145–161. See also Carolyn Korsmeyer and Barry Smith, "Visceral Values: Aurel Kolnai on Disgust," the introductory essay to Aurel Kolnai, *On Disgust*, eds., Carolyn Korsmeyer and Barry Smith (Chicago: Open Court, 2004), pp. 1–25.

13. For further discussion about overcoming repugnance in taste, see Aurel Kolnai, "The Problem of Overcoming Disgust," *On Disgust*, eds. Korsmeyer and Smith, pp. 86–90.

19

Japanese Whisky

"It's Called Queen George, and It's More Bitched Up Than Its Name"

Chris Bunting

The first record we have of foreigners tasting Japanese whisky goes back to a curious set of events in 1918. The port of Hakodate, on Japan's northern island of Hokkaido, was an isolated outpost of Japan's growing empire. The British woman traveler Isabella L. Bird had passed by a few years before and found it a "cold-blooded-looking grey town, straggling up a steep hillside." The dominant element, she noted, was the wind. Every roof was "hodden doun" with as many stones as its householder could muster to keep the structure from flying off in the gales.[1]

Foreigners were not unknown. Hakodate was an important fueling station for ships in the northern seas. But when two gargantuan U.S. military transport ships sailed unannounced into harbor in September 1918, Hakodate's residents might have been forgiven a jolt of panic.

The boats were full of American soldiers chosen for one of the more obscure and unsuccessful adventures in U.S. military history. As the butchery in the trenches of Europe entered its final awful weeks, this forgotten expeditionary force was being shipped to Siberia, where it would spend the next two years fighting cold, disease, and both sides of the Russian civil war.

Hakodate itself had nothing to fear from the seasick soldiers. Japan and the United States were on the same side at the time. At least one waterfront entrepreneur seems to have overcome her shock quickly enough to have recruited a foreigner with a sense of humor, perhaps one of the first soldiers off the ships, to write a sign in English for the doughboys given shore leave. The sign read:

> Notice!! Having lately been refitted and preparations having been made to supply those who give us a look-up, with Worst of Liquors and Food at a reasonable price, and served by the Ugliest Female Savants that can be Procured. This establishment cannot boast of a proprietor, but is carried on by a Japanese lady whose ugliness would stand out even in a crowd. The Cook, when his face is washed, is considered the best looking of the company.[2]

The place was soon packed, as were all the other drinking holes and brothels in Hakodate, and it was at that moment, for the first time in recorded history, that a large group of Western consumers got to try Japanese whisky.

Major Samuel L. Johnson, who had been sent ashore with the enlisted men, was soon back on the transports reporting chaotic scenes to his fellow officers: "All the cheap bars have Scotch whiskey [sic] made in Japan," he said. "If you come across any, don't touch it. It's called Queen George, and it's more bitched up than its name. It must be eighty-six per cent corrosive sublimate proof, because 3,500 enlisted men were stinko fifteen minutes after they got ashore. I never saw so many get so drunk so fast."[3]

Captain Kenneth Roberts, who was part of a team sent to round up the paralytic soldiery, recalled: "Intoxicated soldiers seemed to have the flowing qualities of water, able to seep through doorways, down chimneys, up through floors. When we slowly edged a score of khaki-clad tosspots from a dive and started them toward the ships, then turned to see if we had overlooked anyone, the room would unbelievably be filled with unsteady doughboys, sprung from God knows where, drunkenly negotiating for the change of American money or the purchase of juss one more boll of Queen George."[4]

The American ships left Hakodate as soon as the last drunk could be thrown aboard, and that is the last we hear of that gloriously cross-dressed brand Queen George in the annals of Japanese whisky history. We can get some sense of the stuff if we discard any notion of traditional distillation. Olive Checkland describes a typical manufacturing process in this period as involving the "judicious mixing of a wide range of alcohol, sugar, perfumes, spices and flavourings."[5] It seems to have been common for these unstable concoctions to suddenly explode while sitting on shop shelves. Indeed, the young chemist Masataka Taketsuru, of whom we will hear more later, is supposed to have made his early reputation by producing ersatz whiskies that did not blow up!

Everything about these early Japanese whiskies was fake. Bottles that survive to us all show what might charitably be described as a playful relationship with authenticity: Holy whisky proclaimed itself a "Special Quality Old Scotch Whisky" that was "distilled and bottled" by the Eigashima company in Japan. Lady Brand, displaying what looks like a European operatic diva against a backdrop of the hills of the Lowlands of Scotland, was also an "Old Scotch Whisky," and it comes as no surprise that the Rock Crystal brand "supplied to the market of the world" by Tojima and Company of Japan, was a "Very Fine Old Scotch Whisky," too. The one phrase that is a constant feature on these bottles is a portentous declaration "Registered Trade Mark," usually in a font at least as large as the brand name itself. Even that most legalistic of phrases seems to have been grist for the mill: part of a ragbag of facsimile symbols thrown together to create a playful illusion of the real thing.[6]

Bar Zoetrope, Tokyo, 2008

Fast forward ninety years and Atsushi Horigami, the landlord of Bar Zoetrope in Tokyo's bustling Shinjuku district, lovingly pours a glass of Japanese 20 year old Yoichi single malt whisky. It is the best single malt in the world.

That overreaching claim is not authorial hyperbole. In April 2008, at the World Whisky Awards in Glasgow, the Yoichi beat the best that Scotland or any other country had to offer in a tasting by some of the world's top judges. The news earned banner headlines. The *Sun* newspaper in London announced breathlessly: "Scotland has been overtaken by Japan as the maker of the world's best whisky." The *Times* of London could not resist a pun or two: "Like English wine, it has suffered from the taint of inauthenticity and has been the butt of condescending jokes. Now Japanese whisky has finally scotched all criticism by being voted the best in the world, ahead of its Highland rivals." Japan had won not only the top single malt prize but also the award for the best blended whisky in the world, which went to a 30-year-old Hibiki blend.

The Japanese coup was not a surprise. Ever since a 10 year old Yoichi whisky won the Best of the Best Award in an international tasting organized by *Whisky Magazine* in 2001, the country's two top producers, Nikka (which makes Yoichi) and Suntory (distillers of Hibiki) as well as smaller Japanese brands such as Fuji Gotemba, Ichiro's Malt, and Karuizawa have regularly been among the medals at world tastings. An award ceremony that does not include a Japanese maker has become the exception.

Japanese whisky bars have also moved on considerably since the days of ugly "female savants" and comely cooks. Taylor Smisson, a man who has tried more than four thousand single malts in Tokyo's bars (and has the tasting notes to prove it), describes the Japanese capital as a "single malt drinker's heaven on earth." Smisson says: "It probably has the world's largest selection of Scotch single malt whiskies to choose from, with over 50 bars with selections of over 100 malts each and several with over 500."[7]

These bars, perched in the high-rise entertainment districts of Japan's big cities, can be disorienting spaces. On the street outside, crowds of baggy pants– and miniskirt-wearing young revelers barge shoulders with sozzled salarymen; but open the door to Bar Argyll in Shinjuku or the Crane in Ikebukuro and you are in a sort of whisky library of record, with hundreds of expressions neatly stacked around the walls. It is easy to forget you are in Japan, although Japan is probably the only place where you could have the experience. The barmen wear impeccable tartans or formal suits. The shelves are lined with evocative place names from half a world away—Brora, Caol Ila, Ardbeg, Knockdhu.

You could spend months exploring this rich drinking culture, but if I had to recommend only one bar to a visitor to Tokyo, it would be Bar Zoetrope. It specializes in Japanese whiskies—250 of them at the last count—and its style is unique. While other Japanese whisky bars attempt to transport you to an imagined space in Scotland not fundamentally dissimilar to that played out on bottles of Queen George and Lady Brand, Zoetrope plasters one of its walls with a continuously played loop of old silent movies. The place's name comes from a nineteenth-century device that prefigured motion pictures. Horigami keeps one under his bar for anyone who is interested: a cylinder perforated by slits, allowing the viewer to see drawings of a jumping frog arrayed around the inside of the drum. As the zoetrope spins, the rapid succession of images framed by the slits produces an illusion of the frog leaping.

There is nothing to remind the drinker of the old country at Zoetrope. There are no sporrans or maps of the Highlands. The names on the bottles have no Gaelic in them: Yoichi, Miyagikyo, Yamazaki, Chichibu. And yet, no modern whisky expert would contest that the 20 year old Yoichi that Horigami serves his customers is an authentic Scotch-style single malt whisky, as authentic as anything produced by

Royal Lochnagar or Glen Mhor. The addition of the word 'style' to that description is a nod to the commonsense view that a whisky made in Japan is not, strictly speaking, Scotch, but for all intents and purposes it is. For example, while American and Irish whiskeys are typically judged in separate categories from Scottish single malts in international competitions, Japanese whisky is almost always categorized as part of the Scotch tradition. In some contemporary whisky guides, the Japanese distilleries are listed almost as if they constituted a new Scottish whisky region, somewhat to the east of Speyside.

How did we get to this odd situation? For the answer, we have to go back to a remarkable journey begun a few months after the Americans' encounter with the redoubtable Queen George.

Glasgow, 1919

On Thursday April 17, 1919, Masataka Taketsuru, the promising young chemist with a reputation for making nonexplosive fake whisky, boarded a Caledonian Railway train heading north out of Glasgow's Buchanan Street Station. He must have made a strange sight: a lone Japanese traveler mumbling traditional songs from his homeland to calm himself as he traveled toward whisky's promised land. He changed at Perth and took the North Highland Railway to Elgin, at the heart of the world-famous Speyside whisky region.[8]

Taketsuru had been in Scotland barely five months, carrying out orders from his bosses in Japan to find out as much as he could about the drink they were trying to copy. He had prepared himself with courses in chemistry at Glasgow University and the Royal Technical College, but the journey north to Elgin marked his first attempt to access the centuries-old distilling lore guarded by Scotland's distilleries. It must have been a nerve-racking experience. He was alone, a twenty-five-year-old chemist from what was then regarded as a developing country. He had brought no money or promises of lucrative partnerships to open the doors of the Scottish distillers, just an imperfect command of English and a well-thumbed copy of *The Manufacture of Spirit as Conducted in the Distilleries of the United Kingdom* by J. A. Nettleton. The first person he called on in Elgin was Nettleton himself. It seems to have been a disappointing interview. The author asked for a large sum of money for his help. Instead, despite warnings from Nettleton that getting an apprenticeship would cost a small fortune, Taketsuru began knocking on the doors of the Speyside distilleries. He was rewarded when the Longmorn Distillery, three miles south of Elgin, agreed to give him five days' practical experience.

It would be easy to portray Taketsuru's time in Scotland as an audacious industrial espionage mission. In fact, it appears Taketsuru was perfectly straightforward about his purpose. The distillery workers, for their part, went out of their way to share their knowledge. Taketsuru was allowed to keep detailed notes of all he saw. In early summer 1919, Taketsuru spent a further three weeks working and taking a similarly precise record at Bo'ness Distillery in West Lothian, where he learned about grain whisky. He secured an extended five-month "apprenticeship" in the Hazelburn Distillery at Campbeltown the next year.

On his return to Japan in 1920, Taketsuru was frustrated at first. His employer, Settsu Shuzo, was reluctant to invest in a proper distilling operation and put him in charge of an unchanged ersatz spirits production line. Soon, however, another businessman named Shinjiro Torii, the founder of the empire that would become Suntory, heard of Taketsuru's expertise, and the two set up Yamazaki Distillery near Osaka in 1924. Yamazaki's first whisky hit the shelves in 1929 under the brand name Shirofuda ("White Label"), which is still sold today.

In 1934, Taketsuru set up his own business, which was to become Suntory's great rival Nikka. He bought land at Yoichi on Hokkaido, and that distillery's first whisky was released in 1940. There are all sorts of interesting byroads to be explored in Japanese whisky history. For instance, the role of Japanese military demand in helping the whisky companies find their feet in the 1930s and 1940s is intriguing (the Imperial Japanese Navy drank whisky like the British Navy drank rum. During the war, Yoichi was designated as an Imperial Navy installation).[9]

After 1945, whisky managed to reinvent itself as the glamorous drink of the occupiers and, later, of the business class that established Japan as a world economic power. With protectionist policies limiting foreign imports to the elite, the string of domestic distilleries that are now stunning the world with their single malts were set up to slake a raging domestic thirst for a more ordinary sort of drink sold for a few yen a shot. In 1956, the Karuizawa Distillery came on line, and between 1969 and 1973, the opening of Miyagikyo (Nikka), Fuji Gotemba (Kirin), and Suntory's Hakushu Distillery, the biggest distillery in the world at the time, significantly increased productive capacity.

Throughout this development, spanning a period of militaristic isolation, a devastating world war, a humiliating occupation, and a dizzying economic resurgence, Japanese whisky stayed remarkably loyal to its Scottish lineage. There have been experiments with Japanese bourbons but, by and large, Japanese whisky has always tried to be Scotch, using Scotch methods and ingredients. The product has not always been as pure as it is now. In the 1960s (when, incidentally, Jean-Paul Sartre and Simone de Beauvoir developed a taste for the stuff), Japanese blended whiskies often contained neutral spirit rather than grain whisky[10] and there are accounts of significant amounts of wine being found in some bottles.[11] However, throughout this period, hundreds of distillery workers were sent to follow in the footsteps of Taketsuru to learn their trade in Scotland, building a reserve of knowledge that is now serving the industry well.

Following the collapse of the bubble economy in the early 1990s, the Japanese mass whisky market has declined precipitously. A younger generation has looked elsewhere for its drink—notably, the indigenous distilled spirit shōchū—and the old protectionist rules have gone, allowing reasonably priced and extremely high-quality Scotch onto Japan's supermarket shelves. It is in this crucible that the Japanese producers have been forced to develop the excellent products that are now receiving international attention. The fourth largest whisky industry in the world (behind the United States, Scotland, and Canada, but producing three times more whisky than Ireland in 1999),[12] Japan is now competing fiercely for a shrinking but increasingly sophisticated domestic market and an emerging export market that demands the highest quality.

What Is Authentic Whisky?

That is a historical account of how Japan has become an accepted and "authentic" producer of Scotch-style whisky: a combination of historical circumstance and lots of hard work has produced a product that is within the Scotch tradition and rivals the home country's spirits in quality. However, this same issue of authenticity can be approached from a more conceptual angle. Unfortunately, this means hacking our way into the thicket of jargon that surrounds much contemporary theory about commodity culture, but I think it offers some intriguing insights into the future development of the global whisky business.

In the late 1960s, Jean Baudrillard developed the idea that modern commodities could not simply be understood as physical products that are valued by consumers because of their practical usefulness (for instance, a bottle of Coke might be practically useful because it quenches the buyer's thirst).[13] The meanings attached to modern commodities go far beyond their practical use, Baudrillard said, and often have very little connection to the physical product itself. For example, a bottle of Coke might be desired as much for its connection to the youth and attractiveness of the young people used in its marketing campaign (something not related to the drink as a physical object) as it is desired for its taste (something clearly related to the drink as a physical object).

It is a simple enough observation with some intuitive appeal to anyone with experience of modern consumerism: a space alien would find it impossible to understand what a bottle of Suntory's premium Hibiki 30 year old whisky ($800 US) *means* to its consumers, indeed, to get any accurate idea of what it is at all, if he were to adopt a simple model that the words and images associated with the commodity (for example, the advertisements, the brand, the shape of the bottle, and so on) referred *only* to the physical product and to its usefulness. According to Baudrillard, the Hibiki brand has to be understood as something with no reliable connection to the physical product itself. The value given to it in the marketplace may be more closely related to exclusive images ascribed to it in marketing campaigns, to nostalgia associated with the brand's history, or simply to its high price (creating a valuable sense of exclusivity). It might be desired because it reinforces its consumer's identities as prosperous and discerning citizens, rather than for anything unique about its taste. In other words, words and images are related to more than the physical things to which they refer.

In Sophia Coppola's film *Lost in Translation*, the point is neatly illustrated when the main character, a foreign actor named Bob Harris (played by Bill Murray), who is doing a television commercial for Hibiki, is harangued by the director for failing to understand the nature of the product. At no point does the director talk about the whisky. Instead, at the height of his fury, he screams (in Japanese): "Cut, cut, cut. Don't you understand? You playing dumb? This is Suntory's Hibiki, the most expensive of all Suntorys. Give a higher class feel! This isn't an everyday whisky." The director instructs the bemused Bob Harris: "You're not just talking about whisky. You understand?"[14]

In his later thought, Baudrillard went further, not merely separating words and images from the physical product, but arguing that in the hyperreal world of modern capitalism, the meanings associated with a product (e.g., Hibiki's "higher class feel") have become not just part of the meanings but moreover that they have become *the thing* that was being bought. The nature of the physical product is no longer a determinant of its value to the consumer. The words and images are the commodity. Baudrillard wrote in "Simulacra and Simulations" (1981): "The age of simulation thus begins with a liquidation of all referentials—worse: by their artificial resurrection in systems of signs. . . . It is no longer a question of imitation, nor of reduplication, nor even of parody. It is rather a question of substituting signs for the real for the real itself."[15] We can use a simile to try to sum up Baudrillard's vision and it is conveniently close to hand: the zoetrope after which Atsushi Horigami named his bar. Just like the viewer of a zoetrope, the contemporary consumer is bombarded by a constant succession of interrelated signs and images that overwhelm her ability to process them individually, constructing a world in which the simulated image floats free from reality.[16]

How does this account of an increasingly phantasmagoric consumer culture, in which the Nike logo on the side of a cheaply produced training shoe massively increases its market value, fit with what we know of the development of Japanese whisky? Curiously, our narrative seems to have traveled in roughly the opposite direction from Baudrillard's account. We saw that in 1918, in a small market in which tiny local producers predominated, everything about Japanese whisky was a simulation. The Japanese economy at the time was a cornucopia of the bogus and the phony: of Japanese-produced Lea & Perrins sauces,[17] of exquisite perfumes made in "Fulorida" in the United States, and of fine whiskies made in "Leith, London."[18]

The point here is that what was driving this early sham-consumerism was the sign rather than the product itself. These fakes got their value not from the exploding liquids inside their bottles but by reference to symbols of authenticity and desirability in the market. Baudrillard sees late capitalism as being characterized by a substitution of "signs for the real for the real itself," but there are aspects to the nascent Japanese market for whisky that are suggestive of this. As we have seen, "Holy" whisky's label described itself as "Special Quality Old Scotch Whisky" and immediately went on to proudly declare in large script that it was "distilled and bottled" by the Eigashima Company in Japan.

Since 1918, Japanese whisky, and the whisky market in general, has increasingly strictly defined its commodity in terms of its product. In Baudrillard's terms, rather than seeing the sign floating free from its referent and coming to embody the commodity itself, the whisky market has connected its branding, marketing and the discourse about desirable whisky more and more tightly to the physical product. Although single malt whiskies, defined as malt whiskies made at a single distillery, have been around for centuries, the current fascination with single malt whisky, which has come to dominate the premium end of the Scotch whisky market (though it does not dominate the overall market in sales), is a relative novelty. It tells drinkers precisely which factory made their whisky and what its ingredients were.

The trend has been toward an even closer definition of each bottle's contents. The year a whisky was laid down, the history of the barrel in which it was aged (e.g., sherry cask, bourbon cask, etc.), what wood the barrel was made from, the size of the barrel, and any barrel in which it was finished are not only recorded on labels but can define the marketing of a whisky. Single cask whiskies not only specify the distillery but the number of the casks they come from. In fact, the premium whisky market has become so obsessed with these manufacturing details that a headline-grabbing single malt released by Nikka in 2007 sold itself almost entirely on the basis that it had been distilled in a Coffey still,[19] which is usually associated with grain whisky and is technically different from the more common pot still.

The fanciful evocations of imagined highland landscapes and glamorous consumers that adorned early Japanese whisky bottles have largely disappeared from their modern single malt successors, replaced by relatively plain labels prominently carrying the name of the distillery in Japanese characters. Some of the single cask whiskies use labels that look more like factory classification stickers than branded marketing.

Have we stumbled across a counter example to Baudrillard's vision of an increasingly abstracted, hyperreal commodity culture? It is not quite as simple as that. Theorists of contemporary consumerism, including Baudrillard, have long noted a preoccupation with authenticity in modern luxury markets and a tendency in such markets to define authenticity very closely.

Arjun Appadurai wrote:

> In a general way, we can suggest that with luxury commodities, . . . as the distance between consumers and producers is shrunk, so the issue of exclusivity gives way to the issue of authenticity. That is, under pre-modern conditions, the long distance movement of precious commodities entailed costs that made the acquisition of them in itself a marker of exclusivity. . . . The only way to preserve the function of these commodities in the prestige economies of the modern West is to complicate the criteria of authenticity. The very complicated competition and collaboration between "experts" from the art world, dealers, producers, scholars and consumers is part of the political economy of taste in the contemporary West.[20]

Although Appadurai's focus on the West seems a little outdated in a world in which a prosperous East is consuming authentic products from Scotland, his point about the importance of experts in vouchsafing tightly defined concepts of authenticity is persuasive when applied to whisky. While many blended whisky brands have lost market share, a bevy of magazines and international awards have been prospering mightily from the rise of single malt whiskies in consumer consciousness. For the average Japanese consumer in the 1980s, finding the best whisky in a shop was a simple matter of reaching for the most expensive bottle of Johnnie Walker. Now, a complex matrix of connoisseurship, weighing up the relative merits of hundreds of different single malt and single cask bottlings from dozens of distilleries, must be negotiated.

Baudrillard observed that premodern artists routinely used collaborators to help paint their canvases but that ideas of authenticity associated with the rise of modern art criticism changed this: "[Previously] the act of painting, and so the signature as well, did not bear the same mythological insistence on authenticity—that moral imperative to which modern art is dedicated and by which it becomes modern."[21] Similarly, identification with a single distillery has become a touchstone among many whisky drinkers and the expert gaze associated with the rise of this concept of *terroir*[22] now peers into minute details of the manufacturing process.

There is a paradox here. At the height of this obsessive focus on authenticity, at a time when that concept has never been more codified and more closely identified with particular localities in Scotland, we have seen Japanese whisky carve its odd status as a new and "authentic" region producing Scotch-style whisky. The idea of single malt seems so tied to the shorelines of Scotland and yet it is largely through the success of its single malts in international tastings that Japan has asserted its authenticity.

Is this an anomaly? It may not be. By so tightly defining what it means to be an authentic Scotch-style whisky: specifying the ingredients it must contain, focusing the attention of the consumer on specific locations (rather than on the much vaguer and more defensible blended Scotch brand names that the Japanese were vainly trying to imitate in 1918), and, most important, by allowing a priesthood of experts to be built around this complex idea of what is authentic, the Scots may have made top-quality Scotch whisky production portable. The consumer, taught to focus not on a familiar brand but on a highly codified set of criteria for authenticity (e.g., malted barley only, a single distillery, long aging, and so on) and to listen to experts extolling certain abstracted qualities in the whisky, can be forgiven for concluding that it hardly matters whether the whisky is made in Hokkaido or Speyside. Importantly, the expert tasters lose nothing by opening the door to the newcomer. In fact, they may gain attention for themselves and the publications that publicize their opinions, while strengthening their claims to objectivity.

Of course, the conceptual shift that has permitted Japanese whiskies to be crowned the best Scotch-style whiskies in the world in 2008 is not limited to Japanese whisky. There is now no bar in principle to authentic single malts being made in, say, China or Russia, both of which have expanding markets for Scotch. If something is feasible in principle, capitalism has a way of making it happen in practice: in May 2008, the *Moscow Times* reported that Dagestan had opened its first Scotch-style whisky distillery.[23] Don't laugh. They would have laughed at Yoichi in 1934.

NOTES

1. Isabella L. Bird, *Unbeaten Tracks in Japan* (Tokyo: ICG Muse, 2000), pp. 208–209.
2. Robert L. Willett, *Russian Sideshow: America's Undeclared War 1918–20* (Dulles, VA: Brassey's US, 2004), p. 168.
3. Ibid.
4. Ibid., p. 169.
5. Olive Checkland, *Japanese Whisky, Scotch Blend* (Edinburgh: Scottish Cultural Press, 1998), pp. 31–32.
6. These references to bottle labels are from photographs in the author's collection.
7. Chris Bunting, "To the Whiskopolis," Nonjatta, http://nonjatta .blogspot.com/2008/02/took-bit-of-getting-used-to-but-this.html (accessed June 10, 2008).
8. Details of Taketsuru's Scottish journey and his return to Japan are from Olive Checkland, *Japanese Whisky, Scotch Blend*, pp. 1–56.

9. For discussion, see Chris Bunting, "Japanese Whisky and War (I)," Nonjatta, http://nonjatta.blogspot.com/2007/12/japanese-whisky-and-world-war.html (accessed June 3, 2008).

10. Inge Russell, *Whisky: Technology, Production and Marketing* (Boston: Academic Press, 2003), p. 20.

11. Nihon Shohisha Renmei, *Honmono no sake wo* (Tokyo: Sanichi Shobo, 1982), p. 128.

12. John Wakely, *The International Spirits Industry* (Cambridge: Woodhead, 2000), p. 73.

13. Mark Poster, *Introduction to Jean Baudrillard—Selected Writings* (Palo Alto, CA: Stanford University Press, 1988), pp. 1–6.

14. Translation based on a discussion at http://forum.wordreference.com, August 2005 (accessed June 30, 2008).

15. Poster, *Introduction to Jean Baudrillard—Selected Writings*, 167.

16. Jonathan Crary argues that the zoetrope and similar devices helped create a modern, subjective observer increasingly engaged in an abstracted visual world with no certain connection to "objective" reality. For further discussion, see Jonathan Crary, *Techniques of the Observer: On Vision and Modernity in the 19th Century* (Cambridge, MA: MIT Press, 1992), pp. 100–113; p. 149.

17. See discussion in the *Japan Weekly Chronicle* (March 8, 1923): p. 316.

18. See discussion in the *Japan Weekly Chronicle* (April 19, 1923): p. C138.

19. See, for example, discussion at Asahi Beer Web site, www.asahibeer.co.jp/news/2007/1012.html (accessed June 30, 2008).

20. Arjun Appadurai, *The Social Life of Things: Commodities in Cultural Perspective* (Cambridge: Cambridge University Press, 1986), p. 44.

21. Jean Baudrillard, *For a Critique of the Political Economy of the Sign* (St. Louis, MO: Telos Press, 1981), p. 103.

22. For an excellent discussion on whether the idea of *terroir* in whisky itself has some mythological elements see "Terroir-ism," originally posted on scotchblog.com.

23. See Dmitry Solovyov, "Dagestani Firm Tries Hand at Whisky," *Moscow Times*, www.themoscowtimes.com/article/1009/42/362533.htm (accessed June 3, 2008).

Whisky and Culture
From Islay to Speyside

Susie Pryor and Andrew Martin

The proper drinking of Scotch whisky is more than
indulgence: it is a toast to civilization, a tribute to the
continuity of culture, a manifesto of man's determination
to use the resources of nature to refresh mind and body
and enjoy to the full the senses with which he has been
endowed.

—*David Daiches*

The pub at the Port Askaig Hotel on the Isle of Islay is typical of
port pubs. With its glossy wooden bar, small fireplace, and
whisky-inspired furnishings, it offers the dark, dependable
intimacy of the traditional Scottish pub. A small window
offers a view of the bright, quiet bustle of port activity outside.
A small line of unmanned cars queue patiently for the ferry
to the neighboring Isle of Jura. Their drivers, presumably,
are drinking in the salty air or picking up necessities in the
small general store. We, too, must catch the ferry—the last
of the day. We have just enough time for a pint and are considering the half a dozen or so varieties of the local ale. We are

thus employed when we are joined by three Englishmen. They know the local ales well, they tell us, and recommend the Black Rock. We settle onto our stools with pint glasses and bottles and they spread out across a corner booth. "What brings you to Port Askaig?" we ask. "Whisky," they say with smile.

It is whisky that has brought us here, too, and whisky, the bartender tells us, that brings most tourists to this remote island off the west coast of Scotland. We are on the last leg of a journey begun nine years earlier, a cultural odyssey of sorts, taking us on distillery tours and to whisky festivals and to many conversations over a "wee dram"—all in quest of a greater understanding of a Scottish staple and the people who give it life. It is a journey that regrettably will end here on Islay, at the Feis Ile, the Islay Festival of Malt and Music, on the upcoming Saturday.

So we talk to our newfound friends about whisky. We talk about the limited quantities of specialist bottles of whisky available at the festival and the rising value of collectible whiskies. It is the second day of the festival and already whiskies bought yesterday have tripled in price. We talk about the Macallan 60 years old, which in the summer of 2002 sold at auction in Glasgow at the then unprecedented price of £20,150 (more than $40,000). In that moment, the market for collecting rare malt whiskies came, itself, of age. The Englishmen had narrowly missed purchasing yesterday's specialty offering at Lagavulin. "What would you have done with the whisky, had you bought it?" we inquire. "Kept it, unopened, undrunk?" "No. Whisky," they insist, "is to be enjoyed." They, like so many others we have talked to over the years, would have consumed it, shared it with friends. The consumption of whisky is a social activity.

Their cab arrives and they are off to a ceilidh[1] (it roughly rhymes with daily) in the nearby village of Portnahaven. We have the ferry to catch. We say our good-byes, exchange e-mail addresses, promise to keep in touch—friendships newly formed and quickly cemented through a shared understanding of Scottish whisky.

In this essay, we discuss two whisky regions, the Isle of Islay and the Malt Whisky Trail in central Scotland, and the social activities and processes of each that play a part in defining the views that consumers globally share concerning Scotch whisky and the things they associate with it.

Scotland's Whisky Regions: A Sense of Place

Scotch whisky is a whisky product that has been distilled and matured in Scotland for at least three years. It is important to Scotland's economy. The industry not only contributes substantially to the balance of trade, but it also drives tourism and produces jobs—many in economically fragile rural areas. Single malt production continues to grow and thrive in an increasingly complex and competitive global economy, and the broad appeal of the industry continues to stimulate entrepreneurial enthusiasm.

Whisky may, then, be understood as a commodity, an export, and a veritable economic engine. But economic activity is, always, social activity, and it has been said that whisky comprises not merely its own world but also "a world with worlds within."[2] Today, those worlds include more than 2,500 individual brands of Scotch, each attempting to create a distinct brand identity.[3] These brand identities are often derived from local or regional history, geography, or mythology, reflecting the extent to which the place of origin is viewed as intrinsic to the product itself—just as the identity of Scotch is intrinsically enmeshed in the identity of Scotland. Whisky is a powerful and iconic symbol of Scottish culture.[4]

These varied worlds of whisky in Scotland exist within clusters of distilleries in the distinct whisky regions that mark her landscape.[5] We set out to understand these regions, adopting the research methods of cultural anthropologists, who study the culture, habits, and customs of societies, to do so. In researching this project, we conducted extensive fieldwork, interviewed consumers and producers of whisky, and systematically analyzed books, news articles, and Web sites about Scotland's whisky and whisky regions.

Cultural studies examine, among other things, how societies come to assign values to goods. Some of these values are purely economic and are reflected in the purchase price of a product or service. Other values, however, are less easily evaluated. They include, for example, the prestige value associated with owning a particular product or brand. Cultural studies have shown that these diverse values arise from shared social beliefs and behaviors of people and that these are both visible and predictable. In some cases, individuals become intensely attached to a particular product class (such as whisky) or a particular brand. If enough individuals share this passion, they may form a subgroup of enthusiasts, creating clubs, rallies, and festivals. These groups play a role in developing a unique language related to the good as well as consumer rituals that prescribe how the good is used. These groups are often important in defining standards of authenticity, fostering deep connections between individuals and product classes or brands, and in determining how goods or brands are perceived by others.

One highly visible example is that of the Harley Owners Group (HOG), formed of Harley-Davidson fanatics. Members adhere to the idea that "the Harley Owners Group is much more than just a motorcycle organization. It's one million people around the world united by a common passion: making the Harley-Davidson dream a way of life."[6] Over time, members have developed a unique language, a shared ethos, norms of dress, and ritualized behaviors and events. Moreover, they have successfully created a set of associations with the brand that are pervasively understood. Whether one is a member of HOG or not, one still understands Harley to be associated with freedom, American productivity and heritage, quality, and antiestablishment principles, among other things. Scholars of consumer behavior have found similar enthusiast groups supporting such diverse brands as Star Trek, Apple computers, and a wide range of automobile makers. This essay considers enthusiasts of two Scottish whisky regions, examining the traditions, habits, and customs of each, and the varied values associated with regionally established whisky brands.

It is the convention of Scotch whisky connoisseurs to describe an individual brand's attributes in terms of nose, color, flavor, finish, age, distillation, strength, and other similar descriptors. Experts also discuss distilleries in terms of their malting processes, physical location, access to water, and historic properties (changes in ownership, periods during which the distillery was dormant, and so on). Very little has been written, however, that examines the relationship between whisky and the communities that produce it. Yet we contend that the ideas we have about whisky and the things we associate with whisky are rooted in the place and culture of its production. Although other studies of brand and product enthusiasts have not considered the effects of local or regional culture on goods or brands, there is a precedent for this view among connoisseurs of wine, coffee, and tea. In these industries, one speaks of *terroir*—a French term that loosely translated means "a sense of place" and is used to convey the idea that these goods embody unique qualities that reflect the sum of the characteristics of the local environment. *Terroir* comprises not merely topography, climate, and soil conditions but also human processes and inputs. Arguably, it is through the concept of *terroir* that wine, coffee, and tea have become goods not just related to the place where they are produced and the processes by which they are produced but also related to the people and cultures that produce them.

We illustrate our argument by examining consumers' and producers' descriptions of whisky in two of Scotland's distinct whisky regions, the Isle of Islay, off the southwest coast of Scotland, and Scotland's Malt Whisky Trail, in the Moray area of Scotland, stretching between Aberdeen and Inverness. Eight working distilleries operate on Islay, and eight on the Malt Whisky Trail. Both areas have spawned internationally recognized brands, including Laphroaig and Ardbeg on Islay and Glenfiddich and Glenlivet on the Malt Whisky Trail.

The Scottish Enlightenment

Underlying this work is some quintessential Scottish economic and philosophical thought, including a body of scholarship that emerged in the mid-1700s from the work of Adam Smith, Adam Ferguson, John Millar, and the historian William Robertson, which is collectively referred to as the Scottish Enlightenment. These scholars argued that man is preeminently social and best understood through observing him at home, at work, and at leisure. Their interest was in studying not individual behavior but social, political, and economic institutions, organizations, and groups. Much of their work anticipated what we refer to today as social capital. They suggested, for example, that it is through the adoption of habits and customs that social reinforcement occurs in social entities, such as communities, schools, and churches. It is sympathetic treatment of group members, emotional identification with group members, and reciprocity among group members that results in social cohesion. For these Scottish theorists, man was always and simply best understood as the product of his (social) environment.[7]

Alas, those involved in the Scottish Enlightenment never turned to the topic of whisky and its consumption, but it is worth philosophizing about, nonetheless. Iain Banks, a contemporary Scottish social commentator, echoes many of the sentiments of the Enlightenment and associates these with Scotch:

Drinking whisky is never about just drinking whisky; we're social creatures and we tend to drink in a social context, with family, friends, or just accomplices. Even if we resort to drinking alone, we drink with memories and ghosts.[8]

The consumption of whisky, like all social activities, is affected by the setting in which it occurs. The following sections explore the varying associations people attribute to the whiskies of Islay and the Malt Whisky Trail and the activities in each region that play a part in reinforcing these over time and in developing a sense of bonding and identification among these whisky consumers and between consumers and whisky regions.

Localizing Whisky

It is possible to contrast the whiskies of Islay with those of the Malt Whisky Trail, not merely in terms of taste (as most whisky writers do) but also in terms of the legends that surround each and the consumer sentiments expressed. These distinctions are based in geography, history, and culture. Hence, Scotch whiskies may be viewed as bearing the cultural attributes of the region in which they are produced.

Although the small Isle of Islay covers only 250 square miles, it has been home to as many as twenty working distilleries. Today, there are eight, including Ardbeg, Bowmore, Bruichladdich, Bunnahabhain, Caol Ila, Lagavulin, Laphroaig, and, most recently, Kilchoman. Of these, only Bruichladdich and Kilchoman are locally owned; the rest are part of larger conglomerates.[9] Each distillery is uniquely beautiful and each enjoys a remarkable setting. Most are a brilliant white, their names proclaimed in large black letters, set in stark relief against the sea.

Islay's history is curious. It is an island that has historically been owned by "outsiders" who have sought to make money off its agriculture, so Islay has always been subject to outside market forces. For current residents, however, this reality is remote. Whisky, from the viewpoint of those we talked with when visiting, has opened the door to the outside world in recent years in more immediate ways. The increase in trade has led to the enhancement of ferry services. Increased interest in whisky distilleries has led to a larger influx of tourists.

There is a natural and symbiotic relationship between the isle and its whisky. Rich in peat, but lashed by wind, rain, and sea, the small island's pockets and coves provide harbors for its distilleries. The sea and the soil contribute to the distinct character of the single malts, which are noted for their sea-weed, peat-rich flavor. The island's relative remoteness leaves it dependent upon the sea for favorable conditions for movement of goods to and from the mainland.

The sea, peat, and the remoteness of Islay feature in the daily life of Islay and in the vernacular of its residents. The sea provides both challenges and a source of livelihood. Peat is an abundant natural resource, used to dry barley and heat homes. Plumbing the sea for its treasures, cutting peat, and, to a lesser extent, working in production in distilleries, all require physical strength and stamina. On Islay, these are largely the activities of men. Women work in the service industries, in the shops, restaurants, and pubs. It is predominantly men who vie for coveted positions in the distilleries and men who have most immediately experienced changes in the industry. As distilleries become increasingly efficient, the need for manual labor has been reduced. Moreover, cultural practices, such as drinking a dram at the beginning and end of one's shift, have been dropped or altered. The camaraderie created by groups of men sharing the rigors of the work and then enjoying together its rich rewards was unique; the stuff of legends. The glory days of work in the distilleries are gone, we are told by those who lived them.

David, our tour guide at Laphroaig, has worked for the distillery nearly three decades. He tells us a strong sense of community remains in the relationships among those work-ing the various and competing distilleries. Those working the distilleries went to school together, know one another socially, and help one another. Distilleries loan one another their expertise and manpower, in times of need. They collaborate annually to help Islay produce her Feis Ile, the Islay Festival of Malt and Music. A young man on our Laphroaig tour arrives wearing a T-shirt depicting Bowmore's Black Bottle. A Laphroaig worker stops him, thumps him soundly on the chest with the stub of a finger, "Aye, thee's the Black Bottle!"

he shouts, with apparent approval. David turns to the group to explain this enthusiastic reaction to a competitor's brand. "Bowmore supports our island's pipe band," he tells us proudly. "We just won first place in the national championship." In fact, though the Port Ellen Pipe Band bears the name Black Bottle, the band receives financial support from most of Islay's distilleries.

Islay's distilleries share a closed and close-knit social structure. This is apparent as one spends time on the small island, traveling her narrow winding roads, hiking her rugged open spaces, shopping in the small communities' business districts, and enjoying her restaurants and pubs. If there are, indeed, worlds within worlds of whisky, the world of Islay is distinctly communal. One is immediately drawn into the community of three thousand, nearly all of whom wave to you as you share those precipitous roads. Faces become familiar as you ride the local buses. An apparent bond transcends the differences that might otherwise create barriers among the tourists, who hardly share a common language but for an appreciation of the malts of Islay. It is evidenced in the stories shared by distillery tour guides, at ceilidhs, and in daily interactions.

The legends that surround the Islay malts are often tales of adversity, sometimes set against the sea, other times against market forces. Some stories depict daring sea exploits, others daring entrepreneurial ventures. Each situates tiny Islay against daunting and more powerful opposition, and Islay comes through with aplomb.

Banks wrote following his arrival at Port Ellen on Islay:

> The first signpost you see coming off the ferry . . . has only two words on it; it points right to ARDBEG and left to BOWMORE. Brilliant, I thought; a road sign that is made up 100 per cent of distillery names; a proclamation that you are on an island where the making of whisky is absolutely integral to the place itself, where directions are defined by drink![10]

While Banks found Islay defined by its distilleries, it would be as true to say, conversely, that the distilleries are defined by the towns from which they derive their names. Andrew Jefford thought so, as the following quotation illustrates:

Among malt whiskies, these [Islay malts] are more palpably marked with the place of their birth than any others. Savage, stern, uncompromising: Islay is the conscience of Scotch.[11]

Our own impression of Port Ellen from the ferry was of a little row of black-and-white buildings, looking like miniatures of the distilleries themselves, standing small and stoic, silently regarding our departure like figures in a painting by Lowery. Islay affects her visitor, and her whiskies are so intertwined with the place that it is impossible to understand the product without reference to the place.

In contrast to the culture associated with Islay, Scotland's Malt Whisky Trail was initiated as a tourism venture in 1972. In response to increased public interest in whisky making, distilleries in Speyside began offering visitor centers. Under the auspices of the regional tourist association, a promotional brochure for the region's attractions made reference to the three distilleries of Glenfiddich, Glenfarclas, and Strathisla, whose locations delimit what was referred to as the Whisky Trail. Subsequently renamed the Malt Whisky Trail, the association sought to promote awareness of participating distilleries and their products, and to encourage visitors to explore the countryside away from main tourist routes. Today, the Malt Whisky Trail comprises eight distilleries—Benromach, Cardhu, Dallas Dhu, Glen Grant, Glen Moray, Glenfiddich, Glenlivet, and Strathisla—and the Speyside Cooperage.

This region, between the cities of Inverness and Aberdeen, is considered the heartland of malt whisky distillation. Geographically, it features granite mountains, fertile countryside, and lush forestation. Speyside exhibits a pretty tidiness that is made all the more lovely by its natural symmetry. Its countryside

327

is crisscrossed by narrow lanes bracketed by hedgerows and stone fences, dotted with tidy cottages and equally tidy hamlets, made brilliant by its golden foliage, and punctuated at intervals by medieval castles and, of interest here, whisky distilleries.

The distilleries of the Malt Whisky Trail, though varied in physical appearance, are imposing and substantial and possess a sort of gravity and a sense of entitlement. Some, like Glen Grant and Glen Moray, are baronial in appearance. Others, such as Benromach, feature the white, stark appearance of the Islay distilleries. Speyside single malts are noted for their elegance and complexity, and often a refined smokiness, which reflects the architecture from which they arise.

Although six of the eight operating distilleries on Islay are owned by large conglomerates, her distilleries are perceived as less corporate than those of the Malt Whisky Trail. Consumers suggest this is due, in part, to the greater sense of transparency offered by the Islay distillers. The Islay distillers, for example, all offer tours and tastings and allow photography. Although the distilleries on the Malt Whisky Trail also offer tours and tastings, many of their neighbor distilleries do not. The distilleries of Speyside are criticized for limiting photography. This confirms and perpetuates the view that the Speyside distilleries are less accessible, more corporate, and less local.

But there is something about these landlocked distilleries that is both compelling and reassuring. One feels one is walking through the halls of something substantive, historic, and meaningful. We had the great fortune to visit Strathisla on the last day of the tourist season and enjoyed a virtually private tour with Tom, retired from production, but still young and smiling in the many photographs that adorn the distillery's walls. As he guided us on the familiar distillery tour, he lovingly stroked the copper kilns, shared tales from his youth, stopped to speak to a local farmer, and eventually pulled out a bottle of a very fine, very old whisky. We sat in the country house comfort of the Strathisla reception area, before a dying fire, and felt that life is very good indeed.

When informants speak of Islay, they emphasize stoicism, tradition, simplicity, and rugged independence. They arrive in Land Rover Defenders and on Harleys. They talk of the soil and the sea. They talk of community-mindedness, collective responsibility, and the extraordinary means taken to reopen mothballed distilleries on the isle. They share with the novice consumer their own views, experiences, and knowledge. In contrast, consumers and distillery staff on the Malt Whisky Trail speak of barley, economic viability, regional concerns, agriculture, growth, the global economy. Those we interviewed on the street of the Malt Whisky Trail described whisky as a drink to be consumed in the evening, at home. Connoisseurs talk of whisky and water and speak knowledgeably of the very best of brands. Visitors arrive in tour buses and leave laden with branded goods.

But apart from these contrasts, there are similarities. On Islay and on the Malt Whisky Trail, common tensions are found. Both regions struggle to modernize without compromising traditions. In both areas, for example, distillery tour guides decry the replacement of traditional stenciling on casks with bar codes. Both regions struggle to satisfy local needs while adapting to an expanding global marketplace. Both are unselfconsciously Scottish while acquiescing to the needs of an increasingly diverse consumer base. Both appear conscious of the natural resources upon which they are dependent and their responsibility to preserving the quality of the ecological environment.

Distillery Tours, Whisky Festivals, Brand Communities, and Brand Ambassadors

We sought to understand both the culture associated with whiskies and the activities engaged in by consumers and firms within the whisky regions that affect them. While in both regions the distillery communities are relatively close knit, this is far truer of Islay, owed at least in part to its small size.

Moreover, on Islay cooperation among distilleries is informal and occurs at will. In contrast, the distilleries on the Malt Whisky Trail have entered into a structured arrangement through which activities are coordinated and overseen (to some extent), data regarding distillery tourism is shared, and agreements are worked out regarding contributions to and allocation of a pool of marketing funds. But in both cases (and in other regions visited but not reported here), the social structure contributes to the values held in this industry—values that favor tradition over modernization and reflect a strong sense of social responsibility to the local communities.

As in the case of the Harley Owners Group, these regions have developed specific customs and traditions that reflect and reinforce the way whisky is understood and used. Many of these are highly ritualistic and adhere to an unvarying script. They also include identifiable roles by key participants and the use of symbolic objects. (These ritualized consumer behaviors are found in a variety of social settings, from church services to ball parks. For example, the ceremonial first pitch is a longstanding American baseball ritual. It marks the end of the preseason and is performed by a notable individual, and the symbolic object is the ball itself.)

In Scottish whisky regions, similar rituals are apparent in distillery tours and festivals. There is a pattern to the distillery tour and a structure to the festival that consumers internalize and rely upon. Distilleries use regional symbols such as local landmarks, retired employees as tour guides, the Gaelic language, Celtic art and music, and other Scottish symbols to reinforce whisky as embedded in its local and national heritage. Moreover, through scripted distillery tours, appropriate behaviors are passed from distilleries to consumers, and reinforcement of these occurs through consumer interactions. Consumers play a significant role in educating one another about whisky, its consumption, history, and culture.

The festivals provide a means of creating in consumers a sense of identification with individual distilleries as well as with the product class of Scotch whisky. They also facilitate, through ceilidhs and opportunities for informal interaction, the sense of a bond among consumers. As in other consumer groups (think of the Harley riders again), these processes transfer values, teach appropriate behaviors, and create and sustain habits and customs.

Festivals and distillery tours also offer consumers opportunities to clothe themselves in branded apparel and accessories. Some consumers display their allegiance to the region by wearing festival T-shirts. Others create a deeper sense of legitimacy by wearing the T-shirts of previous years' festivals. Finally, it is not uncommon to see consumers make connections between whisky and other goods by combining garments that reflect attachment to multiple brands. For example, Harley riders from Germany and Land Rover Discovery owners from England both donned identifiers from these brands as well as from Islay's distilleries.

Other symbolic objects are also available for purchase. At distilleries, commonly found objects include lapel pins and whisky glassware. In both regions, these include local pottery, soaps, and art. In some cases, the wares are more distinctive. On Islay, for example, attendees at the annual whisky festival look forward to enjoying oysters provided by local fishermen and doused in local whisky as well as what is billed as the world famous Bruichladdich burgers, local beef seasoned with malt. On the Malt Whisky Trail, consumers noted a preference for local produce, notably the region's Angus beef and baked goods.

More recently, individual distilleries have sought to create brand communities, widening the opening for consumer input into how whisky is understood and used, and increasing interaction with other whisky enthusiasts. One can, for example, be a "friend of Laphroaig," an Ardbeg "committee member," enjoying privileges of membership, not the least of which is a sense of deepened identification with the brand. Through these mechanisms, brand loyalists can share experiences with one another as well as with the distillery. These marketing initiatives (began as a lark, according to one tour guide) may be the means of creating a more sustained and less fleeting sense of attachment than the camaraderie that occurs at the festival ceilidh.

A similar—and similarly effective—device is the emergence of brand ambassadors. Our departure from Laphroaig was interrupted by a young man who dashed after us, inquiring if one of us was American. He was Laphroaig's brand ambassador to the United States, he explained. It felt as if a minor royal had just appeared and bestowed upon us his blessings! We bought the festival bottling and noted the code on the back that would allow us to become "friends" with Laphroaig upon our return home.

Consumers have increasingly sought opportunities to contribute to the dialogue about Scotch whisky outside the official means offered by distilleries, maintaining extensive Web sites and blogs[12] and contributing photographic and video material to the Internet. These contributions add to how whisky is understood, and it may be anticipated that these forums will have substantial influence on the way whisky's consumers view and use the product. These forums are a means by which new consumers gain information about how to consume whisky and which whiskies are best suited to reflect the individual consumer's sense of personal identity. Past studies in other branded contexts have shown that consumers play a significant role in defining a brand's identity, and this has forced firms, in some cases, to adhere to consumers' beliefs about the brand.

Conclusion

The nature of consumer goods has changed, and branded goods have assumed a more central role in consumer life. Products and brands offer a means of defining identity and act as a shorthand way through which consumers may communicate complex belief and value systems. Brands allow us to recognize others like ourselves, who share our values, beliefs, and interests. We throng to "brandfests," where we celebrate the ostensible uniqueness of owning a Harley, watching *Star Trek*, or consuming—knowledgeably—Chivas Regal. Yet, studies show that despite our brand loyalty, we are generally unable to distinguish one cola (or one beer) from another.[13]

Scholars of consumer behavior argue that consumers increasingly seek to engage in consumption rituals, both in daily life (e.g., by adding a splash of water to whisky) and through participation in larger events (such as whisky festivals and ceilidhs).[14] There is evidence of this in Scotland's whisky regions. Moreover, within these, whisky consumption reflects regional ways of life that are evident in and outside of the marketplace, in the activities, language, foods, music, and dress of a group of people, and in their relations with others.[15] Hence, the cultural—and ultimately economic—values of Scottish whisky are created, in part, through the activities in which marketplace actors engage—at distilleries, at festivals, in public and in private, online and interpersonally, juxtaposing history, media representations, and locally relevant material.

Scotland's whisky regions shape—and are shaped by—their natural and economic environments; they impact social relations and influence cultural interpretations. With the explosion of interest in Scotch whisky, these regions have emerged as important sites of consumer activity, helping to define and position individual brands and regionally prescribed brand clusters, and providing consumers with information about cultural attributes of individual brands. In this study, those cultural attributes are another means by which consumers distinguish Islay malts from those of Speyside.

NOTES

The chapter epigraph is taken from David Daiches, *Scotch Whisky: Its Past and Present* (London: Macmillan, 1970), p. 163.

1. A ceilidh is a traditional Scottish social event including Scottish music, dancing, and refreshment.

2. Stuart Delves, *Great Brand Stories: Scotch Whisky; Creative Fire: The Story of Scotland's Greatest Export* (London: Cyan Books, 2007), p. 10.

3. Ibid.

4. See, for example, Andrew Martin and Geoff McBoyle, "Scotland's Malt Whisky Trail: Management Issues in a Public-Private Tourism Marketing Partnership," *International Journal of Wine Marketing* 18.2 (2006): pp. 98–111. See also Geoff McBoyle, "Culture and Heritage: Keys to the Success of Scottish Malt Whisky Distilleries as Tourist Attractions," in *Tourism and Culture: Culture as the Tourist Product*, ed. Mike Robinson et al. (Newcastle, UK: University of Northumbria Press, 1996), pp. 279–295.

5. These distinctions may be historically traced to the Wash Act of 1784, which delineated the industry simply between Highland and Lowland distilleries. By the mid-1800s, four regions were identifiable, including Highland, Islay, Campbeltown, and Lowland, although some writers simply referred to Eastern and Western malts. The whiskies of Speyside, known frequently as Glenlivets, were written about from as early as 1820. Today (with some variation) authorities typically classify malts as Highland (North, South, East, West, and Central), Lowland, Islay, and Speyside (and divide Speyside into Glenlivet, Strathsepy, Dufftown, Rothes, and Elgin). Some continue to classify Campbeltown as a region, though where there were once thirty-two distilleries, there now remain but two.

6. HOG Web site, available at www.harley-davidson.com/wcm/Content/Pages/HOG/HOG.jsp?locale=en_US (accessed July 29, 2008).

7. For a helpful discussion of the Scottish Enlightenment, see Alan Swingewood, "Origins of Sociology: The Case of the Scottish Englightenment," *British Journal of Sociology* 21.2 (1970): pp. 164–180.

8. Iain Banks, *Raw Spirit* (London: Random House, 2004), p. 3.

9. Diageo, Fortune Brands, Moet Hennesey, Morrison Bowmore Distillers, and Burn Stewart Distillers Ltd. all have an interest in Islay's whiskies. For more on whisky and conglomerates, see Andrew Jefford, "Scotch Whisky: From Origins to Conglomerates," pp. 21–39 (this volume).

10. Banks, *Raw Spirit*, p. 27.

11. Andrew Jefford, *Peat Smoke and Spirit: A Portrait of Islay and its Whiskies* (London: Headline Book Publishing, 2004), p. 3.

12. See, for example, Malt Maniacs, www.maltmaniacs.org (accessed July 5, 2008); For Scotch Lovers, www.forscotchlovers.com

(accessed July 5, 2008); and Dr. Scotch, www.drscotch.com (accessed July 5, 2008).

13. See Brand Solutions, Inc., "A Short Introduction to Branding," brand.com, www.brand.com/intro.htm (accessed June 30, 2008).

14. Ibid. See also John Sherry, Jr., "A Sociocultural Analysis of a Midwestern American Flea Market," *Journal of Consumer Research* 17 (1990): pp. 13–30.

15. Janeen A. Costa and Gary Bamossy, *Marketing in a Multicultural World: Ethnicity, Nationalism, and Cultural Identity* (London: Sage, 1995).

APPENDIX A

Whiskey Tasting Notes

Islay

LAGAVULIN 16 YEAR OLD

Appearance: Pale gold

Nose: Salty nose with peat

Palate: Smoke, sea salt; intense peat and medicinal notes

Finish: Mild finish with nice lingering smoke

Notes: Lagavulin 16 year old, from Diageo's Classic Malts Selection, brings a smooth transition from palate to finish, which is equally pleasant from beginning to end. The intense peat-smoke flavors nicely blend with the crashing sea-salt notes. Lagavulin is an exceptional Islay whisky.

BUNNAHABHAIN 18 YEAR OLD

Appearance: Full gold

Nose: Salt and sweet nose with nuttiness

Palate: Slightly floral and fragrant; caramel and wood with hint of salt

Finish: Finish continues the palate and ends pleasantly

Notes: This whisky from Bunnahabhain brings a twist to what one generally expects from Islay as it has minimal peat flavor.

Nonetheless, it is an excellent whisky and a fine example of Islay whisky without pungent peatiness.

Speyside and Highlands

THE MACALLAN 15 YEAR OLD

Appearance: Light straw

Nose: Sweet with butter

Palate: Floral and perfumed fragrant notes; toffee

Finish: Sherry and citrus

Notes: The Macallan 15 year old is a delightfully well-made Highlands whisky. The marriage of bourbon and sherry casks is flawless in this whisky. This is the gold standard for Highlands' flavor.

OLD PULTENEY 17 YEAR OLD

Appearance: Light amber

Nose: Sweet nose with hint of salt; fruity

Palate: Floral; hint of salt

Finish: Surprising finish that endures

Notes: Old Pulteney 17 year old from Inver House is a great whisky. Strangely, it is not as well known as some of its competitors, but we found that it held its own and beat out the majority of the Highlands' region in our tastings. Old Pulteney's line is unique for the Highlands' style given its coastal location. The finish is a delight and quite a surprise as well for the Highlands.

GLENFIDDICH 18 YEAR OLD

Appearance: Pale/full gold and amber

Nose: Full-bodied nose, slightly drying with new wood notes

Palate: Woody overtones, especially oak

Finish: Old wood finish, slightly spicy and a bit of pepper

Notes: This is our favorite of the Glenfiddich line. It is a wonderfully aged single malt with a nice amount of complexity and fine wood notes throughout from nose to finish.

OBAN 14 YEAR OLD

Appearance: Bright chardonnay

Nose: Salty, slightly sharp nose with citrus zest

Palate: Full-bodied with fruity notes

Finish: Progressive finish with hints of salt and seaweed

Notes: Oban 14 year old is a balanced, full-flavored whisky. It has a unique flavor profile since it is from the West Highlands and thus incorporates two regions: the Highlands and the Islands. The result is a delicious whisky that brings together the best of the Highlands' sweetness and the Islands' saltiness.

Bourbon

A. H. HIRSCH 16 YEAR RESERVE BOURBON

Appearance: Dark amber

Nose: Sweet with slight citrus and wood

Palate: Rich, balanced, full flavor; woody with thick texture

Finish: Long-lasting finish that continues on the palate; hint of fresh fruit

Notes: This is the best bourbon we've ever tasted. Beyond the historical significance of Hirsch 16 year, the bourbon itself is like none other. From its enveloping nose to its vibrant palate, this bourbon is on the level of the best whiskeys in the world.

FOUR ROSES SINGLE BARREL

Appearance: Full copper

Nose: Sweet, nutty nose

Palate: Winey, nutty flavor with new wood notes

Finish: Sweet finish lingers nicely with a small amount of spiciness

Notes: This bourbon is very well balanced and easy to drink. It isn't a complicated bourbon for a single barrel, but it is a great bourbon in its price range (around $35–$45). What it might be lacking in complexity it makes up for in the finish. Overall, a great bourbon.

ELIJAH CRAIG 12 YEAR BOURBON

Appearance: Dark amber red

Nose: Fruity nose with faint vanilla

Palate: Full flavor; intense warming with rich flavors of fresh fruit, new wood, and vanilla

Finish: Smooth, continuing finish; Woody

Notes: This is an amazing, full-bodied whiskey; our favorite from Heaven Hill. This is not your average bourbon. Elijah Craig is arguably the best bourbon under $30.

Other American

WASMUND'S SINGLE MALT

Appearance: Dark old gold and copper

Nose: Earthy with strong wood bark with very slight smoke; hint of black tea

Palate: Woody with light smoke and hint of sherry

Finish: Wood continues with warming finish

Notes: This single malt whisky from Rick Wasmund at Copper Fox Distillery is much darker than most single malts with an appearance almost like a bourbon. The nose is much more complex than any other American whiskey, with intense earthy notes. The flavor is exceptional and multifaced with a clean finish. A unique American whiskey.

STRANAHAN'S

Appearance: Rich gold

Nose: Sweet with butter and toffee

Palate: Floral notes with a hint of honey

Finish: Lingering finish

Notes: This Colorado whiskey from Jess Graber took us by surprise. The nose has a sweetness reminiscent of a bourbon, but the palate brings a delightful complexity with a smooth texture. The finish is mild with a pleasant aftertaste. An excellent whiskey that adds a unique addition to the American whiskey enthusiast's collection!

Rest of the World

MACKMYRA PRIVUS:03

Appearance: Light straw

Nose: Salt with strong peat

Palate: Light texture, intense smoke and peat

Finish: Smoke continues in finish; drying

Notes: Remarkable whiskey from Sweden with intense flavor. The strong peat flavors are especially delightful, but though peaty the flavor is quite different from that of an Islay whisky. The texture, also, is different from an Islay and represents a further departure from the Islay style—a departure that is quite enjoyable, though.

CROWN ROYAL XR

Appearance: Golden bright sunlight

Nose: Sweet nose; slight solvent and hint of cream soda

Palate: Wood notes with pepper and spice

Finish: Mild finish with exceptional smoothness

Notes: This rare bottling from Crown Royal represents whisky from the closed Waterloo Distillery. The whisky is very well balanced, beginning in a very mellow fashion but finishing with a dynamic spiciness. Certainly the best Canadian whisky we've tried!

BUSHMILLS BLACK BUSH

Appearance: Pale gold

Nose: Sweet; nutty and sherry

Palate: Medium texture with fruit and especially a hint of cherry

Finish: Mild finish with slight wood, smooth but fades quickly

Notes: Black Bush from Bushmills is great Irish whiskey in this price point (approximately $25–$35). It has moderate complexity, but it is exceptionally smooth with subtle hints of fruit and wood. It brings the sweetness anticipated in an Irish whiskey, but its subtle notes provide a more experience than your average Irish.

APPENDIX B

Our Favorite Whiskey Cocktails

While some of the more serious essays in this book are best read with a dark and brooding Islay whisky, some of the more farcical ones call for a cocktail. Great cocktail books abound, so we will hardly be comprehensive, but let us offer five of our favorite whiskey cocktails.[1] These will, as the spelling suggests, all be made with American whiskeys, though not necessarily with bourbon. Our neglect of Scotch partially emanates from the bias and agenda suggested in the book's introduction, but we do think that the flavor profiles of American whiskey are more congenial to these cocktails than those of Scotch. Irish whiskey over ice can be a casual sipper, perfect for summer evenings or while playing poker, but Scotch, especially single malt, is almost always best served neat. There are Scotch cocktails—such as the Rob Roy, a Manhattan made with Scotch instead of rye—but we'll take American whiskey in our cocktails. Note also that there are many American whiskeys widely available under $30, whereas Scotch can be more limited in this price range. There is usually no point in using expensive bottles for these drinks, though that's not to suggest that quality isn't important. Herewith are our five favorites, mostly traditional but with some innovations as well.

Manhattan

3 ounces rye whiskey
1.5 ounces sweet vermouth
3 dashes bitters
1 brandied cherry

The Manhattan is, without a doubt, a great cocktail—and especially for the purposes of this book, since it deserves a lot of thought and reflection. Few drinks are as complicated or nuanced as the Manhattan, or have a similar history. We have an entire essay devoted to this drink:[2] How many other cocktails could command such a forum? And what makes the Manhattan so great? Rumor has it that it was invented in 1874 in, of course, Manhattan. The story goes that Winston Churchill's mother was hosting a party in honor of New York's then governor Samuel Tilden, and that the drink debuted there.

The Manhattan should be made with rye whiskey and not with bourbon; this reversal is a common, yet to our minds inexcusable, mistake. Bourbon, made predominantly with corn, is rich and reminiscent of summer; the Manhattan should be a gloomy drink reserved for winter nights. Rye is darker, spicier, and less effusive than bourbon. The Maker's Manhattan, so named for its eponymous whiskey, is better suited for its alliterative merits than for the proper choice of whiskey. If you have to use a bourbon, though, Maker's isn't a disaster, because it uses red winter wheat in the mash bill; this gives it a profile more appropriate than some other high-corn bourbons. Bulleit has a high proportion of rye and is another reasonable alternative.

But, if you want to do it right, go find a bottle of rye. You can make a completely serviceable Manhattan with Wild Turkey Rye, which is widely available. Rittenhouse is another good one worth seeking out, though we'd suggest you stay away from Jim Beam, Old Overholt, or other less expensive variants since the Manhattan is a fairly unadulterated drink, and the quality of the whiskey is therefore important. Canadian whiskies have a lot of rye but, we think, the wrong flavor profile. Go American. Strong mid-range options are Sazerac Rye and Van Winkle Family Reserve Rye. The Sazerac, while unlabeled on the bottle, has been aged for six years, and the Van Winkle has been aged for thirteen years; the latter is therefore a couple of dollars more expensive.

There might even be more variation among vermouths than ryes, so try a bunch. To keep your Manhattan traditional, make sure to use sweet vermouth, though various combinations with dry vermouth are worth exploring as well. The standard is Martini & Rossi Rosso, but vermouth quickly gets better from there. One of our favorites is Noilly Prat, which adds a lot of depth to the drink and makes a great complement to the rye. Punt e Mes is a bruiser, powerful and astringent. Some love this one, some hate it; we suggest drinking it straight over ice as it might overwhelm your whiskey in a cocktail. Carpano, which makes Punt e Mes, also makes Carpano Antica, widely regarded as one of the world's best vermouths. This formula dates from 1786 and will take your Manhattan to a new level. Vya, from California, is another option, though it's very different from the French and Italian versions, and we prefer it over ice as well.

And then come the oft-forgotten bitters. One thing that makes the Manhattan so great is that it uses three different ingredients, all of which make significant impacts on the final drink. Angostura, which comes from Trinidad & Tobago, is the most traditional. But play around with other possibilities, especially orange bitters. Fee Brothers West Indian Orange Bitters and Regans' Orange Bitters No. 6 are great, though different; Fee's has more straightforward orange, while Regans' has more spices, including cinnamon. Fee Brothers also makes an Old Fashioned Bitters that you can use in place of Angostura. Bitter Truth bitters, made in Germany, are now available worldwide and are also worth seeking out, especially its Aromatic Bitters. Try incorporating some orange bitters: one of our favorite combinations is to use two dashes of Fee Brothers Old Fashioned Bitters and one of its West Indian Orange Bitters. This blend comes off lighter and more subtle than straight Angostura, and the hints of orange really work well with the drink.

The best Manhattan we have ever had? The Violet Hour in Chicago, without a doubt. This is one of the best whiskey bars in the country and head mixologist Toby Maloney puts together some amazing concoctions. Maloney uses 3 ounces Sazerac 18, 1 ounce Carpano Antica, .5 ounce Noilly Prat Dry, and 3 dashes homemade bitters. Sazerac 18 is brilliant and, while more expensive than the standard bottling, you can still find it for around $60. The dry vermouth takes this drink toward a Perfect Manhattan (equal parts sweet and dry vermouth), but the 2:1 sweet to dry ratio still shows respect for tradition. In place of the homemade bitters, try the Fee Brothers approach suggested above.

While you might not make your own bitters, do brandy your own cherries. Get 1 cup sugar, 2 whole cloves, 1 cinnamon stick, and 4 cardamom pods. Combine these and heat with 1 cup of water until sugar is dissolved. Add 4 ounces brandy and as many cherries as you can keep submerged; let them macerate for two days.

Stir the ingredients together in a shaker, then strain into a chilled cocktail glass and serve up. Add your brandied cherry at the end.

Mint Julep

2 ounces bourbon

4–6 sprigs mint

2 tablespoons mint syrup

The Mint Julep isn't the most sophisticated of whiskey drinks, but it's among the most enjoyable. The reason that we chose to write it up for this book is because it's a very well-known whiskey cocktail even if not one that's very widely available. The Mint Julep's home is the Kentucky Derby, where almost 120,000 juleps are made every year during the event. Its history, though, extends beyond the first running of the Derby in 1875: the word 'julep' derives from an ancient Arabic and Persian drink called 'julab', which translates as "rose water." That drink was made from crushing rose petals into water, but the roses were replaced with the more widely available and economic mint once the drink moved to the Mediterranean. Alcohol was thereafter added, and Juleps have been made with a range of different alcohols, including vodka, rum, brandy, and others. The American South, though, Kentucky in particular, is where the whiskey variant gained popularity, especially through its ubiquity at the Derby.

Because of the amount of ice in this drink—and because it's either crushed or shaved, which releases more water—the kind of whiskey that you use is not as important as it is in other drinks.

The Old Seelbach Bar probably makes more Mint Juleps than any other bar in country; it's in Louisville, Kentucky, and only a few miles from where the Derby is run. A historic bar inside a hotel dating from the early 1900s, it's a must-visit if you're ever in the area. They use either Maker's Mark or Woodford Reserve in their Juleps, and we had good success with both. There is somewhat of a debate whether to use bourbon or rye whiskey, but we preferred bourbon because of the sweetness of the drink. Bulleit, because of its high rye content, might be a reasonable compromise. Maker's was our favorite, perhaps because of the wheat used in it.

The key to this drink is to get a lot of mint into it; many recipes call for as many as 4 to 6 sprigs, and you really do need a lot. Use spearmint rather than peppermint, which gives a softer flavor and is better suited for cocktails. We use mint syrup, which you make by starting with simple syrup: combine 1 cup sugar and 1 cup water, then heat and stir until all of the sugar is dissolved. Add a few sprigs of mint to this, and refrigerate overnight. (This mint syrup is good to have around for other drinks, too, like Mojitos.) You don't have to make the syrup in advance, but it will get you more mint, a little better flavor, and save you from having to dissolve sugar in the glass. If you aren't using mint syrup, use 2 teaspoons of sugar, preferably demerara or turbinado as opposed to refined sugar, and add a couple more sprigs of mint. If you have the syrup, add 2 tablespoons to the glass and if you're using sugar add 2 teaspoons and 1 ounce of water. Put in the mint, muddle it gently, then let it stand for a couple of minutes to integrate. Finally, pour in the whiskey and stir.

The Julep might be the only cocktail to have a dedicated service vessel: the Julep cup. Other drinks, like the Old Fashioned, have their own glassware, though that glassware has now been co opted for myriad other purposes. The Julep cup, though, is used only for Juleps. These are metal cups, which therefore stay very cold, and they range from silver-plated or pewter all the way up to sterling silver at $200 or more. If you're going to make a lot of Juleps, get a couple of these glasses; options exist at around $20 each. Otherwise, though, use a double–Old Fashioned glass. Add crushed or shaved ice to fill it, then stir the drink and add more ice to return it to the original level.

Old Fashioned

2 ounces bourbon
1 sugar cube
1 to 2 dashes Angostura bitters
1 to 2 dashes orange bitters
1 slice orange
1 brandied cherry

The Old Fashioned is a classic cocktail from the 1880s that still enjoys a great deal of popularity today; this isn't surprising since it tastes so good. The cocktail originated in a gentlemen's club called the Pendennis Club, and the legend goes that it was the invention of a bartender there and a local bourbon producer, Colonel James Pepper.[3]

As you prepare this drink, you'll see that it's a fun drink to discuss both while making it and later while drinking it. Given the drink's longevity, there are myriad recipes available, but we have a few favorites. First, let's talk about the main ingredient—whiskey. As with the Mint Julep, there is some controversy here as some recipes suggest bourbon while others suggest rye. We argue that bourbon is a better choice for two reasons: first, historically the drink has been made with bourbon, and we think that keeping within that historical lineage adds to the appreciation of the finished product; and second, the drink just tastes better with bourbon. Regarding the latter, we preferred Buffalo Trace bourbon in our tastings, but for those of you out there who simply must have rye, we thought Rittenhouse made the best complement to the drink.

Beyond the whiskey you choose for the Old Fashioned, there is also the issue of what sweetener to use. We use a standard sugar cube, at least partially for tradition. You could try brown sugar instead, though the latter will make the drink seem to have a heavier sweetness; some of the other sugars suggested in the Mint Julep recipe are also possibilities. Finally, while the drink is customarily made with Angostura bitters, we like to use orange bitters as well, just as in our Manhattan recipe. You could use the Fee Brothers options we discussed in that recipe—Old Fashioned Aromatic

Bitters and West Indian Orange Bitters—though the quantities should be equal for this drink. We actually like Angostura, though; there's something about keeping this drink more traditional that just resonates with us. Regans' Orange Bitters No. 6 makes a great complement to Angostura.

Now let's talk about making the cocktail. Start with a chilled Old Fashioned glass. Add the sugar cube to the bottom of the glass and the bitters to the top of the sugar cube. Let the bitters soak into the cube for a bit, and then crush the sugar cube with a muddler. Next, cut the orange slice in half (save the other half for later) and place it in the bottom of the glass on top of the crushed cube. Lightly muddle the orange slice but be careful not to be too forceful as the main point of this step is to extract orange juice and oils from the slice. Now stir these items together being careful not to stir too vigorously.

Next you will begin to form the cocktail, introducing the bourbon and ice to the glass in two steps. First, add 1 ounce of bourbon and 2 medium-size ice cubes. Stir continuously as you pour in the bourbon; the goal is to dissolve completely the sugar so that you get the proper texture for the drink. Now remove the used half orange slice and continue stirring as you add the rest of the bourbon. When the sugar is completely dissolved, add a handful of ice to the glass. With all this stirring, the drink will take on some water from the ice, but this is how the Old Fashioned should be enjoyed—after all, it's mostly bourbon! Finally, take the remaining half orange slice and use it as a garnish, first running it around the rim of the glass. Add a brandied cherry for garnish; details appear in the earlier Manhattan recipe.

For a variation on the above, try the following recipe used at Bourbon & Branch, a Prohibition-style whiskey bar in San Francisco and one of our favorite whiskey bars in the country. Bourbon & Branch bar manager Yanni Kehagiaras recommends first rubbing the inside and rim of the glass with the skin side of a lemon peel. Next, drench the sugar cube in Fee Brothers Whiskey Barrel Aged Bitters, which are, as the name suggests, aromatic bitters aged in used whiskey barrels; these give a fantastic flavor and depth to the drink. Add about 3/4 ounce of soda and muddle well. Next, add 2 ounces of Knob Creek, which lacks a lot of the sweetness of other bourbons. Finally, add ice, stir gently, then add more ice to restore the original level. Garnish with a wide lemon twist and serve.

Smoke, Vanilla, and Coke

2 ounces bourbon or corn whiskey
4 ounces Mexican Coca-Cola
3 dashes liquid smoke
1 teaspoon vanilla extract

Jack Daniel's and Coke is a classic American drink, if not a terribly cerebral one. As good as these drinks are, it almost seems like an insult to our readership to write up: 2 ounces Jack Daniels, 4 ounces Coke, add ice and stir. If you really want to take this drink to a new level, there are some great options. Ours is inspired by a drink called the Waylon, designed by Eben Freeman at Tailor, a Manhattan restaurant and bar. That version uses Old Forester, liquid smoke, regular Coke, and a preserved lemon for garnish, though we came up with something a little different.

Mexican Coke is sweetened with cane sugar, whereas domestic Coke uses high-fructose corn syrup; using real sugar gives the Mexican version a cleaner, sweeter flavor. It is carried at almost any Mexican market and is available online. For the whiskey, you really want something corn based, which complements the sweetness of the Coke. Rye whiskey, or even bourbon using much rye, clashes with the Coke rather than integrates. Our favorite for this drink is Buffalo Trace, which harmonizes perfectly with the Coke. Another option is using 100% corn whiskey—most bourbons are around 70%–75% corn, which is almost too sweet to drink on its own. Our favorite is Mellow Corn, made by Heaven Hill.

Any sort of liquid smoke is fine, though a little goes a long way. Freeman makes his own by smoking Coke syrup over cherrywood, but you can easily buy it already made. We really liked Lazy Kettle's Hickory Liquid Smoke, which has a somewhat meaty taste. Finally, inexpensive vanilla extract is fine, but it might be worth trying to find the good stuff. Nielsen-Massey makes one called Organic Madagascar Bourbon Pure Vanilla Extract that is fantastic.

Stir thoroughly, then serve in a double–Old Fashioned glass over large ice cubes.

Whiskey Smash

2 ounces rye whiskey

2 tablespoons simple syrup

1 to 2 dashes orange bitters

6 mint springs

3 lemon wedges

The Whiskey Smash is an amazing whiskey cocktail that is sadly underappreciated. If you like the flavor of a whiskey sour, we suggest you try this classic cocktail. An early recipe for the Whiskey Smash is from Jerry Thomas's 1862 *How to Mix Drinks*,[4] which was more of a variation on the Mint Julep than anything else. Our recipe incorporates lemon as well as simple syrup rather than granulated sugar, both of which we believe improve the flavor and texture of the drink. Various recipes suggest using bourbon, but, as with the Manhattan, we suggest using a rye whiskey for added complexity and flavor.[5]

If you can't find rye whiskey, you can try a bourbon such as Maker's Mark or Bulleit, but a rye such as Sazerac or Rittenhouse will make a wonderful Whiskey Smash; Sazerac was our favorite. To make the simple syrup, dissolve 1 cup of sugar into 1 cup of boiling water by stirring continuously. Remove from the heat, let it cool, and then refrigerate in a covered container.

So here's how you make Whiskey Smash. First, take the lemon wedges and muddle them in the bottom of a shaker glass. Make sure you leave the peel on the wedges to get the essential oils into the drink. Next, add 4 sprigs of mint on top of the lemons. Slightly bruise the mint with the muddler, but be sure you don't use too much force. Next, add the rye, simple syrup, and orange bitters. Shake very well with ice in a shaker, and then strain into a chilled Old Fashioned glass filled with medium-size ice cubes; make sure that the large chunks of mint and lemon pulp do not get through the strainer. Then, add 1 mint sprig to the drink as a garnish, breaking off the bottom of the sprig before adding it to give added mint flavor. Finally, spank the final sprig of mint over the drink (i.e., break the sprig in half and then clap it in your hands over the drink).

There are a lot of variations worth exploring, so try playing around with these as well. At Bourbon & Branch—one of our favorite bars that we met above in the Old Fashioned recipe—a dash of soda is used instead of bitters. This gives the drink a slight effervescence and, without the bitters, a lighter feel. Fresh fruit can also go in it during summertime; try, for example, using ripe peaches or cantaloupe. Whether you make it traditionally or with some contemporary flair, there's a lot to like in this drink.

NOTES

1. One of the best is Harry Craddock, *The Savoy Cocktail Book* (London: Pavilion Books, [1930] 1999). Craddock was a bartender at the Savoy Hotel London, and this book has been a classic since its first printing. Gary Regan's *The Joy of Mixology: The Consummate Guide to the Bartender's Craft* (New York: Clarkson Potter, 2003) is both contemporary and outstanding.
2. See Hans Allhoff, "The Manhattan and You: Thinking about a Classic Whiskey Cocktail," pp. 90–105 (this volume).
3. For the historical background, see Ian Wisniewski, "Nothing Wrong with Old Fashioned Values," *Whisky Magazine* 46 (October 2005): p. 31.
4. Jerry Thomas, *How to Mix Drinks or the Bon Vivant's Companion* (New York: Dick & Fitzgerald, 1862). The entire book is available on Google Books since it is no longer under copyright restrictions.
5. Toby Maloney of the Violet Hour (see his other recipe under the Manhattan on page 344) provides a demonstration of how to make the Whiskey Smash in a video on YouTube. See Toby Maloney, "Cocktail Minute with Toby Maloney: The Whiskey Smash," YouTube, www.youtube.com/watch?v=1yi9UnrO28g (accessed September 30, 2008).

Contributor Biographies

Marcus P. Adams, M.A. Marcus P. Adams is a Ph. D. student in the Department of History and Philosophy of Science at the University of Pittsburgh. He has graduate degrees in both philosophy and religious studies, and his papers have appeared in philosophy journals such as *Synthese* and the *American Journal of Bioethics* and in religious studies journals such as the *Journal for the Study of the Pseudepigrapha* and *Vetus Testamentum*. His research interests are in epistemology, the philosophy of psychology, and applied ethics. He enjoys a wide range of whiskeys, but he is particularly partial to Speyside whiskies.

Fritz Allhoff, Ph.D. Fritz Allhoff is assistant professor in the Department of Philosophy at Western Michigan University and a research fellow in the Centre for Applied Philosophy and Public Ethics at the Australian National University. He has held visiting fellowships at the Center for Philosophy of Science at the University of Pittsburgh and at the Brocher Foundation (Geneva, Switzerland). Fritz's primary research interests are in applied ethics, ethical theory, and the history and philosophy of science. He has edited nearly twenty books, including *Wine & Philosophy* (Blackwell, 2007) and *Food & Philosophy* (with Dave Monroe; Blackwell, 2007). He might be one of the few to prefer bourbon to Scotch, even if sometimes making an exception for Islay.

Hans Allhoff, J.D. Hans Allhoff received an undergraduate degree in political science from Brown University, an M.Sc. in Philosophy, Policy and Social Value from the London School of Economics, and a law degree from Stanford University. He has been a research assistant at the American Enterprise Institute for Public Policy Research in Washington, D.C., and a commercial litigation associate in San Francisco. His academic interests lie in criminal law and procedure, the First Amendment, and armchair law and economics. In his spare time he writes op-eds and book reviews, cycles and runs, and pairs cocktails with iPod playlists and sartorial norms.

Robert Arp, Ph.D. Robert Arp is a research associate with the National Center for Biomedical Ontology and works with the Ontology Research Group at the New York State Center of Excellence in Bioinformatics & Life Sciences doing research in foundational ontology and ontology development related to the biomedical domain. His areas of specialization include biomedical ontology, philosophy of biology, and philosophy of mind. His first book, *Scenario Visualization: An Evolutionary Account of Creative Problem Solving*, was published by MIT Press in 2008. He thinks that philosophy and pop culture books are one important way to get people to do philosophy.

Thom Brooks, Ph.D. Thom Brooks is reader in political and legal philosophy at the University of Newcastle and founding editor of the *Journal of Moral Philosophy*. He is author of *Hegel's Political Philosophy: A Systematic Reading of the Philosophy of Right* (Edinburgh, 2007) and *Punishment* (2009). Brooks is editor of *The Legacy of John Rawls* (with Fabian Freyenhagen; Continuum, 2005), *Rousseau and Law* (Ashgate, 2005), *Locke and Law* (Ashgate, 2007), *The Global Justice Reader* (Wiley-Blackwell, 2008), and *The Right to a Fair Trial* (Ashgate, 2008). He is currently writing a book on global justice and enjoying breaks between writing by thinking about how Hegel would view a great glass of Scotch.

Ada Brunstein, M.A. Ada Brunstein's academic acronyms include an M.S. in science writing from MIT, an M.A. in linguistics from New York University, and an unfinished Ph.D. at Boston University. She is currently the senior acquisitions editor for linguistics and computer science at MIT Press. Her writing has appeared in the *New York Times, Discover, Wired, New Scientist*, and *Technology Review*, and in her column Ada's Ardor (the *Vocabula Review*), she dissects the language of love and science. Ada was pleasantly surprised to have discovered feminism through whiskey.

Chris Bunting. Chris Bunting is a Tokyo-based journalist. He has written for a variety of UK publications, including the *Independent*, the *Times*, the *Times Higher Education Supplement*, and the *Times Educational Supplement*. He is currently writing a book about Japanese alcohol culture and runs a Web site about Japanese whisky at www .nonjatta.blogspot.com. His last brush with philosophy was a B.A. degree in philosophy, politics, and economics at Merton College, Oxford University.

Douglas Burnham, Ph.D. Douglas Burnham is professor of philosophy at Staffordshire University (UK). He is the author of several books and papers on Kant and on Nietzsche; other research interests include the relationship between philosophy and the arts. He is coauthoring *The Universal Nose: Wine and Aesthetics* with Ole Martin Skilleås. Although displaying geeklike properties in other fields, he is neither a wine nor a whiskey geek; he just enjoys a thoughtful tipple.

Ian Buxton. Ian Buxton, a former marketing director of Glenmorangie, lives on the site of a former distillery! Ian began work in the industry in 1987 and now runs his own consultancy. He was elected Keeper of the Quaich in 1991 and is also a member of the Worshipful Company of Distillers. He is director of the World Whiskies Conference and serves on the tasting panel for the World Whisky Awards. He writes regularly for *Whisky Magazine*, the *Malt Whisky Yearbook*, *Scottish Field*, *Whisky Etc.*, and others. Ian was a coauthor of Eyewitness Companion *Whisky* (Dorling Kindersley, 2008), recently completed a new facsimile edition of Aeneas MacDonald's 1930 classic *Whisky* (Canongate, 2006), and is currently working on a history of John Dewar & Sons.

Jerry O. Dalton, Ph.D. Jerry O. Dalton received a Ph.D. in physical chemistry from the University of Louisville. He is a retired master distiller, most recently for Jim Beam. In his twenty years of distilling, he has been involved in the production of over 200 million proof gallons of bourbon. He has appeared in many bourbon documentaries, conducted hundreds of bourbon tastings, and has written for *Malt Advocate*. He is also author of *Backward Down the Path* (Humanics Publishing, 1998), an interpretation of the Tao Te Ching, a classic of Chinese philosophy. Jerry is passionate about bourbon and likes to think that the worst he ever made was wonderful.

Ian J. Dove, Ph.D. Ian J. Dove is assistant professor of philosophy and director of Logic and Critical Thinking at the University of Nevada, Las Vegas. His efforts to aid in drought relief in Las Vegas include drinking his whisky neat. When he isn't thinking about whisky or water, he writes about mathematics, logic, and conditionals.

Steven F. Geisz, Ph.D. Steven F. Geisz is assistant professor of philosophy at the University of Tampa. He received his Ph.D. from Duke University. He works in philosophy of mind, Chinese philosophy, and political philosophy. One of his best whiskey experiences occurred on a bus on the road outside of Beijing. The whiskey itself wasn't great—just some blended stuff with a dry cork, bought at a twenty-four-hour Korean convenience store in the city—but a bunch of folks shared the bottle, drinking from disposable cups while picking pieces of cork from their teeth and watching the landscape of northern China roll by. Perhaps it wasn't whiskey the way its makers intended, but it surely was whiskey as it was meant to be.

Andrew Jefford. After undergraduate studies at the University of Reading (UK) and postgraduate studies at the University of East Anglia (UK), Andrew Jefford worked in publishing before becoming a freelance writer and broadcaster in 1988. His twelve books include *The New France* (Mitchell Beazley, 2002) and *Peat Smoke and Spirit: A Portrait of Islay and Its Whiskies* (Headline, 2004). He is a columnist for *Decanter* and *The World of Fine Wine* and broadcasts on BBC Radio Four in the United Kingdom. The relationship between the physical facts of place and the agricultural products brought into being in those places is a particular professional interest. During 2009, he will be wine writer-in-residence at Adelaide University, enabling him to research a book about Australia's distinguished vineyard sites.

Jason Kawall, Ph.D. Jason Kawall is associate professor of philosophy and of environmental studies at Colgate University. He has published extensively in the areas of ethical theory, environmental ethics, and epistemology. When not engaged in deep thought, he has been known to enjoy an occasional dram, with a special fondness for Ardbeg and Laphroaig (where he has planted a Canadian flag somewhere near his Friends' plot). He also especially enjoys, and can sometimes properly spell the name of, Bunnahabhain.

Charles MacLean, M.A. Charles MacLean has been researching, writing, and lecturing about whisky since 1980. He is the author of ten books on the subject, including *Scotch Whisky: A Liquid History* (Cassell, 2005)—the only spirits book ever to be acknowledged as Wine & Spirits Book of the Year (2005) in the James Beard Awards. In addition to a law degree (LL.B.), he is a writer to Her Majesty's Signet (W.S.) and a fellow of the Society of Antiquities (F.S.A.) of Scotland. He is a consultant to the Scotch whisky industry and to Bonhams International Auctioneers, sits on the judging panel of the International Wine & Spirits Awards, and has lectured at *inter alia* the Smithsonian Institution, Massey College (University of Toronto, where he is an honorary fellow) and Champlain College (University of Trent). He was founding editor of *Whisky Magazine* and is the *Sunday Times*'s whisky correspondent.

Andrew Martin. Andrew Martin is the director of the Scottish Centre of Tourism in the Robert Gordon University, Aberdeen, Scotland. Prior to joining higher education, Andrew held three consecutive hotel general management positions. He has published in the area of whisky tourism. Andrew has also led three multimillion-pound projects to identify skills gaps in the hotel sector, and has developed innovative online products to bridge these gaps. Andrew currently holds the post of vice chairman for the regional hotel association and has a regular radio slot.

Richard Menary, Ph.D. Richard Menary received his Ph.D. from King's College London. He is an expat Pom, living and working in Australia, where he lectures at the University of Wollongong. He lives on the New South Wales coast with his wife, Sarah, daughter, Sophie, and two cats. He is the author of *Cognitive Integration* (Palgrave Macmillan, 2007) and the forthcoming the *Philosophy of Cognition* (Acumen). He has also written journal articles on the philosophy of mind and cognitive science. He reckons the best way to end a day is to settle into a comfortable chair and share a few drams with his wife.

Dave Monroe, M.A. Dave Monroe is a teetotaler who hates the taste of whiskey and never understood how people could stand it, being more of a beer guy back in the day. Nevertheless, he supports the right of individuals to make their own choices about poisoning themselves with firewater. Monroe is an adjunct instructor of

357

Applied Ethics at St. Petersburg College, an adjunct instructor of philosophy at University of Tampa, and is the cofounder and current president of the Lighthearted Philosophers' Society. Dave also coedited (with Fritz Allhoff) and contributed to *Food & Philosophy: Eat, Think, and Be Merry* (Blackwell, 2007), another anthology in this series. In his spare time, he allows sports to ruin his good humor far more than is appropriate, and hangs out with his lovely new bride, Rhonda.

Thomas W. Polger, Ph.D. Thomas W. Polger is associate professor of philosophy at the University of Cincinnati, 235 kilometers (approximately 146 miles) from Bardstown, Kentucky. He is the author of numerous articles concerning the philosophy of mind, philosophy of science and metaphysics, and of the book *Natural Minds* (MIT Press, 2004). He prefers his whiskeys on the rocks and is a Maker's Mark ambassador.

Susie Pryor, Ph.D. Susie Pryor is assistant professor of marketing at Washburn University. Her research interests include social capital and its operation in rural areas and central business districts. She is widely published in these areas. Prior to working for Washburn, Susie owned a series of successful retail stores and consulted extensively with small businesses in rural Kansas and Nebraska. For the past several years, Susie has worked with and studied farm wineries and distilleries. Most recently, she has been appointed to serve on the state of Kansas's Wine and Grape council, as an adviser on marketing-related issues. She is passionate about both the wines of Kansas and the whiskies of Scotland!

Harvey Siegel, Ed.D. Harvey Siegel is professor and chairman of the Department of Philosophy at the University of Miami; he did his graduate work in a joint program in philosophy of education and philosophy at Harvard under the direction of Israel Scheffler. He has written extensively in epistemology, philosophy of science, and philosophy of education. His books include *Relativism Refuted: A Critique of Contemporary Epistemological Relativism* (Springer, 1987), *Educating Reason: Rationality, Critical Thinking, and Education* (Routledge, 1988), and *Rationality Redeemed?: Further Dialogues on an Educational Ideal* (Routledge, 1996), and he is editing the forthcoming *Oxford Handbook in Philosophy of Education* (Oxford). He has enjoyed drinking Scotch of one sort or another since childhood, and he used his single malt collection to help teach his daughter to read.

Ole Martin Skilleås, Ph.D. Ole Martin Skilleås is professor of Philosophy at Bergen University (Norway), where he previously also taught English. He is the author of *Philosophy and Literature* (Edinburgh, 2001), as well as several articles in journals such as *British Journal of Aesthetics, English Studies,* and *Metaphilosophy,* and he writes on wine for the Norwegian journal *Vinforum.* His tastes in whisky center around the Highlands region. He is coauthoring *The Universal Nose: Wine and Aesthetics* with Douglas Burnham. He is a certified wine geek and the father of two young children.

Kevin W. Sweeney, Ph.D. Kevin W. Sweeney teaches philosophy in Florida at the University of Tampa. He received his Ph.D. in philosophy from the University of Wisconsin–Madison, writing a dissertation on aesthetics. His research interests include topics in modern philosophy, philosophy of literature, film theory, and the aesthetics of silent film, particularly the films of Buster Keaton. He has published several articles on the aesthetics of taste, most recently, "Is There Coffee or Blackberry in My Wine?" in *Wine & Philosophy* (Blackwell, 2008).

Mark Waymack, Ph.D. Mark Waymack teaches philosophy at Loyola University in Chicago. He was introduced to single malt whisky by a University of Edinburgh medical student on a cool, blustery, March day in 1976 on the Atlantic shore of the Isle of Lewis. His long-term philosophical passion has been understanding values. His work has primarily been in the history of ethics and in applied ethics and the philosophy of medicine. With James F. Harris, he is the coauthor of *Single-Malt Whiskies of Scotland* (Open Court, 1992), as well as *The Book of Classic American Whiskeys* (Open Court, 1995).

David Wishart, Ph.D. Director of statistics at the Scottish Executive, David Wishart is a fellow of the School of Management, University of St. Andrews, where he works on marketing and the Scotch whisky industry. His book *Whisky Classified, Choosing Single Malts by Flavour,* 2nd edition (Pavilion, 2006), is published in six languages, with *Whisky Analyst,* his unique computer system for profiling and classifying whiskies by flavor. He was elected Keeper of the Quaich in 2006, and writes regularly for *Malt Advocate, Whisky Etc.*, and elsewhere. David hosts whisky tastings from Melbourne to New York, and he lectures widely at whisky festivals on the heritage of Scotch whiskies and the diversity of their flavors.

Index